Nine Nights of Power

SUNY series in Hindu Studies

Wendy Doniger, editor

Nine Nights of Power

Durgā, Dolls, and Darbārs

Edited by

Ute Hüsken, Vasudha Narayanan,
and Astrid Zotter

SUNY
PRESS

Cover image taken by Ina Marie Lunde Ilkama.

Publication of this book was made possible in part by the generous support of the Department of Culture Studies and Oriental Languages (IKOS) at the University of Oslo and the Heidelberg Academy of Sciences and Humanities.

Published by State University of New York Press, Albany

For information, contact State University of New York Press, Albany, NY
www.sunypress.edu

Library of Congress Cataloging-in-Publication Data

Names: Hüsken, Ute, editor. | Narayanan, Vasudha, editor. | Zotter, Astrid, editor.
Title: Nine nights of power : Durgā, dolls, and darbārs / Ute Hüsken, Vasudha Narayanan, Astrid Zotter.
Description: Albany : State University of New York Press, [2021] | Series: SUNY series in Hindu Studies | Includes bibliographical references and index.
Identifiers: ISBN 9781438484075 (hardcover : alk. paper) | ISBN 9781438484068 (pbk. : alk. paper) | ISBN 9781438484082 (ebook)
Further information is available at the Library of Congress.

10 9 8 7 6 5 4 3 2 1

Contents

Gendered Identities in Navarātri

Navarātri as Instrument of Power

Illustrations

Figures

Tables

Acknowledgments

This publication was generated in the international working group Navarātri, Navarātra, and Durgāpūjā in South Asia and Beyond, which was initiated by Ute Hüsken in 2014 (then at the University of Oslo; at Heidelberg University since 2017) and has extended over several years with participants from all over the world, including a collaboration with the University of Texas at Austin. Most of the papers in this volume were presented at two meetings of the group in 2016: a workshop at the University of Texas at Austin and an exploratory session on Navarātri at the Annual Meeting of the American Academy of Religion in San Antonio. The present volume is the companion to the group's first volume, *Nine Nights of the Goddess: The Navarātri Festival in South Asia,* edited by Caleb Simmons, Moumita Sen, and Hillary Rodrigues and published by SUNY Press in 2018. The editors wish to express their gratitude to the Department of Culture Studies and Oriental Languages (IKOS) at the University of Oslo and the Heidelberg Academy of Sciences and Humanities, whose generous financial support enabled us to include numerous color plates throughout this volume. We would also like to thank Douglas Fear for revising the English; Malini Ambach for her help in formatting the volume; Chris Ahn, James Peltz, and the SUNY Press team for their professional work; and Wendy Doniger and the editorial board of the SUNY series in Hindu Studies for accepting this volume as part of the series.

Nine Nights of Power

Durgā, Dolls, and Darbārs—An Introduction

UTE HÜSKEN, VASUDHA NARAYANAN,
AND ASTRID ZOTTER

The autumnal Navarātri festival—also called Durgā Pūjā, Dasarā, or Dasaĩ—is an important event celebrated all over South Asia and wherever Hindus settle. This nine-day-long festival, often understood as a celebration in honor of the goddess Durgā, ends with the "victorious tenth" (*vijayadaśamī*), the tenth day. Traveling through Hindu homes, temples, and neighborhood community halls in South Asia and all over the world during this festival is a journey through Hindu traditions and practices that have originated at different times and different places. Local and pan-Hindu stories and performances found in different parts of the subcontinent and in many parts of the world are layered, interconnected, and sometimes blended together into a diachronic assemblage of practices, ideas, and material culture. Many of these traditions have been amplified while others have been marginalized, jettisoned, or recycled over the centuries. Indeed, as the diversified materials in the chapters in this volume show, the festival of Navarātri, the nine nights and ten days of rituals, performances, and celebrations of Durgā, Rāma, or other Hindu deities, can well function as a hologram of the history and practices of the Hindu traditions.

No wonder, then, that the stories of Navarātri are legion. Simmons and Sen (2018, 3–8) discuss some of the multiple textual narratives attested to in the epics and Purāṇas, also including modern inversions, especially as concerns the character and role of the goddess's antagonist Mahiṣāsura, the buffalo demon, who becomes an identificatory character for marginalized groups. In textual traditions, too, Mahiṣāsura is not just the villain that any good story needs. In the *Kālikā Purāṇa,* for example, he is also seen as a form of Śiva and as the foremost devotee of the goddess; he would rather die by her hands than forgo union with her (Stietencron 2005, 129–30). In her newly released study of Durgā, Bihani Sarkar (2017, 221–71) traces the early history of the festival back to an amalgamation of traditions. Clearly, the constant making and remaking for ever-new and specific contexts has been at the core of the festival right from its beginning. Brahmanical texts cover elite versions, which typically take place at royal courts, but even these texts attest to the presence of popular traditions.

Yet Navarātri is not just an expression of specific local traditions. In this volume, it is also viewed through the lens of individual participation and experience: the individual participant in the festival oscillates between their ordinary life and the special festival time. Religious and quotidian realities intermingle, and, simultaneously, the private becomes public, and the other way around (Simmons and Sen 2018, 8–13). People live from festival to festival through both memory and anticipation, as the festival is not only enacted but also takes place during the act of remembering and in imaginative anticipation. In this volume, scholars have written from multiple perspectives about how celebrants shape and reconstruct Navarātri through their material, mental, physical, ritual, emotional, and, as many describe it, spiritual participations and remembrances, in multiple realms of sovereignty and of domestic, communal, and professional well-being and order. And the festival, in turn, shapes and reconstructs the celebrants.

All the contributors to this volume look at one festival, albeit from different perspectives and in different settings, highlighting similarities and differences. When different sets of values confront one another, it creates an occasion to appreciate and celebrate together but also to disapprove and resist. Both individually and taken together, the chapters address questions of meaning (re)making and efficacy, probing into the values underlying the festival; exploring criticism, conflict, and resistance; and paying attention to questions of ritual agency and competence.

The present volume is an outcome of the international working group Navarātri, Navarātra, and Durgāpūjā in South Asia and Beyond and a direct continuation of the group's first volume, *Nine Nights of the Goddess* (Simmons, Sen, and Rodrigues 2018). In this first volume, spatial aspects—the different spaces and spheres of Navarātri—were a special focus, establishing that the festival is constantly moving between spaces and therefore transcending them. This "'everywhere'-ness" (Simmons and Sen 2018, 12) is also highlighted by Hillary Rodrigues (2018) in his conclusion to the same volume, which stresses the goddess's presence in multiple material forms and in female humans. The necessity to negotiate diverse agendas is another red thread of the first volume: Navarātri, as a festival for all people, is increasingly democratized, so that the number of actors and interest groups that have a say in shaping the festival multiplies. This development is in line with what has been seen as an important feature of the festival ever since Burton Stein's (1983) and Nicholas Dirks's (1993) analyses of Navarātra practices in the Vijayanagara empire and Madeleine Biardeau's (1981, 2004) groundbreaking studies of Navarātri in village contexts in South India: the festival brings together all strata of society and becomes a stage where roles, status, and hierarchies are displayed, negotiated, and reconfirmed. Navarātri may have historically been domestic or royal, but regal pomp and splendor came to overshadow domestic worship by the sixteenth century. Recent democratizations, however, differ from more traditional examples in their authority structures and have opened up new, hybrid spaces for performance and display. Regarding display, the ludic aspect and conspicuous consumption continue to play major roles but also assume modern forms (Rodrigues 2018, 322–25). Such newer spaces keep pace with social organization, social hierarchies, nationalism, and local ethnic-pride movements. *Garbā* dancing, for instance, moved from the home and the village center to community halls in India and in the diaspora, and the dances are now mega spectacles involving tens of thousands of participants at commercially sponsored sites in Gujarat (see Shukla-Bhatt's contribution to this volume). The United Way of Baroda's *garbā*, for instance, has about forty thousand "players" every night, and the circular dance moves like a universe expanding from the goddess in the center.[1] These mega displays are now held in club grounds, or "playgrounds," of large social clubs, where, in some cases, women who enter wearing traditional Gujarati attire are exempt from the hefty registration fees. In metropolises, large areas of the city are transformed into dancing sites. The space is ethnically marked, and as such the Navarātri here becomes distinguished from other Navarātri spaces in other parts of India because of the insistence on local attire. As in many other cultures, women's bodies become the sites that are the carriers and markers of ethnic pride.

These insights are the starting points for the present book project, which delves deeply into the performative, material, and visual aspects of the festival as it manifests itself in specific local and temporal contexts. We explore the ways that Navarātri becomes the ground on which social integration and separation are negotiated in South Asia in four clusters. We attend to this constructing, enacting, assessing, and revising through Navarātri by studying the festival at both the back and front of the stage. The festival is understood here as contact zone between individuals, groups, and spheres and as a mediator between past, present, and future. Through the prism of diverse perspectives on the annual Navarātri, the volume addresses the work this festival does. Navarātri as we conceive it here is not just as an expression or staging of the social, or of religious beliefs, but an agent that accomplishes important tasks. We employ a concept developed in ritual theory that sees ritual agency not as confined to individuals asking how they use rituals for "political" or "strategical" purposes but more broadly conceived as "the ability to transform the world" (Sax 2006, 473–74).[2] Navarātri has the transformative power, the agency, to render a king victorious, to rejuvenate the world (Rodrigues), to transform women into goddesses (Ilkama; Sen), to initiate men into manhood (Saul; Zotter), or to create girls' class belonging (Ortegren). It is not an individual actor or clearly defined group of actors who brings about this transformation. Agency is complex and diffuse and arises from an interplay of different constituents of a ritual, such as actors, texts, and material in specific settings. Even more so, the abandonment of the "'intentional sovereignty' of the individual agent" (Sax 2006, 478) seems to be a precondition, as shown in the example discussed by Sen, where actors vehemently deny their intention to render a politician into a goddess. So, we set out to explore how the agency of and in the festival comes about, how it materializes, but also how it is challenged or denied.

Looking at different aspects of the festival as it is celebrated in diverse regions of South Asia and other locations where South Asian traditions have taken new roots, the individual contributions to this volume address common questions: What does this festival do? What does it achieve, and how? What are the various criteria for evaluating Navarātri? What contexts and conditions determine whether these aspects thrive or fail? How does the festival reflect cultural conditions, and how does it produce new cultural realities? How is this festival one festival and many different festivals at the same time?

In responding to these questions, strong emphasis is laid on images, since we look at the festival as a practice and as a performance rather than as a text. Not only are material religion and its enactment and efficacies often better represented in visual form, but we also conceptualize the images as a potential way of knowing. Sometimes, in pragmatic terms, a picture is a shorthand for a lot of description. Even more importantly, the intermediality produced by the close interlocking of the images and the texts brings the field alive; allows a more nuanced, multilayered storytelling; and gives the reader more resources than the author might initially have intended. One might miss an object in a ritual scene while analyzing it, but a reader can reuse this source and analyze it differently. The images included in the contributions are thus not simply illustrations but a way of conveying arguments, enabling the reader to grasp how the festival's work is accomplished through interaction, material culture, and performances, along with texts and narratives.

The present volume tells the festival's stories through understanding (1) Navarātri as agent of renewal and transformation, through the juxtaposition of (2) propriety and creativity in Navarātri, through looking at (3) gendered identities in Navarātri, and through acknowledging the role of (4) Navarātri as instrument of power.

Navarātri as Agent of Renewal and Transformation

While festivals are important vehicles for maintaining cultural continuity and passing on tradition, they are also valuable instruments employed in situations of cultural and religious renewal. In his chapter "Ritual of Revitalization: The Transformative Power of the Durgā Pūjā," Hillary Rodrigues discusses the potential of Durgā Pūjā and of several of its rites, concluding that they stand for and are performed at a time of annual and cosmic revitalization and that they also accompany or even accomplish transformations in the performers, on both personal and transpersonal levels. While the charter myth of the festival celebrates a death—in this case, the death of the demon Mahiṣa—the rituals are concerned with birth, fertility, and renewal. Specifically, the festival's Tantric underpinnings show that it serves not only as an expression of devotional reverence but as a rite of transformative empowerment.

Especially when Navarātri is adopted by new sets of performers, or when it is transferred to new cultural, geographical, historical, or virtual contexts, the festival itself can be fundamentally transformed and gain an entirely new character, even though key elements may remain recognizable. Neelima Shukla-Bhatt demonstrates this with the example of the *garbo* dance performed by women in Gujarat in her chapter "Straddling the Sacred and the Secular: Presence and Absence of the Goddess in Contemporary *Garbo*, the Navarātri Dance of Gujarat." When it is transposed from what was a neighborhood context into new public and commercial arenas, this dance is fundamentally transformed. Some participants are not at ease with the fact that the *garbo* now seems to be taken over by larger agencies and corporate entities, whereas others view these new forms of *garbo* "as valid components of *Navarātri* celebrations" (Shukla-Bhatt 42, this volume). Similarly, in South India, the festival has become more popular with corporate power moving the traditional *kolu* doll displays into public spaces. Has the festival been transformed into an ethnic or folkloristic show rather than being a religious celebration? Issues of power, prestige, and financial prowess connected with cultural productions are all intricately blended with notions of piety and national pride in such moves. These threads blend into the next section of the volume, which focuses on propriety and captures voices that criticize commercialization and the disentanglement from what is conceived as the more traditional performance.

Propriety versus Creativity in Navarātri

Clearly, Navarātri, like other festivals, has a pronounced ludic dimension (Rodrigues 2018, 322–25), providing creative space that leaves room for individual expressions. Just as many Hindu traditions think of the creation of this universe as the play, or *līlā,* of the deity, so, too, is Navarātri an act of play and creation. Importantly, it is this creative space that allows for competition, subversion, and critique. It seems that Navarātri gives occasion to simultaneously adapt to and resist political, social, and cultural changes. Different subjective realities with their attendant values, practices, and histories meet or confront one another, forcing celebrants to cope with diversity. This is no recent phenomenon, as can be seen from the many texts on dharma as well as the Purāṇas composed in the first millennium CE and their hugely diverging prescriptions for festival performance, such as the many ways of waking up or bringing the goddess to life and of propitiating and appeasing her (Einoo 1999; Sarkar 2017, 210–71; Kane 1958, 158–59). These texts also place significant stress on allowing people of all castes—and even those "beyond the pale of the caste system" (Kane 1958, 157)—to celebrate this festival with sacrifices. Here, the texts are not shy about specifying the animals most suitable as offerings for specific days during this festival. Above all buffaloes but also birds, turtles, antelopes, deer, rhinoceros, crocodiles, bulls, goats, and even human beings are all considered suitable sacrificial victims. Yet the same texts also allow for the substitution of these animals with offerings of fruits and cooked food (Kane 1958, 164–65). Thus, what is and what is not considered appropriate are ultimately negotiated by the celebrating communities.

The two contributions in this section investigate the slippery dynamics of the competing agendas of the stakeholders in Navarātri, providing a window into such processes of ritual creativity and interpretations of propriety. Here we see how aspects of the Navarātri festival are deployed as instruments of social critique and how they are agents of change as well as how this critique and change meets resistance and how the participants are reined in. These processes of contestation, acceptance, and rejection are key to understanding what matters most to the celebrating communities and individuals in Navarātri. In "Can Didi Truly Become Durgā? The Riddle of the Two Goddesses," Moumita Sen discusses the rapid process of both politicization and secularization of the Durgā Pūjā of Kolkata and the sometimes-contradictory demands of ritual propriety and of spectacle or novelty through looking at 2016 *paṇḍals* in Kolkata, which take the chief minister of West Bengal, Mamata Banerjee, as their theme. Sen shows that there exist parallel discourses over images and their worship, which, however, do not interfere much with each other. Sen's interest is with the agents behind these processes of reinvention and the negotiations they involve. In "Limits of Creativity: *Kolu* in Brahmin Vaiṣṇava Households in Kāñcipuram," Ute Hüsken discusses a creative and intentionally innovative form of *kolu*, a display of dolls on stages typical for Navarātri in South Indian homes, which has received mixed responses. While the themes of this *kolu* are very traditional, replicating the festivals and scenery of the temple next door in every minute detail, its material (waste material) evokes the *kolu*'s rejection. We can see here how, even when conscious reinvention explicitly reaches back to what is perceived as traditional and authentic, this appropriation and reinterpretation of the past becomes culturally productive and controversial at the same time. Cultural creativity is risky, so there is always a certain uncertainty in festivals like Navarātri. However, this risk is part of a festival's attraction. While changes in the place of manufacture of the dolls of *kolu* from little towns like Panrutti in Tamil Nadu to China (resulting in cheaper dolls but with better finish) have been accepted, Mr. Sundarajan's *kolu* made with recyclable materials is rejected by Kāñcipuram's Brahmin Vaiṣṇava community.

Gendered Identities in Navarātri

Agency in festivals is complex and diffuse. Participants in Navarātri are celebrants as well as witnesses, actors as well as spectators. The focus in the three contributions to this section is on gendered identities and agencies in private and public domains, oscillating between urban and rural settings, and between caste and class identities. Often, Navarātri is said to be a women's festival, especially as the goddess plays a crucial role: many texts reiterate the importance of the story of Mahiṣāsuramardinī—the goddess Durgā, the personification of female energy who slays the buffalo demon. This story is the best-known charter myth for Navarātri in many parts of India. However, sometimes the goddess also takes the back seat. Despite the overwhelming popularity of the narrative of Durgā's victory,

Rāma's battle with Rāvaṇa is also commemorated with considerable gusto in many villages and towns of North India. Known as Rām Līlā (the sports of Rāma or the play of Rāma, an incarnation of Viṣṇu), it can last anywhere from a day to a month. The best-known performance is in Ramnagar, near Varanasi (Schechner and Hess 1977, Sax 1990, Kapur 2006). The Rām Līlā includes participants from many sectors of the local communities and culminates during the days of Dasara. At that time, the ritual victory of Rāma over Rāvaṇa is enacted, and the effigies of Rāvaṇa and other demons are burned or blown up with fireworks. In 2008, UNESCO recognized the Rām Līlā in its "Representative List of the Intangible Cultural Heritage of Humanity." Less widely known, yet celebrated locally with no less fervor, is the worship of Hanumān, the faithful facilitator of Rāma's victory, as Jeremy Saul illustrates in his chapter "Navarātri as a Festival of Hanumān and Male Asceticism." Focusing devotion on the helper of the goddess's devotee rather than on the goddess herself, young men adopt Hanumān as a role model in practices of embodiment. Centering an athletic, chaste, and youthful male body advances a concept of masculinity that distances itself from prevalent stereotypes, such as the Indian *babu* or the rapist. Saul shows how individual participation is an empowerment strategy and even has an initiatory potential for men within their peer groups and within the whole social fabric—similar to the masculinity displayed by the actors in blood sacrifices in Nepal (see Zotter's contribution to this volume). The Hanumān-style self-constructed ascetic in Saul's case study, however, is a very different character than the Nepalese worshipper of Durgā who sheds blood in heroic devotion.

Jennifer D. Ortegren focuses on the implications of the urban/rural divide for middle-class women. In "Going Home for Navarātri: Negotiating Caste, Class, and Gender between Rural and Urban Rajasthan," she analyzes the ways in which middle-class and religious identities are mutually constructed in relationship to localized communities by examining differences in Navarātri celebrations among upwardly mobile Hindu women whose lives move between urban and rural Rajasthan. In the city, Navarātri plays an important role in fostering cross-caste bonds between diverse urban neighbors whose relationships are rooted in shared class identities. Yet Navarātri is also a time when many urbanized families return to their ancestral homes to reinforce their identities with their family and clan (as in Bengal) or to rural homes to worship local goddesses within caste-homogeneous communities. Here, women feel more comfortable precisely because of shared caste identities but still perform their urban middle-classness vis à vis their caste fellows. In this way, Navarātri also serves to reinforce family, clan, and caste identification as well as to introduce class distinctions. Ortegren's focus is on perceived appropriateness of behavior and on how participants perform gendered class identities.

Unlike the prominence of public spaces in the celebration of Navarātri in northern India, until recently, it is in domestic spaces that the festival came to life in southern India. Here, the *kolus* were not just domestic but largely a festival celebrated with women's agency (Sivakumar 2018; Narayanan 2018; Wilson 2018). Ina Marie Ilkama, in "Female Agency during Tamil Navarātri," compares these settings with the Navarātri celebrations in the temples. Navarātri is celebrated in most goddess temples and in homes across the South Indian temple town Kāñcipuram. Here, women not only perform the domestic rituals for the *kolu*, but their role is also prominent in the temples, seen, for example, in *pūjās* directed to or performed by women. However, women's roles are expressed very differently in the temples and in the homes, and they also differ significantly among the diverse temples. Ilkama's contribution looks closely at these differences, exploring important details of Navarātri's alleged nature as a women's festival.

Navarātri as Instrument of Power

The last cluster of contributions explores how changing political realities affect Navarātri and how Navarātri provides an occasion to claim, solidify, or reorder political power. The focus here is on space, spatial practices, negotiations between communities, and negotiations between state authority and practices on the ground, as manifested during the annual festival celebrations. How did kings and those traditionally charged with the protection of the land and its people propitiate the goddesses for victory and prosperity? The performative commentaries and the multiple rituals include those connected with the royal courts. They display, in addition to valor and conquest, a sense of the lingering nostalgia of imagined victories and, literally, the boast of heraldry and the pomp of power presented in frames of frayed splendor (Simmons 2018; Skoda 2018; Zotter 2018).

Dealing with one material aspect of state practices in Nepal, the buffalo sacrifices, Astrid Zotter, in "Who Kills the Buffalo? Authority and Agency in the Ritual Logistics of the Nepalese Dasaĩ Festival," explores the logistics and agency that become obvious from official paperwork on the provision, killing, and further use of buffaloes. These attest to a huge mobilization of resources and a tremendous administrative effort. The largesse staged by the state on this occasion underpins the splendor of the goddess and the king as her prime worshipper. The ruling class celebrated themselves as masters over life and death, thereby enacting a strong parallelism of sacrifice and war. By enshrining buff consumption as a touchstone for state-sanctioned caste grading, with consumers of buffalo meat ranking below nonconsumers, schemes for the partition and redistribution of sacrificed buffaloes reflected and reinforced social hierarchies. Official directives, channeled and performed through agents of the state from above, were, however, also mediated, enacted, and challenged by actors on the ground.

Elsewhere, it was instead a democratic impulse to level caste distinctions and have larger numbers of the population participate in the festival that led to recasting it in secular frames: in some states, like Karnataka and Tamil Nadu, this has become a folk-craft or Tamil festival without religious overtones. Yet here, too, its reframing has made it, like commercial athletics, into a celebration of statehood that is performed in public spaces.

While the Nepalese case deals with a phase in history when Hindu kingship was still in place, the next two contributions look at royal Navarātri traditions without ruling kings. In the chapter "Domains of Dasara: Reflections on the Struggle for Significance in Contemporary Mysore," Caleb Simmons explores Mysore's Dasara as a site through which various kinds of social power are negotiated, drawing from ethnographic work conducted during Mysore's 2013 celebration of Dasara. Looking at the movements of the festival and the image (*mūrti*) of the goddess from the palace to the temple and back to the palace, from the beginning of the festival to its close on Vijayadaśamī, Simmons carefully considers the parallelism between the traditional rituals performed in the temple and the palace and between the temple priests and the mahārāja's staff. Clearly, contemporary Dasara reflects early modern forms of subversion against the British government, but these continue vis-à-vis contemporary Indian political structures. Through this case study, Simmons reflects on Navarātri as a time in which various powerful institutions continue to carve out socially significant domains of power and authority.

Uwe Skoda, in "The Ups and Downs of Competing Power Rituals: Dasarā and Durgā Pūjā in a Former Princely State of Odisha," deals with the dynamics of Durgā worship in a former princely state in northwestern Odisha. Skoda contrasts two different types of *pūjā* performed largely simultaneously: inside the raja's fort, the older rituals commonly referred to as Dasara are conducted, whereas in the market area a relatively recent tradition of Durgā Pūjā has been established. In the former, Goddess Durgā appears primarily in the form of iron swords and with a permanent seat. Though the royal sacrificial polity involving various communities including Adibasis is disintegrating, some elements such as the worship of the Goddess Kant Debī, associated with Durgā as well as the Adibasis, are very or even more popular than during state time. In contrast to the fort-centered rituals, Durgā Pūjā that is closer to the Bengali tradition with a temporary idol has until recently seen a considerable rise in popularity due to donations specifically from sponge-iron factory and mine owners, who are the nouveau riche of the area. While they have offered new spectacles to the local audience, at times challenging or even overshadowing the older tradition, the ongoing slowdown of extractive industries has recently led to a downsizing of Durgā Pūjā celebrations. With the Rashtriya Svayamsevak Sangh, a third player has recently entered the stage, reappropriating formerly royal ritual space with its own overtly political agendas. Skoda's case study shows how different actors launch different rituals at different places and create new spaces competing with older spaces, whereas in Simmons's and Zotter's case studies different actors contest over the same ritual or its interpretations and implications. Clearly, the decline and rise of worship traditions are not linear processes.

Conclusion

Navarātri's different elements speak to one another. The stories of Navarātri laid out in this volume show that the different layers and performance genres of the festival are purposefully used by several sets of agents but also dynamically interact with one another. Importantly, religion and religious practice do not take place in a neatly carved-out sphere or institution in society but are entangled, built into and inseparably bound to other social institutions, including economics, politics, and consumerism. We might ask, then, what precisely is religious about these festival practices? Does it make sense at all to delineate religion as a separate sphere? It might be more appropriate to deal with festivals as "special events" (Taves 2011) that are in many ways distinct from everyday practices. This distinctness unfolds differently for different participants—the specific creative powers activated during Navarātri, for example, also encompass the possibility or even necessity of violence. Materiality and abundance are further important features of the festival: from extensive bloodshed to dolls overpopulating the living room, abundance signals social bigness and thus corresponds to social capital, which in turn increases access to and mobilization of resources. Navarātri is a peak time of overexpenditure and conspicuous consumption, amounting to a display and performance of status and power, which, however, is also critiqued as commercialization or politicization. These critiques point to the ways competition can unfold within the frame of the festival. Abundance often also implies messiness, working against attempts to script and dictate proper order and meaning. Similar to other festivals that are celebrated transregionally, by appropriating and reinterpreting the past and the Other, Navarātri is culturally productive and transformative, on the individual as well as the collective level. The festival is more than the sum of its parts, developing its own dynamics and creating new and unexpected forms, thereby retaining its importance for the lives of the celebrants.

Notes

1. See "Top Gujarati Garba Events to Celebrate Navaratri" by Sharell Cook, *TripSavvy*, https://www.tripsavvy.com/gujarati-garba-venues-for-navaratri-4136013; and "Garba Mahotsav," *United Way of Baroda*, https://unitedwaybaroda.org/3-our-work/events/annual-fund-raiser/; both accessed April 30, 2020.

2. Based especially on a performative approach to ritual (Kapferer 1983; Schechner 1977; Tambiah 1979). For agency in rituals and the difference between actors and agents, see also Sax (2013).

References

Biardeau, Madeleine. 1981. "L'arbre *śamī* et le buffle sacrificiel." In *Autour de la déesse Hindoue*, edited by Madeleine Biardeau, 215–43. Paris: École des Hautes Études en Science Sociales.

———. 2004. *Stories about Posts: Vedic Variations around the Hindu Goddess*. Translated by Alf Hiltebeitel, Marie-Louise Reiniche, and James Walker. Chicago: University of Chicago Press.

Dirks, Nicholas B. 1993. *The Hollow Crown: Ethnohistory of an Indian Kingdom*. Ann Arbor: University of Michigan Press.

Einoo, Shingo. 1999. "The Autumn Goddess Festival: Described in the Purāṇas." In *Living with Śakti: Gender, Sexuality and Religion in South Asia*, edited by Masakazu Tanaka and Musashi Tachikawa, 33–70. Osaka: National Museum of Ethnology.

Kane, Pandurang Vaman. 1958. *History of Dharmaśāstra: Ancient and Mediaeval Religious and Civil Law in India*. Vol. 5.1, *Vratas, Utsavas and Kāla etc*. Poona, India: Bhandarkar Oriental Research Institute.

Kapferer, Bruce. 1983. *A Celebration of Demons: Exorcism and the Aesthetics of Healing in Sri Lanka*. Bloomington: Indiana University Press.

Kapur, Anuradha. 2006. *Actors, Pilgrims, Kings and Gods: The Ramlila at Ramnagar*. London: Seagull Books.

Narayanan, Vasudha. 2018. "Royal *Darbār* and Domestic *Kolus*: Social Order, Creation, Procreation, and Re-Creation." In Simmons, Sen, and Rodrigues 2018, 275–97.

Rodrigues, Hillary. 2018. "Conclusion." In Simmons, Sen, and Rodrigues 2018, 317–30.

Sarkar, Bihani. 2017. *Heroic Śāktism: The Cult of Durgā in Ancient Indian Kingship.* New York: Oxford University Press.

Sax, William S. 1990. "The Ramnagar Ramlila: Text, Performance, Pilgrimage." *History of Religions* 30 (2):129–53.

———. 2006. "Agency." In *Theorizing Rituals,* edited by Jan Snoek, Jens Kreinath, and Michael Stausberg, 473–81. Leiden, Netherlands: Brill.

———. 2013. "Agency." In *Ritual und Ritualdynamik: Schlüsselbegriffe, Theorien, Diskussionen,* edited by Christiane Brosius, Axel Michaels, and Paula Schrode, 25–31. Göttingen, Germany: Vandenhoeck & Ruprecht.

Schechner, Richard. 1977. *Essays on Performance Theory.* New York: Drama Books Specialists.

Schechner, Richard, and Linda Hess. 1977. "The Ramlila of Ramnagar (India)." *The Drama Review* 21 (3): 51–82.

Simmons, Caleb. 2018. "The King and the Yadu Line: Performing Lineage through Dasara in Nineteenth-Century Mysore." In Simmons, Sen, and Rodrigues 2018, 63–82.

Simmons, Caleb, and Moumita Sen. 2018. "Introduction: Movements of Navarātri." In Simmons, Sen, and Rodrigues 2018, 1–22.

Simmons, Caleb, Moumita Sen, and Hillary Rodrigues, eds. 2018. *Nine Nights of the Goddess: The Navarātri Festival in South Asia.* Albany: State University of New York Press.

Sivakumar, Deeksha. 2018. "Display Shows, Display Tells: The Aesthetics of Memory during Pommai Kolu." In Simmons, Sen, and Rodrigues 2018, 257–73.

Skoda, Uwe. 2018. "Dasara and the Selective Decline of Sacrificial Polity in a Former Princely State of Odisha." In Simmons, Sen, and Rodrigues 2018, 83–102.

Stein, Burton. 1983. "Mahanavami: Medieval and Modern Kingly Ritual in South India." In *Essays on Gupta Culture,* edited by Bardwell L. Smith, 67–90. Delhi: Motilal Banarsidass.

Stietencron, Heinrich von. 2005. "The Goddess Durgā Mahiṣāsuramardinī: Myth, Representation, and Historical Role in the Hinduization of India." In *Hindu Myth, Hindu History: Religion, Art, and Politics,* 115–172. Delhi: Permanent Black.

Tambiah, Stanley J. 1979. "A Performative Approach to Ritual." *Proceedings of the British Academy* 65:113–69.

Taves, Ann. 2011. "Special Things as Building Blocks of Religions." In *The Cambridge Companion to Religious Studies,* edited by Robert A. Orsi, 58–83. Cambridge: Cambridge University Press.

Wilson, Nicole. A. 2018. "Kolus, Caste, and Class: Navarātri as a Site for Ritual and Social Change in Urban South India." In Simmons, Sen, and Rodrigues 2018, 237–56.

Zotter, Astrid. 2018. "Conquering Navarātra: Documents on the Reorganisation of a State Festival." In *Studies in Historical Documents from Nepal and India,* edited by Simon Cubelic, Axel Michaels, and Astrid Zotter, 493–531. Heidelberg, Germany: Heidelberg University Publishing. https://doi.org/10.17885/heiup.331.454.

Navarātri as Agent of Renewal and Transformation

1

Ritual of Revitalization

The Transformative Power of the Durgā Pūjā

HILLARY RODRIGUES

Introduction

One of the most popular and widespread religious festivals celebrated by Hindus is Navarātri, the "nine nights" dedicated to the goddess. Also known by various other names, such as Navarātra, Dasain, and Dussehra, it typically includes a tenth day known as *vijayādaśamī*, the "tenth for Victory." Given its ancient origins, regional diversity, and long duration, there are rich variations in how Navarātri is celebrated in the Hindu world. People may visit temples, chant scriptural texts ritually, perform rites of devotional worship, engage in austerities, undertake pilgrimages, install colorful displays, prepare special meals, and so on. In this chapter, I wish to focus on the Durgā Pūjā, an elaborate ritual of worship that occurs during Navarātri, in order to highlight its capacity to enact change. In this I align with the intent of this volume, which is to illustrate how rituals have agency, the capacity to affect reality.

Although the term *Durgā Pūjā* is often used by certain Hindus as a synonym for Navarātri, my use of it is narrower. I am using it primarily to refer to the constellation of worship rites (*pūjā*) that occur during Navarātri, centered on the temporary establishment and veneration of the goddess (Devī).[1] The boundaries of the term are by no means solid, because there are peripheral activities that one might wish to include or exclude for consideration. My analysis draws heavily on the Bengali style of Durgā Pūjā celebrations, which, because of its Tantric orientations, offers more robust indications of transformative action.[2] However, one may readily extend the analyses to most other types of Durgā Pūjās, with the obvious stipulation that intent is a crucial proviso in the analysis of ritual. Moreover, my sphere of inquiry is not exclusively on the Durgā Pūjā ritual but on rites of worship that adhere to or correlate with it. I shall use the term *festival* for Navarātri. I use *ritual* for the academically constructed category of religious actions as well as for the whole complex of Durgā Pūjā, which is composed of both small-scale religious actions (rites) and more complex structured activities, for which I use the terms *rituals* and *rites*, sometimes interchangeably. I shall not engage in fine-grained theorizing on ritual in this chapter. A simple example of the playing of a national anthem may suffice to draw out some of the complexities entailed in the intention behind and participation in public rites. For instance, the persons or parties that initiate the playing or singing of a national anthem may do so not only to elicit patriotic sentiments; they may wish to induce some initial sobriety and solemnity in a crowd of excited participants, such as at sporting events. In schools, the ceremonial activity of playing and singing the national anthem may be a method through which it is taught and learned. Anthems may of course be used to induce or celebrate feelings of national pride, such as at victory celebrations, or to confer symbolic status upon leaders during inaugurations. For participants, the responses and degrees of participation may be mixed. Depending on the context, some may gladly hop to their feet, stand at attention, hand on heart, and sing out wholeheartedly; others may participate reluctantly, pressured by the actions of the crowd around them. Others may offer some symbolic resistance by being slow to rise, not singing along, or making other bodily gestures such as moving shiftily. The behaviors and emotional states during the playing of a national anthem are even more complex for benign nonnationals, rivals in athletics, economic or political adversaries, and so on. In short, ritual is not one thing. It does not have an express purpose or uniform effects. The discussion and analyses that follow of the Durgā Pūjā and ancillary worship rites are by no means comprehensive. Its aim is to extract specific strands of meaning embedded within the broader complexities of the ritual actions to highlight how these affect people and their world.[3]

General Comments on *Pūjā*

Pūjā is the term typically applied to the constellation of activities entailed in invoking, worshipping, and dismissing a deity. In typical settings, the deity is already established in a temple or home shrine, and the *pūjā* consists of the rites of worship, more technically known as *upacāra*. The simplest form, typically a five-part *pūjā*, or *pañcopacāra*, conventionally entails offerings of fragrant paste (*gandha*), fresh flowers (*puṣpa*), incense (*dhūpa*), an honorific flame (*dīpa*), and an edible (*naivedya*). This is followed by an honorific exclamation, such as "Om, homage to deity *x*" (*Om x namaḥ*), and the food offering is regarded as consecrated or blessed (*prasāda*) through the process. Waving the honorific flame is a high point in the rite and is often known as *ārati* (from the Sanskrit *ārātrika*) when performed by a priest (*pūjāri*) in a temple setting.[4] Such a simple *pūjā* may be completed in a few minutes. By contrast, the Durgā Pūjā includes elaborate rites to install the goddess into a variety of different abodes as well as to dismiss her. And the rites of veneration are also extensive. The *pūjā* spans several days and mirrors royal consecration rituals. Such elaborate *pūjās* are not exclusive to Durgā worship. There are complex rituals to worship the great gods Śiva and Viṣṇu, although these tend to occur within temple settings.[5] While anyone may perform the simple type of five-part *pūjā* described above, complex rites require that the ritualist has received appropriate initiation. In fact, initiation enabling a ritual specialist (*purohita*) to perform a Tantric Śākta *pūjā*, such as the Bengali style of Durgā Pūjā, requires that one already has initiated capacities to perform both Vaiṣṇava and Śaiva rites. The Tantric Śākta *purohita* is a ritualist par excellence.

Before proceeding to our analysis, it is useful to briefly examine a typology of *pūjās* and an abbreviated overview of the Durgā Pūjā's main components. Obligatory (*nitya*) *pūjās* stand in contrast to optional (*kāmya*) *pūjās*, which are often undertaken to satisfy some desire or to attain some personal favor. For instance, the daily rites of purification for a Brahmin priest are classified as *nitya*. The so-called morning or evening *āratis* at temples could be classified as *nitya*. Occasional (*naimittika*) *pūjās* are those that occur when the situation arises and typically refer to festival (*utsava*) *pūjās*. The Durgā Pūjā may therefore the categorized as a *naimittika pūjā*. This is also because it is not obligatory. Families may or may not choose to celebrate it in any given year. Evidently, there may be substantial overlap among these categories. For instance, the Durgā Pūjā may be commissioned by a patron in order to obtain some special power or for a specific goal. As such it would be a *kāmya* rite. However, of course it also entails several obligatory rites of purification that the ritualists must undertake to cleanse themselves and the offerings, disperse pernicious forces, sanctify the ritual space, and so on. The goal of a *kāmya pūjā* may be made explicit in the declaration of intention, or *saṅkalpa*, recited by the priest at the start of most rituals conducted on behalf of a patron. However, such a desire-driven rite resonates more with the transactional attitudes we associate with ancient Vedic *yajñas* than with rituals deriving from devotion. In the proper spirit of *bhakti*, the fruit (*phala*) of the ritual arguably should be offered back to the deity. Such a *pūjā* would then be regarded as *niṣkāmya*, or "without attachment" to the fruits of the ritual.

The Durgā Pūjā superbly illustrates the complexities in ritual analysis alluded to in our brief theoretical introduction. A narrow analysis would focus exclusively on the activities of the priest and the patron. However, even when it is celebrated within a domestic milieu (and these are disappearing as costs and logistics expand), the rite has a collective religious and festive reality. At the very least, the patron's extended family members are participants in the rite. More often than not, members of the local community, friends, and so on also show up to participate in segments of the rite. For some, there may be purely devotional fervor, an opportunity for *bhakti* to the Devī. However, for others, the *purohita*'s ministrations to bring the Devī into a variety of accessible, embodied forms is an opportunity to encounter Durgā, their Cosmic Mother or Divine Sovereign, and often to plead for some sort of blessing, favor, or empowerment. For most worshippers at the Pūjā, beyond the patron, the most important days of the Durgā Pūjā occur toward the end of Navarātri's nine days, on the so-called Great Seventh (*mahāsaptamī*), Great Eighth (*mahāṣṭamī*), and Great Ninth (*mahānavamī*). Of course, preparations for the ritual have begun months in advance with the purchase of food and other items for offerings by the patron and his family, the commissioning and building of the clay image, and so on. Songs to invite the Devī begin on the first day of Navarātri, and the *purohita* typically begins the process of invoking and establishing the goddess from a wood-apple (*bilva*) tree branch into an earthen jar as early as the sixth day. The Devī will subsequently be established in a cluster of nine plants (*navapattrikā*); an unbaked, anthropomorphic clay image; a cosmograph; and even a prepubescent girl (*kumārī, kanyā*). The worship rites are extensive, with lengthy baths and at minimum a sixteen-part set of offerings (*ṣoḍaśopacāra*). However, even more offerings may be made, such as of cooked food (*bhoga*). The Durgā Pūjā generally includes a blood sacrifice (or substitute), known as *balidāna*, offered to the goddess. At the end of the nine days, the goddess is dismissed from her abodes, which are carried in procession on the tenth day with great fanfare for immersion in a body of water. Detailed descriptions of the Durgā Pūjā procedures are found in Ghosha (1871) and Rodrigues (2003), and a summary treatment is provided in Rodrigues (2018).

Communal Revitalization

In this paper, I wish to point to how the Durgā Pūjā functions as a ritual of revitalization, renewal, and transformation at communal, personal, and cosmic levels. This is not to say that features such as transformation are the Pūjā's only function. Contrasting with the notion of transformation, the Durgā Pūjā functions to provide not change but a sense of social stability through its annual celebration. This is a long-standing and widely held perspective on ritual, articulated as early as by Émile Durkheim ([1915] 1965), who theorized on the socially unifying function of religious activities. The collection of papers on the Devī-centered Dasain festival in Nepal edited by Krauskopff and Lecomte-Tilouine (1996) offers many examples of the so-called social solidarity thesis. The papers most notably demonstrate how the ritual activities during Dasain—Nepal's Durgā Pūjā, if the term is understood in its broadest meaning—have been patronized by various royal dynasties (Malla and Shah) in order to unify the country of Nepal.[6] Zotter (2016a) explores how this dynamic is being negotiated in the context of the secular state after Nepal abolished its monarchy in 2006.[7]

Victor Turner's (1969) influential theory of the ritual process as a movement from social structure through the transitional period of antistructure to its return to structure, which added nuance to the social solidarity thesis, is also applicable to the Durgā Pūjā. Festival periods could arguably be regarded as periods of antistructure because they cordon off from their mundane dimensions a sacralized time and space, within which the festival celebrations may occur. The joyful exuberance of the festivities, marked by feasting, dancing, musical performances, creative design, and so on, which will be discussed in some detail later, are illustrative of the license granted by antistructure. Within the shared experience of the state of antistructure, the spirit of what Turner called *communitas* cannot be sustained for long and typically serves as a portal that ushers participants back to their structured social milieus, but with a transformation in their statuses. Indeed, Navarātri is a festival period that offers an orchestrated and limited period of antistructure in order to establish norms, affirm hierarchies, and so on. However, these, too, may be understood as a revitalization of a stagnating status quo. In this respect there are significant transformations that occur on various fronts, some of which will be outlined in this chapter. Thus, in tandem with the complex functions of the Durgā Pūjā to preserve social structure, forge a link with tradition, unify people, and so on, the dynamics of social and communal renewal are evidently also especially strong, particularly in the outer, public manifestations of the rite.

Textual references, such as verse 12.11 in the *Devīmāhātmya* (*Glorification of the Goddess*) of the *Mārkaṇḍeya Purāṇa*, offer solid evidence that the ritual worship of the Devī in the autumn was well established by the ninth century CE, and probably much earlier. Bihani Sarkar (2017) examines the development of the royal worship of the Devī as Durgā from the third to the twelfth century CE. Ritual manuals (*paddhati*), Dharmaśāstra digests (*nibandha*), and other texts testify to the continued worship of the goddess in various ways. Sarkar (2012) has also traced the historical layering of some of these rites from prescriptions in the Smārta Brahmin *nibandhas* dating from the twelfth century onward. Traveler accounts, such as by the Italian Nicolo de Conti, describe grand celebrations by the South Indian Vijayanagara kings in the fifteenth and sixteenth centuries, a tradition that has continued to the present within what was once their feudatory state of Mysore, ruled by the Woḍeyars.[8] What forms the autumn celebration of Devī worship took in northeastern India during the Vijayanagara period is unclear, but the distinctive style that we associate with the current Bengali Durgā Pūjā appears to have arisen in that region as Mughal influence began to decline. In the late sixteenth or early seventeenth century, powerful landlords (*zamindār*) initiated elaborate Durgā Pūjās, perhaps to serve as more public expressions of a faith that had previously been repressed. A century later, some of these had grown into flamboyant celebrations to testify to their wealth and princely status. In both cases, the Durgā Pūjā functioned as a locus for the revival of Hinduism in the public arena after centuries of marginalization under non-Hindu rulership. However, when these princely houses again began to lose their power under British rule, the late eighteenth century saw the origin of the so-called Barowari Pūjās, named after the group of twelve friends (*baro-yari*) who collectively sponsored the rite. This marked the beginning of the development of public (*sarvajānīna*) *pūjās*, which are multiplying throughout the Hindu world, particularly where there are substantially sized Bengali communities, which spearhead the ritual style.[9]

These *sarvajānīna pūjās* are especially vivid examples of communal revitalization. They are no longer conducted exclusively in the Tantric style and may follow more conventional forms of orthodox *śākta pūjās*. However, in my casual conversations, I have often heard devotees familiar with the ritual expertise required for an initiated Tantric *purohita* being dismissive of the relatively amateurish activities and training of the priests who preside at many of the public, community *pūjās*. Traditional Bengali styles of clay image clusters include the triad of Durgā, her lion, and the buffalo demon, Mahiṣa, along with the attendant deities Sarasvatī, Lakṣmī, Kārttikeya, and Gaṇeśa crafted into a single tableau, known as the *kaṭhamo*. Figure 1.1 depicts such a tableau, which was built by artisans for the home of Manindra Lahiri in Banāras, where I conducted a close study of the Durgā Pūjā in 1990 and 1991. However, nontraditional styles of depicting the attendant deities separately along with the central triad are now found wherever the Durgā Pūjā is celebrated, including within Bengali milieus. In fact, highly creative, artistic depictions of these images

Figure 1.1. A traditional Bengali-styled image cluster, with the triad of Durgā, her lion mount, and the buffalo demon Mahiṣa flanked by attendant deities and situated in a single tableau (*kaṭhamo*), stands completed in the nearby workshop where it was commissioned by the patron Mr. Manindra Mohan Lahiri (Bengali Tola quarter, Banāras, 1991). Photo by author.

and the temporary shrines (*paṇḍal*) that enclose them are now the norm in the larger venues.

The *sarvajānīna pūjās* may be sponsored by businesses or public service groups, staged by religious organizations, and so on. However, the vast majority are staged by neighborhood communities. It is often young Hindu men in a community who form an ad hoc Durgā Pūjā club and spend months preparing for and mounting the ritual celebration. The club members face several challenges, certain complexities of which are great for fledgling organizations. Without an established donor base, Durgā Pūjā club members need to go door to door soliciting donations from their community. They must find an artisanal workshop and commission the construction of the unbaked clay images. There will have to be regular visits to the workshop to check on the progress of these images, which will form the centerpiece of the Pūjā. They need to ensure that the space where the Pūjā will be held (*pūjālaya*) is available and that the appropriate permits are obtained. Quite importantly, a ritualist with the appropriate abilities must also be commissioned to conduct the rite. As the popularity of these public celebrations grows, so do the complexities in securing what is needed. In Banāras, for instance, where there is an excellent representative combination of Bengali and non-Bengali *pūjās*, there is a growing shortage of spaces in which to erect the temporary shrines (*paṇḍal*) to stage the ritual. The city has been limiting the number of permits that it issues, although that has not stopped the staging of dozens of illegal *pūjās*. In 1990, there were about two hundred licenses granted in Banāras, but I knew of several *paṇḍals* operating without permits just within my circuit of observations. The numbers of both legal and unauthorized *paṇḍals* have grown substantially in the last decades. Naturally, the artisan workshops are surfeited with work, and, most importantly, competent ritualists are also in progressively higher demand. In the Bengali communities, the food offerings must ideally be prepared by an initiated woman, but these, too, are harder to find.

As the days of the Pūjā approach, club members must arrange for the erection of the *paṇḍal* and for transportation to move the images (*mūrti*) from the workshops to the places of worship. Extreme care must be taken when moving the unbaked clay *mūrtis*, since any damage would render them useless. The *purohita* would not establish a deity within a damaged image. During the Pūjā, it is crucial to manage the crowds and ensure the smooth functioning of the ritual activities. Care must be taken that the *paṇḍal* is kept safe from vandalism, for instance. Finally, when the Pūjā concludes, there are the duties to transport the images to a body of water for immersion. Due to mounting concerns about river pollution as the number of *pūjās* increases, cities have now placed restrictions on what is to be immersed and where such immersions can take place. A few years ago, in an effort to diminish river pollution, manage crowds, and diminish accidents, immersion in the Gaṅgā was prohibited in Banāras. It is now restricted to some natural ponds and two artificially created tanks (*kuṇḍa*). For the same reasons, state and municipal governments throughout India now dig thousands of ponds for immersion rites in rural communities.

This summary account of some of the tasks and responsibilities of the Durgā Pūjā clubs partly ameliorates the typical accusations occasionally lodged at their members: that the boys squander much of the money they collect on drunken revelry. It is true that some liquor and revelry may accompany the organizational meetings of the young men, as well as their after-parties for a *pūjā* well accomplished, particularly during the immersion (*visarjana*) festivities. However, for the most part, their communities are forgiving and pleased if the clubs have managed to stage an impressive celebration. The pride and sense of accomplishment is evident in figure 1.2, which captures the mood of many of the members of the Durgā Sporting Club, which set up their *paṇḍal* close to the Durgā Kuṇḍ temple in Banāras. For two successive years, in 1990 and 1991, I was able

Figure 1.2. The Durgā Sporting Club members, mostly young men, take pleasure in their successful staging of the unbaked clay images (*mūrti*) at the temporary shrine (*paṇḍal*) erected for their community's Durgā Pūjā celebration (Durgā Kuṇḍ quarter, Banāras, 1991). Photo by author.

to follow the club's activities closely—their challenges, setbacks, and successes—because the sons of my research assistant, Om Prakash Sharma, were active members of the group. Their trials were fairly typical of a relatively new community *paṇḍal* group, and although they now have decades of experience under their belt they face new challenges, such as maintaining and expanding their donor base, securing more funds to keep up with rising economic costs, and striving to improve upon the previous year's display.

Navarātri is one of the largest festivals in the annual religious cycle for Hindus and functions economically akin to the way Christmas does in Christian-dominated societies. The economic impact on the community is marked. There is a substantial redistribution of wealth during Durgā Pūjā. Priests and artisans earn a good portion of their annual income servicing the needs of their communities at this time of year. Merchants profit because people buy food, fine clothes (both to wear and as gifts), ritual implements, and so on. The young men in the *pūjā* clubs, some often unemployed, have found work, learned organizational and management skills, and enhanced their status within their neighborhoods. The communities themselves feel proud when people from adjacent neighborhoods or further afield come to look at their displays. The aura of friendly competition makes them want to do better with each passing year. Neighborhoods are united with feelings of solidarity, because the community *pūjās* are like giant block parties, bringing people together and offering them a venue for social interaction.

In Bengali households, Navarātri is also a time when married daughters traditionally return to their paternal homes; they typically reunite during the climactic final days of the Durgā Pūjā. Thus, the ritual functions as an opportunity for the reestablishment of family bonds. When a daughter marries, she typically leaves home to live with her husband's family. During Durgā Pūjā the returning married daughters may bring their husbands and children with them, allowing these to forge relationships with their in-laws. From family reunions to neighborhood solidarity, the Durgā Pūjā works to bring people together and to establish or reestablish bonds. Money circulates, stimulating the economy. Artistic creativity is valued and on display. Music, dance, and other cultural performances are widespread, and people seize the opportunity to dress in their finest, feast, and revel. The Durgā Pūjā has an unmistakable socioeconomic impact on the communities where it is staged. It clearly revitalizes families and neighborhoods while renewing people's confidence in their abilities, talents, work, livelihoods, and accomplishments.

Of the four goals that are valued in Hinduism, academic studies on *dharma* (righteousness) and *mokṣa* (liberation) far surpass those on *kāma* (pleasure) and *artha* (accomplishment). The latter tend to get relegated to discussions of the *Kāmasūtra* and the *Arthaśāstra*, respectively. Unfortunately, the key role played by festival traditions (*utsava*) in serving the attainment of these latter two goals is generally ignored. In some measure, this may be because *kāma* and *artha* are regarded as the worldly pursuits of the householder and thus are less valued than the other two, more spiritually oriented objectives. However, this is clearly myopic, because festivals are enormously important in the fabric of Hindu life, and the Durgā Pūjā is among the most exuberant of these. It is little wonder, then, that the Durgā Pūjā was embraced by royalty, for it provided an opportunity for rulers to display their power and largesse through the grandeur of their celebrations. In those celebrations, the rituals of worship ran alongside performances by dancing girls and recitals of classical music. Durgā worship, especially, in contrast with *pūjās* to other deities, offered an intersection between *kāma* and *artha,* in that the Devī was intimately connected with sovereign power and authority. Performance, accomplishment, attainment, wealth, and power are all dimensions of *artha.* And the sexually charged celebrations during the immersion (*visarjana*) rites in the style of the Śabarotsava, which the *Kālikā Purāṇa* (1891, 61.21–22) firmly extols, are clear indications of the *kāma*-oriented dimensions of the Durgā Pūjā. Although such explicit expressions of power and pleasure are attenuated in modern celebrations, the implicit thrust of the rite has not changed. The Durgā Pūjā celebrates social life in the world and stands in contrast to a world-denying renunciation. As such, it reinvigorates the social order, renewing and revitalizing it with each annual celebration.

It would, of course, be inaccurate to assert that the goals pursued by renunciation are utterly absent from Durgā Pūjā celebrations. This is because the Devī is regarded as a granter of both worldly wishes and spiritual attainments. In the *Devīmāhātmya*'s frame tale, after rigorous worship, a king named Suratha, disenfranchised from power, and a merchant named Samādhi, who has been similarly set upon, are eventually granted boons by the Devī. Suratha chooses sovereign power, while Samādhi chooses the transcendental understanding that leads to perfect attainment (*saṃsiddhi*). This myth reinforces the goddess's reputation as the bestower of both worldly desires and spiritual liberation (*mokṣa*). Even though the Devī's boon of spiritual attainment is not linked to renunciation, monastic organizations in Banāras (e.g., the Ramakrishna Mission, the Shree Shree Anandamayee Sangha, and the Bharat Sevashram Sangha) are avid actors in Durgā Pūjā celebrations. In the case of the Shree Shree Anandamanyee Sangha, which stages a Bengali-styled Durgā Pūjā during both the spring and autumn Navarātras, there is a tacit identification drawn between the goddess and the female saint Ānandamayī Mā. The

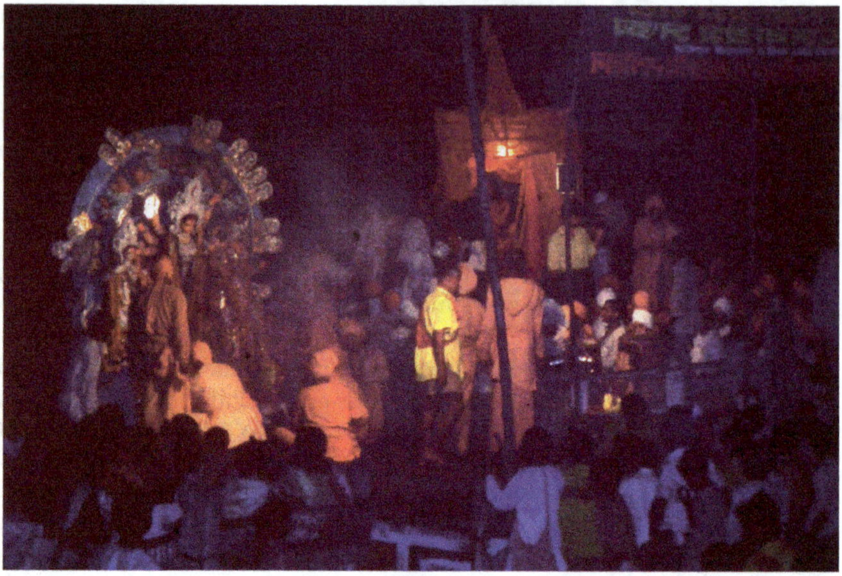

Figure 1.3. Immediately prior to the immersion of the Durgā Pūjā images, ochre-clad members of the Bharat Sevashram Sangha, a spiritual brotherhood of monks, perform an elaborate enactment of myths from the *Devīmāhātmya*, most notably Durgā's defeat of the buffalo demon Mahiṣa (Gaṅgā riverbank, Banāras, 1990). Photo by author.

Bharat Sevashram Sangha stages an elaborate spectacle immediately prior to the immersion of the image cluster into the river Gaṅgā at the end of the Durgā Pūjā. As figure 1.3 illustrates, amid a throng of onlookers, the *Devīmāhātmya* is recited, and saffron-clad monks enact scenes from the text in which the Devī defeats a variety of demons, most notably the buffalo demon Mahiṣa.

Personal Empowerment and Transformation

While the social, economic, and political dimensions of Durgā Pūjā celebrations are prominent to most observers, it is short-sighted to ignore the ways in which the ritual touches individuals. After all, each person experiences the Pūjā uniquely. The Devī is thought to be always available in her temples and other abodes or seats (*pīṭha*), but clearly the Navarātris provide distinct windows of sacred time in which she is especially accessible. A mythic tale recounts how the warrior prince Rāma, an *avatāra* of the great god Viṣṇu, awakened Devī from her slumber to solicit her aid in defeating the demon Rāvaṇa.[10] Indeed, the autumn Navarātri falls during a most turbulent time of the year, when disease and death are believed to be rampant. Rāma's untimely awakening (*akālabodhana*) of the goddess and his worship of her is often cited as the ancient precedent for the autumn Durgā Pūjā. Hence the Durgā Pūjā circumscribes time and space in a distinctive way, creating a sacred window of opportunity for personal renewal and empowerment.

The Durgā Pūjā is often regarded as the Kali Yuga's equivalent of the Vedic *aśvamedha* ritual, which has themes of sovereign empowerment.[11] Doubtless, the pageantry of parades and animal sacrifices might misdirect one's attention away from the personal empowerment that often underscored the intent of the ritual's royal patrons, particularly in days of yore. However, the autumn Durgā Pūjā is celebrated near the end of the rainy season, inaugurating the traditional period of warfare. The goddess was not only worshipped to empower soldiers, armies, and their weapons against their enemies. To embolden a kingdom's subjects to embark on a military campaign, the Devī must first appear to commit her support for the individual sovereign. In versions of the myth of Rāma's worship of the goddess, as testament to his devotion, the exiled prince is willing to tear out one of his lotus-like eyes to substitute for a missing flower in the offering of 108 blue lotuses. This is a model for individual piety and commitment on the part of the king, who must not only convey to his people his magnanimity and largesse but also be seen as having a special relationship with the goddess, or as having secured her personal favor. Only then is the kingdom likely to have hope for its future prosperity, and, more importantly, only then might his armies be willing to follow him into battle. Although such sovereign dimensions have begun to vanish as monarchies yield to democratic governance, the symbolic thrust of such empowerment has been picked up by politicians.[12] And beyond the personal empowerment sought by leaders, individuals, too, seek such boons from the goddess for much more mundane ends, such as to find spouses, pass exams, or have children or well-paying jobs. Just as Rāma had to prove his devotion, devotees need to do the same, because, if gratified, the Devī is widely regarded as certain to reward them with her beneficence.[13]

Although one cannot provide an account of the countless ways in which each and every worshipper may engage with the Devī during the Durgā Pūjā, there are a few general ritual activities that highlight personal objectives and orientations. Besides contributing to community *pūjā* celebrations, families or individuals may sometimes establish the Devī within their own homes. This is most often done by invoking the goddess into a wide-mouthed, narrow-necked, wide-bodied jar, topped with a coconut. The jar is filled with water, its neck adorned with leafed twigs, and it is set upon a small earthen altar, a few inches high. The jar is draped with a red scarf, and grain is often sown into the earthen altar. The jar form of the goddess resembles a sārī-shrouded squatting woman. This jar effigy of the goddess becomes the locus of devotional worship throughout the nine days of Navarātri. The Brahmin ritualists who perform the Durgā Pūjā routinely establish such a jar in their own homes and render it regular worship. However, the capacity for anyone to invoke the Devī into the jar effigy in their own home, where she may be venerated, is enormously empowering. It undercuts the indispensable role of male Brahmin officiants in orthodox rites of worship. Figure 1.4 depicts the wife of the healer Mithai Lal, who had taken over her recently deceased husband's healing practice, establishing a jar in her home shrine room. Mithai Lal's empowerment to divine the cause of his clients' ailments and heal them through his devotion to and possession by the Devī are visually documented in Robert Gardner and Ákos Östör's (1985) classic film *Forest of Bliss* and discussed in some detail in Östör's (1994) essay on the film. The Devī is capable of manifesting anywhere she is invoked by anyone seeking her presence, and even a woman may bring this about.

Figure 1.4. The wife of Mithai Lal, a recently deceased renowned healer, seeks to enhance her own healing empowerment by establishing the Devī in her home shrine in a wide-bodied jar topped with a coconut and draped with a red scarf (Banāras, 1990). Photo by author.

Besides rendering the standard array of offerings to the jar effigy, it is also common for votaries to recite the *Devīmāhātmya* out loud, or to commission someone to do the ritual recitation on their behalf. This is because even merely listening to the text is said to confer blessings. The *Devīmāhātmya* is therefore used in a wide variety of ways. Individuals or groups may commission groups of priests, skilled in Sanskrit, to perform multiple recitations of the text. This may be done in conjunction with offerings into a fire altar, mimicking a Vedic fire sacrifice, or *yajña*. Alternately, specific verses from the text may be selected for specific ends, such as to eliminate illness or for safe travels. These select verses are then recited repeatedly, enveloping (*sampuṭa*) or sandwiching each of the seven hundred verses of the *Devīmāhātmya*. Thus, during Navarātri in North India it is common to see and hear countless numbers of persons in temples and homes engaged in a myriad assortment of ritual recitations.[14] Figure 1.5 depicts ritualists that have been commissioned performing such recitations of the *Devīmāhātmya* for their patrons or themselves at the Durgā Kuṇḍ temple in Banāras.

It is quite clear that a sizeable number of these recitations are not done simply out of pure, loving devotion (*bhakti*) but in order to secure the grace of and thereby a sought-after boon from the goddess. The Devī is especially well-known as a granter of wishes, and this characteristic is

Figure 1.5. On the premises of a goddess temple, ritualists recite the *Devīmāhātmya* (*Glorification of the Goddess*), a revered Sanskrit scripture, as part of their own worship rites or on behalf of patrons who have commissioned them (Durgā Kuṇḍ temple, Banāras, 2003). Photo by author.

what distinguishes rites of worship during Navarātri from more typical devotional worship. In the *Devīmāhātmya* story mentioned earlier (verses 13.11–17), the king Suratha and merchant Samādhi worship the Devī intensely for several years with an earthen image and offerings of their own blood. As a *kṣatriya* and *vaiśya,* respectively, Suratha and Samādhi model the capacities for individuals from those social classes (*varṇa*) to invoke and worship the goddess without the mediation of a *brāhmaṇa* ritualist. They are then graced with a vision, and the Devī grants them their wishes. Following such scriptural models, individuals recite, meditate, fast, perform night-long vigils, and engage in all manner of austerities in order to obtain the Devī's grace. While these practices are not intrinsic to the Durgā Pūjā per se, they most certainly may be part of the practices of priests and certain family members who perform or commission the Durgā Pūjā. They are within the orbit of the Durgā Pūjā, if the term is expanded to encompass ancillary practices. This is why the term is often used synonymously with Navarātri, although Navarātri is more evocative of the festival period of sacred time, while Durgā Pūjā elicits a greater sense of the ritual-worship complex during that period.

One other clear instance of personal revitalization and transformation that takes place within the context of the Durgā Pūjā is evident in the *purohita*'s ritual activities, especially so in the Bengali style, which has Tantric underpinnings. In order to install the goddess into the various abodes where she will be worshipped, such as the earthen jar, the cluster of nine plants, the earthen image, and so on, the *purohita* must first perform a ritual bodily cleansing, which is part of the standard preparatory actions in Tantric worship. This is known as the *bhūta śuddhi*—literally, a cleansing of the constituent elements. Performing *prāṇāyāma,* or control of the vital energy, in tandem with *kuṇḍalinī* yoga, the ritualist purifies all the physical and mental components of his body.[15] Figure 1.6 depicts the master ritualist Pandit Nitai Bhattacharya engaged in the *prāṇāyāma* portion of the *bhūta śuddhi* in the context of the Durgā Pūjā. With the aid of sacred verses (*mantra*) and gestures (*mudrā*), and a complex series of imprints (*nyāsa*), he putatively transforms his body into a vibrational body of sound. Thereupon, through a meditative visualization verse (*dhyāna śloka*), he ostensibly transforms himself into the goddess, or allows his own body to serve as the Devī's temporary abode. After rendering her mental worship in this abode, he finally transfers her to the locales where she will be established, such as the earthen image.[16] Although this procedure is typical in most Tantric rituals to invoke and establish a deity for the purpose of worship, and not exclusively performed in the context of the Durgā Pūjā, the high profile of the Durgā Pūjā and the large number of forms in which the Devī is established and worshipped mean that the *purohita* engages in a marathon performance of self-purifications, meditative

Figure 1.6. Pandit Nitai Bhattacharya, a highly skilled, initiated priest (*purohita*), performs *prāṇāyāma* (regulation of the breath), in tandem with *kuṇḍalinī* yoga, as part of the *bhūta śuddhi* rite, intended to purify the constituent elements of a ritualist's body-mind complex (Lahiri home, Banāras, 1991). Photo by author.

visualizations, and divine embodiments. There can be little doubt that the Durgā Pūjā stands as one of his greatest priestly challenges of the year and leaves the ritualist profoundly empowered when it is completed. In casual conversations with votaries, I have heard many attribute all sorts of supernormal attainments, such as weather prediction or extraordinarily long periods of wakefulness, to Tantric *purohitas* who are skilled in performing the Durgā Pūjā.

Finally, apart from an opportunity for personal growth, material boons, or even fundamental spiritual transformation, the Durgā Pūjā provides a venue for simple enjoyment of the festive dimensions of eating, viewing the artistry of *paṇḍals* and *mūrti* displays, attending music and dance performances, and so on. Durgā is believed to have taken up her abode in the imagery through the *purohita*'s ministrations, and, as she promises in scriptural sources such as the *Devīmāhātmya,* she maintains her protective presence wherever she has been established. Like the visiting daughter who returns from her husband's home, each year Durgā's return revitalizes each neighborhood or home by her presence. Her embodied forms are clearly displayed to everyone. She is both daughter and mother, whose presence is plainly evident and ubiquitous during the festival period. Kinsley (1979) extensively examined the concept of *līlā* in Hinduism, typically understood as a rationale for the activity of the divine as akin to the purposeless play of children. In the Durgā Pūjā we note a differently nuanced and inadequately examined notion of *līlā,* which is centered precisely on the notion of human purposeless play. During the Navarātri festival, it is the Devī's devotees who can enter the Durgā Pūjā's ritually circumscribed arena of sacred space and time to play happily like little children under the protective gaze of their Divine Mother. In this way, they are themselves symbolically rejuvenated, "made young again."

Cosmic Renewal and Rejuvenation

Although rituals serve both personal and broader social needs, one should not forget that within Hinduism there is a long tradition of a ritual's cosmic significance. The paradigmatic symbol for all Hindu rituals, first articulated in Vedic literature, is sacrifice (*yajña*). The world and all within it are created through the sacrifice of the primordial being, Puruṣa; it is sustained through the regular performance of sacrifice and comes to an end in the final sacrificial immolation (*antyeṣṭi*), which is one's own cremation upon death. The Durgā Pūjā evokes these Vedic sacrificial themes very explicitly in that the *homa,* or fire sacrifice, is a crucial rite on the ninth day of Navarātri. On that day, Mahānavamī (Great Ninth), there are hundreds of *homas* of the type depicted in figure 1.7, which is being

Figure 1.7. On Mahānavamī (Great Ninth), the final day of Navarātri, the priest (*pūjārī*) presides over a fire ritual (*homa*) with members of the Durgā Sporting Club, which has staged the Durgā Pūjā for the local community (Durgā Kuṇḍ quarter, Banāras, 1991). Photo by author.

performed by members of the Durgā Sporting Club, occurring in Banāras alone. Moreover, the Pūjā is also centered on an actual blood sacrifice (*bali*) or a symbolic substitute, particularly at the climactic juncture of the eighth and ninth day during the Sandhi Pūjā. The widespread popularity of the Durgā Pūjā ensures that sacrifice is enacted on an unimaginably large scale throughout the Hindu world.[17]

There are other symbolic layers in the Durgā Pūjā that elicit themes of cosmic rejuvenation. The *kalaśa*, the wide-bodied jar in which the goddess is first established, resembles a woman, or, more appropriately, a squatting pregnant woman. It symbolically evokes the notion of the Earth Mother or a cosmic egg, from which the creation will emerge. The *bilva*-tree branch, which together with eight other plants constitutes the *navapattrikā*, another form of the Devī, embodies themes of vegetative growth and abundance. The earthen altar on which the jar form is established is often seeded with grain, which sprouts during the nine days of the Navarātri, again eliciting the themes of fertility and new beginnings. The *navapattrikā* is clothed in a sārī and said by many worshippers to represent a newly married wife, the *kala bau*. In the anthropomorphic clay image, Durgā is represented as the unmarried, voluptuous warrior woman, and in the *kanyā* she is worshipped as a prepubescent girl. We see a vector of forms over each day of the Pūjā that is an inversion of a female's development from girlhood to motherhood. Durgā is worshipped progressively in forms from the pregnant, earthen Cosmic Mother; to the fertile, vegetative married wife; to the unmarried but alluring earthen warrior goddess; and finally to the fresh and pure divine princess, the *kumārī*, unsullied by the ritual pollution of menstruation, sexual union, and childbirth.

This symbolic vector is unequivocally a rejuvenation of the feminine principle. In such symbols of the feminine during the Durgā Pūjā, the goddess, who represents nothing less than the cosmos and all within it, undergoes a transformation and revitalization. Lest anyone doubt that the Devī is indeed the entire creation, she is explicitly represented as such in the Sarvatobhadra Maṇḍala, a cosmograph of all-encompassing auspiciousness, which contains all the goddesses and gods. While people may grow old and accrue the ritual pollution that accompanies life in the world, the goddess and her creation are perennially pure, reborn and reconstituted afresh with the celebration of the great annual festival in her honor.

Concluding Remarks

When theorizing about the study of religion, Jonathan Z. Smith (1988) and Catherine Bell (2009, 267) have observed that words such as *religion* or *ritual* are concepts that we necessarily impose upon facets of human activity to serve intellectual exploratory purposes. In support of this, it certainly would be rare for Hindu celebrants to speak about how much they anticipate the arrival of the "ritual" of Durgā Pūjā and what "religious ritual activities" they will engage in upon its arrival. They generally comment that Durgā Pūjā (or Dasain, etc.) is coming and that they are looking forward to meeting with family and friends, eating delicious food preparations, and celebrating in countless other ways. Nevertheless, when necessarily applying such terminological categories in our academic examination, we noted that Durgā Pūjā is a ritual complex par excellence within the festival of Navarātri, encapsulating most of the features that such activities entail.

Prescriptive descriptions of the Durgā Pūjā appear in a variety of Dharmaśāstra texts, which testify to the dharmic ends that the annual celebration fulfills, as ascertained by Hindu orthodoxy. We also noted that texts such as the *Devīmāhātmya* promote worship of the Devī during Navarātri as the optimal time to secure her grace, which might even include spiritual liberation (*mokṣa*). And while much has been written on the role of Durgā worship in the acquisition and maintenance of sovereignty, our focus was on aspects of the Durgā Pūjā that tend to be overlooked. These are dimensions of *artha* beyond martial success as well as the festive features of the ritual complex, which pertain to *kāma*. In other words, we can see that the celebration of Durgā Pūjā and its ancillary practices, such as scriptural recitation, service all four of the traditional *puruṣārthas*, or goals of life—namely, *dharma*, *kāma*, *artha*, and *mokṣa*.

This multivalent capacity of the Durgā Pūjā is significant because it allows us to understand why it endures, and is arguably even growing in popularity, after the ongoing demise of its patronage by royalty throughout the Hindu world. So much is written, and rightly so, of the worship of Durgā in relation to kingship that its significance to the broader populace is underexamined. The Durgā Pūjā can and does function without a king. This does not mean that it has ceded its associations with political power, for we observe that even within secular states politicians seek out the benefits of aligning themselves with the Devī. However, the exuberance and proliferation of the public (*sarvajānīna*) *pūjās* testify to its popularity among the masses. I have argued that it is insufficient to assert that the Durgā Pūjā solely functions to maintain social stability and preserve the status quo and have pointed to its roles in communal revitalization, personal empowerment and transformation, and cosmic renewal and rejuvenation. These are not hyperbolic assertions but substantiated potencies.

As we clamor for meaning within the mystery of our existence, we are drawn to activities that serve our needs in that regard. Of course, the Durgā Pūjā does function to provide material benefits to a large swath of its celebrants. It is often the most profitable time of year for ritualists, who may be commissioned to perform the *pūjā* or to conduct scriptural recitations, among other such priestly duties. It is also just as economically important for vendors of food, clothing, and ritual implements and supplies; temple priests; artisans who construct the disposable *paṇḍal* images; and so on. However, it is myopic to ignore the sustenance that it provides for other human needs. I have discussed the vital dimension of play (*līlā*) in the context of the Durgā Pūjā, which creates a window of sacred time in which everyone may play within the awakened presence of the Divine Mother. Such play includes the unification of families and communities and the enjoyment of fine food, clothing, and music, not to mention the making and witnessing of the creative exuberance of *paṇḍal* and *mūrti* designs. This joyful spirit is captured by the Sanskrit term for festival, *utsava*, which also has connotations of blossoming and beginning. This dimension of the Durgā Pūjā moves us beyond its capacity to satisfy political and economic (*artha*) needs, or even those concerned with pleasure (*kāma*). At its core, the Durgā Pūjā acts to service a deep metaphysical need—namely, to renew that which has grown old. In such symbols as the jar of plenty (*pūrṇa kalaśa*) and the virgin girl (*kanyā*), both of whom embody the manifest goddess, the Durgā Pūjā affirms that it is through the agency of the feminine principle that individuals, families, communities, kingdoms, the earth, and the cosmos itself can be and are perennially revitalized. And although each new cycle may resemble the previous ones, it reveals the creative potential for transformative change within each manifestation. That no two Durgā Pūjās are ever absolutely identical is a visible testament to the unlimited creativity of the Great Goddess.

Notes

1. Italicized foreign-language words are generally transliterated Sanskrit terms.

2. Many details of my studies of the Bengali Durgā Pūjā are found in Rodrigues (2003).

3. A more comprehensive theoretical discussion of ritual, specifically as illustrated by the Durgā Pūjā, is found in Rodrigues (2003, 303–12), especially footnotes 38–67. Excellent comprehensive treatments of ritual theory and analysis are found in Bell (2009, 1992).

4. The most comprehensive study of orthodox Hindu *pūjā* is found in Bühnemann (1988).

5. For Śaiva worship in medieval temple traditions, see, for instance, Davis (1991).

6. Among its similarities to Bengali Durgā Pūjā, Dasain, also called Mohani or Mvahni, typically begins with the establishment of a pot form (*ghaṭasthāpanā*) of

the Devī on the first day, worship of the Goddess in a cluster of plants known as the Phulpati on the seventh day, and animal sacrifices on the eighth and ninth days.

7. Zotter (2016b) argues that this decision to oust the monarchy from its central role in royal rituals is an instance of the denial of ritual.

8. See Simmons (2014) and Stein (1989, 39).

9. The development of this process is found in McDermott (2011).

10. The myth is recounted in Kṛttivāsa's Bengali *Rāmāyaṇa* but is also found in the *Bṛhaddharma Purāṇa* (1.18–22, according to Kinsley [1986, 109, 234]), the *Kālikā Purāṇa* (1891, 60.25–31), and the *Mahābhāgavata Purāṇa* (1913, 36–48).

11. See *Devī Purāṇa* 22.23 (1973). Also, Kaṃsanārāyaṇ of Tahebpur, who arguably inaugurated the first Durgā Pūjā in 1583, claimed it as a substitute for the Vedic *aśvamedha*, which would consolidate a ruler's rights over an empire (McDermott 2001, 328–29nn86–87).

12. See Moumita Sen's, Caleb Simmons's, and Uwe Skoda's contributions in this volume.

13. Durgā is well known by the epithet *Siddhidātrī* (granter of fulfillment).

14. Coburn's (1991, chap. 5) thorough discussion of the ritual recitation process deals with the limbs/appendages (*aṅga*) that are typically attached to the *Devīmāhātmya*.

15. For details on the *bhūta śuddhi*, see Rodrigues (2003, 96–99).

16. Details on the procedures for *nyāsa* are found in Rodrigues (2003, 98–110), and the invocation of Durgā into the earthen image in Rodrigues (2003, 162–69).

17. For the magnitude of buffalo sacrifice in Nepal, see Astrid Zotter's contribution in this volume.

References

Bell, Catherine. 1992. *Ritual Theory, Ritual Practice*. New York: Oxford University Press.

———. 2009. *Ritual: Perspectives and Dimensions*. With a new foreword by Reza Aslan. New York: Oxford University Press. First published 1997.

Bühnemann, Gudrun. 1988. *Pūjā: A Study in Smārta Ritual*. Vienna: Institut für Indologie der Universität Wien.

Coburn, Thomas B. 1991. *Encountering the Goddess: A Translation of the Devī-Māhātmya and a Study of Its Interpretation*. Albany: State University of New York Press.

Davis, Richard. 1991. *Ritual in an Oscillating Universe*. Princeton: Princeton University Press.

Devīmāhātmya (śrī-durgā-saptaśatī). n.d. Gorakhpur, India: Gita Press.

Devī Purāṇa. 1973. Edited by Pushpendra Kumar Sharma. New Delhi: Kendriya Sanskrit Vidyapeeth.

Durkheim, Émile. (1915) 1965. *The Elementary Forms of the Religious Life*. Translated by Joseph Ward Swain. Reprint, New York: Free Press.

Gardner, Robert, and Ákos Östör, producers. 1985. *Forest of Bliss*. New York: Arthur Cantor Films. 16 mm, color, 90 min.

Ghosha, Pratapchandra. 1871. *Durga Puja: With Notes and Illustrations*. Calcutta: Hindu Patriot Press.

Kālikā Purāṇa. 1891. Bombay: Veṅkaṭeśvara Press.

Kinsley, David R. 1979. *The Divine Player: A Study of Kṛṣṇa Līlā*. Delhi: Motilal Banarsidass.

———. 1986. *Hindu Goddesses: Visions of the Divine Feminine in the Hindu Religious Tradition*. Berkeley: University of California Press.

Krauskopff, Gisèle, and Marie Lecomte-Tilouine, eds. 1996. *Célébrer le pouvoir: Dasaĩ, une fête royale au Népal*. Paris: CNRS Éditions de la Maison des sciences de l'homme.

Mahābhāgavata Purāṇa. 1913. Bombay: Manilal Itcharam Desai.

Mārkaṇḍeya Purāṇa (śrīmanmārkaṇḍeyapurāṇam). 1910. Bombay: Venkateśvara Press.

McDermott, Rachel Fell. 2001. *Mother of My Heart, Daughter of My Dreams: Kālī and Umā in the Devotional Poetry of Bengal*. New York: Oxford University Press.

———. 2011. *Revelry, Rivalry, and Longing for the Goddesses of Bengal: The Fortunes of Hindu Festivals*. New York: Columbia University Press.

Östör, Ákos. 1994. "Forest of Bliss: Film and Anthropology." *East-West Film Journal* 8 (2): 70–104.

Rodrigues, Hillary. 2003. *Ritual Worship of the Great Goddess: The Liturgy of the Durgā Pūjā with Interpretations*. Albany: State University of New York Press.

———. 2018. "Bengali Durgā Pūjā: Procedures and Symbolism." In *Nine Nights of the Goddess: The Navarātri Festival in South Asia*, edited by Caleb Simmons, Moumita Sen, and Hillary Rodrigues, 197–204. Albany: State University of New York Press.

Sarkar, Bihani. 2012. "The Rite of Durgā in Medieval Bengal: An Introductory Study of Raghunandana's Durgāpūjātattva with Text and Translations of the Principal Rites." *Journal of the Royal Asiatic Society* 22 (2): 325–90.

———. 2017. *Heroic Shāktism: The Cult of Durgā in Ancient Indian Kingship*. Oxford: Oxford University Press.

Simmons, Caleb. 2014. "The Goddess and Vaiṣṇavism in Search for Regional Supremacy: Woḍeyar Devotional Traditions during the Reign of Rāja Woḍeyar (1578–1617 CE)." *Indian History* 1:27–46.

Smith, Jonathan Z. 1988. " 'Religion' and 'Religious Studies': No Difference at All." *Soundings: An Interdisciplinary Journal* 71:231–44.

Stein, Burton. 1989. *The New Cambridge History of India: Vijayanagara*. Cambridge: Cambridge University Press.

Turner, Victor W. 1969. *The Ritual Process: Structure and Anti-structure*. Chicago: Aldine.

Zotter, Astrid. 2016a. "State Rituals in a Secular State? Replacing the Nepalese King in the Pacali Bhairava Sword Procession and Other Rituals." In *Religion, Secularism, and Ethnicity in Contemporary Nepal*, edited by David N. Gellner, Sondra L. Hausner, and Chiara Letizia, 265–301. New Delhi: Oxford University Press.

———. 2016b. "The Making and Unmaking of Rulers: On Denial of Ritual in Nepal." In *The Ambivalence of Denial: Danger and Appeal of Rituals*, edited by Ute Hüsken and Udo Simon, 221–56. Wiesbaden, Germany: Harrassowitz Verlag.

2

Straddling the Sacred and the Secular

Presence and Absence of the Goddess in Contemporary *Garbo*, the Navarātri Dance of Gujarat

NEELIMA SHUKLA-BHATT

Introduction

Garbo (plural *garbā*),[1] the worship dance performed by Hindu women of Gujarat around a festival image of the Great Goddess at night during *Navarātri*, has long been known as a distinctive tradition of the region. It was recognized as a significant component of Gujarat's culture also by the British colonial officials and scholars who worked in the region in the nineteenth and early twentieth centuries. Alexander K. Forbes ([1856] 1878, 613–14) took note of it in his *Rās Mālā*, as did Reginald E. Enthoven (1914, 72) in his *Folklore Notes: Vol. 1—Gujarat*. Gujarati scholars have explored the dance's historical links with myths of various Hindu divinities and Tantra-based practices (Pathak and Panchal 1954; Jani 1978). Feminist scholars have discussed it as an embodied self-expression and celebration of femininity in association with the goddess (Hazrat 1981; Shukla-Bhatt 2016). Literary evidence indicates that *garbo* has prevailed in Gujarat as a popular worship ritual performed without priestly presence since at least the seventeenth century and has formed the region's cherished Navarātri tradition. It continues to be performed today as a form of worship.[2] For the entire duration of Navarātri, Gujarati and English newspapers and journals are full of articles highlighting the religious aspects of the dance and reports of performances in temple courtyards and neighborhood communities (see figure 2.1).[3]

Along with the traditional context of devotion, however, new contexts for *garbā* performances have also emerged in contemporary celebrations of Navarātri in Gujarat. In some of these new contexts, the dance's devotional meaning is tangential at best. *Garbā* performances in these contexts are linked to the expansion of the market economy and reflect changing social norms that have layered and often paradoxical cultural, economic, and political implications. The most notable new context is that of professionally organized *garbā* that have little or no ritual relevance but have clearly recognizable business dimensions. The business aspects of professionally organized *garbā* have been sharply critiqued by scholars and feminist groups. Yet, by and large, people still view them as valid components of Navarātri celebrations. Another context is that of neighborhood-organized *garbā*. Following the increasing fascination with professional singing or recorded music and venue decorations in professionally organized *garbā*, leaders in many urban and semiurban communi-

Figure 2.1. A picture highlighting the devotional content of *garbā* dance by Nirbhaya Kapadia, Ahmedabad section *Divya Bhaskar*, September 28, 2017. Photo of the newspaper by author.`

ties are now making concerted efforts to provide similar arrangements for residents in their neighborhoods. They attempt to keep Navarātri *garbā* a neighborhood affair as it has traditionally been while incorporating popular innovations. Today, professionally organized and neighborhood-organized *garbā* thrive simultaneously with their traditional counterparts as worship rituals during the festival.

This chapter examines contemporary Navarātri *garbā* in three different contexts: (1) the traditional context, where the dance is still performed as a form of worship; (2) large, professionally organized events; and (3) small-scale, neighborhood-organized *garbā*. It is based on my field work in Gujarat and Maharashtra in 2004 and 2017 as well as my experience of *garbā* dancing for over twenty-five years and examines the diverse meanings related to devotion, business, politics, cultural identity, and personal or communal aspirations that emerge in these contexts.[4] While the focus of the chapter remains contemporary *garbā*, in order to develop a fuller understanding of the impact of changing historical contexts on a traditional dance, it also makes brief reference to innovations introduced during the British colonial period in India and in the decades following India's independence, each of which had important implications. Examining *garbā* in this way demonstrates that each historical context is marked by ideological, social, and material frameworks within which various meanings are woven by diverse agents around *garbā*'s main components—song and dance. It highlights that, in contemporary times, Navarātri *garbā* performances are influenced by an emphasis on individual choices, democratic processes, and business ambitions, which are all propelled by the power of technology and media and are reshaping religion in the twenty-first century.

Dynamic reshaping and revitalization of religion, once thought to be on the ebb in the wake of modernity, has attracted considerable scholarly attention in recent years. Sociologists explain that the reemergence of religion as a powerful social force, often termed *desecularization*, can be attributed to its ability to offer certainty in the midst of uncertainties encountered by people in the globalized postmodern world and to serve as a platform for community building.[5] Yet, as Peter Berger points out, the form of revitalized religion is essentially different from the traditional one. It is no longer simply a matter of heritage, but operates by making room for individual choices and interactions with secular forces (Berger, Douthat, and Lucken 2015). The contemporary forms of *garbā* in some contexts exemplify Berger's observation in that they intersect with secular forces and with the growing emphasis on individual choices in India. Yet they have not displaced the traditional *garbā* entirely and thrive alongside those. I suggest that since *garbā* have long formed a popular expression of devotion outside of the purview of religious authority, they allow participants to introduce innovations and new meanings without losing their most powerful aspect for millions of performers—the experience of becoming absorbed in a collective movement through dance.

In what follows, I will first give an overview of traditional *garbā*, which have been performed as a form of worship for centuries. Here, I will also discuss their recent instances that I have observed. This will provide the basis for looking at their transformations in some contexts. After this, I will briefly discuss the *garbā* innovations that occurred in preindependence India and other contexts highlighting historical examples of changes introduced in *garbā*'s forms and meanings. I will then turn to contemporary *garbā* organized professionally and by neighborhoods, examining their structures and social implications and the role played by media in enhancing their popularity. This section will bring into focus the reshaping of a ritual with complex and layered meanings by multiple agents. The concluding section will discuss how, with all their transformations, contemporary *garbā* offer a lens to understand religion as an area of social life that is "situated between political power and economic exchange" but is still marked by aspects that "enable people to experiment with what it means to be human," to use David Chidester's (2005, 1) apt words.

Garbo in the Traditional Religious Context

In order to explore the implications of modifications introduced in the form of the *garbo* ritual in recent times, it is important to first look at it in its traditional religious context that has prevailed for centuries. For non-Gujaratis, and many Gujaratis too, the term *garbo* (or its plural *garbā*) generally brings to mind the circular dance performed in honor of the goddess during Navarātri in Gujarat. But, in fact, the term also connotes the festival image of the goddess as well as a song to which the dance is performed. There have been several scholarly explorations of the origins of all the three referents of *garbo*.[6] While conclusive evidence about the exact origins of the term has remained elusive, a lyric by the seventeenth-century Gujarati poet Bhandas—*Ganganmaṇḍal nī gāgarḍī*—indicates that *garbo* as an image, as a song, and as a worship ritual for the goddess has been prevalent in Gujarat at least since that time (Bhandas 1998). The lyric describes the goddess's cosmic dance. It refers to the image and the dance in a way that matches their incorporation in ritual contexts even today.

The primary referent of the term *garbo* is the festival image of the goddess. It is a perforated, globular clay pot with a wide, round mouth. On the first day of Navarātri, women from many families install the image in their homes by putting a lit lamp inside, which is kept alit for the entire duration of the festival (figure 2.2). The clay pot is understood to represent the womb of the goddess. Most Gujarati scholars agree that the term *garbo* is derived from the Sanskrit term *garbha,* meaning "womb" or "fetus," and is a short form of *garbha-dīpa* or *dīpa-garbho ghaṭah,* meaning "[pot] with lamp in its womb."[7] Worshippers refer to the *garbo* image as *jagat-jananī* (world's mother) or an embodiment of *ādyaśakti* (primordial energy), for whom a Gujarati *āratī* (a type of hymn) is sung every day during the festival. The image's association with motherhood is extended to women as well. *Garbo* is often installed in households of expecting mothers or women who have just given birth. During the day, it is offered simple worship by women inside their homes, and it is brought to a space open to the sky at night for the dance ritual.

Once the images (from one or several households) are in the open space, women circle around them and dance, singing *garbā* songs in the Gujarati language. The songs have simple melodies but are sung with upbeat rhythm in a call-and-response manner by the dancing women. The lyrics for the songs, mostly in women's voices, are broadly of three types: expressing devotion to the goddess, about Lord Krishna's dance with the

Figure 2.2. Festival image of *garbo.* Source: WhatsApp video on YouTube, uploaded by Arjun Gorana.

women of Vraj, and related to women's lives. The goddess-worship songs are sung at the beginning of *garbā* performance to mark the dance as a ritual for the goddess. These songs either invite the goddess to dance in *garbā* or describe her beauty as she dances. The dancing women are referred to as the goddess's friends. After a few songs of this type, songs about Lord Krishna as well as those related to various aspects of women's lives—including love, family, and work—are sung. The latter are nonreligious in nature. The explanation often given for singing such songs in the ritual space is that the goddess dances in the *garbā* space along with women as her friends. No theme related to her friends' lives, therefore, is off limits in her presence. As I have discussed in my essay on the *garbo* image, this ritual arena has provided women with a culturally approved space to express their religious agency, self-perceptions, aspirations in life, and angst against their husbands, in-laws, or employers, often in a humorous manner. In however limited a way, it has been empowering for women. Furthermore, because of the incorporation of such themes in the songs, *garbo* has always possessed the potential to be easily transported to nondevotional contexts (Shukla-Bhatt 2016, 100–108).

As dance, *garbo*'s defining feature is its circular form and counterclockwise movement with clapping. Sometimes women also dance with the *garbā* images on their heads. Under a starlit sky, the light coming from *garbā* images at the center and on the heads of moving women creates the visual appeal of a shimmering orbit (figure 2.3). All women who can move around in the *garbā* circle may join or leave it when they wish. It is not uncommon to see a seventy-year-old woman moving in the circle next to a ten-year-old girl for a few rounds. The steps generally involve graceful swinging of the body and are easy to learn. For generations, little girls have learned their first *garbā* songs and steps dancing next to their mothers and grandmothers. Learning *garbā* in this way with neighborhood women has also provided them the first inkling of their feminine identity, a moment they cherish throughout their lives. Kallolini Hazrat considers the simplicity and spontaneity of the dance in the traditional context its greatest strength. They make, she writes, *garbo* appear like "a dance running in Gujarati women's blood-stream" (Hazrat 1981, 37).

Spontaneous learning of the *garbo* dance is possible because its movements are graceful but repetitive. Unlike classical dances, *garbā* do not provide room for individual expression. But through repetitive movements in unison, they "generate collective energies," to use a phrase employed by Richard Schechner, a theater scholar and director. Schechner suggests that in many dances, such as the whirling dervishes, repetition "lifts performers, and often spectators too, into ecstatic trance." He especially highlights such an effect in "all-night dances" with counterclockwise circular movements. They lead, he says, to "an experience of total flow," where, for the

Figure 2.3. Traditional *garbo* dancing by women with images on their heads, Surat city, 2013. Photo by Anil Dave, courtesy: Reuters Image Library, India.

time being, the dancer loses the awareness of individual identity, time, and space and only has the sense of being a part of a collective moving circle. Schechner describes the experience as that of "total low intensity" (Schechner 1985, 11). A. N. Jani, a Gujarati scholar of Shakta (goddess) traditions, offers a similar explanation based on Tantric geometry. According to this explanation, the counterclockwise circular movement of *garbā* can be understood as collective human energy ascending to connect with the transcendent, symbolized by the image at the center (Jani 1978, 88–89). Jani's theological explanation of the experience of collective energy as the core of *garbo* parallels Schechner's description of "total low intensity." My observation from dancing in *garbā* for over twenty-five years confirms that the palpable experience of being a part of almost a collective body through dance is what draws most dancers to them.

Even though there is great enthusiasm for the dance, to large extent, traditional *garbā* have been small neighborhood affairs, coming together without much prior organizational effort. All they require is a set of simple things: *garbā* images brought out from homes to an open space, a few flowers, food offerings for the goddess (generally sugar and nuts), drums when available, and women ready to sing and dance. Traditionally, most neighborhoods are inhabited by a few communities/castes that are at a similar level in social and economic hierarchies. Women know one another well, and dressing up for *garbā* is generally not very elaborate. A woman may bring out a nicer set of attire for *garbā,* but it would not be a dramatic deviation from her everyday apparel. Thus, traditional *garbā* dancing has been a low-budget community affair in which women are the main participants.

The most authentic traditional *garbā* dances I observed during my research were in the potter neighborhood of the village of Naranpura near Ahmedabad, in 2004. Except for the singing by lead singers on the microphone at the center, all aspects in these *garbā* were traditional. There were multiple *garbā* images at the center, circled by female dancers of all ages clad in nicer sets of their everyday attire. The dancing was vibrant but with simple steps. Nothing in the arena distracted from the stunning visual effect of light sieving through *garbā* images that remained the core of all movements around. The participants saw their dance as a ritual. Two women who had brought *garbā* images to the venue stressed that a *garbo* should be installed only in a household in which there is a newborn baby or hope for a child in the foreseeable future. If the flame of the lamp lit inside it remains unextinguished for the duration of the festival, it is an assurance that the goddess will protect the newborn or the child to be born.[8] Association of *garbā* with divine and human motherhood was clear in this community. This type of traditional *garbo* continues to be performed in rural Gujarat and some urban neighborhoods.

Innovations in *Garbā* in the Colonial and Postindependence Eras

In comparison to the small, community-based traditional *garbā* performances, a large number of contemporary Navarātri *garbā* events in urban areas are complex affairs that have thousands of dancers and require enormous organizational effort. There is vast difference between the two. But the incorporation of innovative elements in *garbā* is not a uniquely contemporary phenomenon. The historian Makrand Mehta (2017) has discussed the striking innovations that were introduced in *garbā* songs and venues soon after Alexander K. Forbes published his *Rās Mālā* in 1856. Forbes's closest Gujarati associate, the poet Dalpatram (1820–1898), and his friends who were engaged in social-reform activities, especially those promoting girls' education, used *garbā* as a channel to promote their progressive agenda. Dalpatram composed lyrics for *garbā* in which, instead of goddess worship or women's social lives, girls' education was the central theme. By the end of the nineteenth century, these new types of *garbā* were being performed at several educational and social institutions for women during or after Navarātri. They were part of a network of social processes promoting women's education.

During the 1920s and 1930s, when freedom movements were at their peak, nationalist songs became a powerful vehicle for the expression of patriotic sentiments in the public arena. In 1930, a nationalist poet named Padrakar published a booklet titled *Rāṣṭrīya Navarātra Rās* (Nationalist Navarātri Songs).[9] The image of Durgā with eight arms and a lion on the cover of this booklet ostensibly links the goddess to the motherland—*Bhārat-mātā* (Mother India; figure 2.4). After the salt march

Figure 2.4. The cover of *Rāṣṭrīya Navarātra Rās* booklet published in 1930, photographed from the *Gujarat Samachar Magazine*, September 28, 2017. Photo by author.

led by Gandhi in 1932, the popular music director and songwriter Avinash Vyas and the reputed poet Zaverchand Meghani composed many patriotic *garbā*, which continue to resonate with people even today. Meghani's "*rāj mane lāgyo kasumbī no rang*" (Beloved, I am drenched in the color orange), which refers to the traditional color of valor and bravery—deep orange, provides an example.[10] Older women today who were little girls at that time still recall Navarātri becoming an occasion to express passionate love for the country and aspirations for freedom.[11] Even as the traditional *garbā* continued to be performed, the dance and the festival of Navarātri accrued layers of socially relevant meanings during the time of nationalist movements before India's independence. And the agents who associated new meanings to them were not persons of religious authority; they were poets, reformers, freedom fighters, and female performers.[12]

Even though the social functions served by the innovations in *garbā* and Navarātri during the late nineteenth and the early twentieth centuries are no longer relevant in contemporary times, they are historically significant. The inherent potential of *garbā* to bridge the sacred and the secular was effectively employed by the innovators to articulate liberal and patriotic aspirations within the reformer/nationalist framework. In all subsequent periods, *garbā* performed in nontraditional contexts have engaged changing social norms and aspirations. In the 1950s and 1960s, they began to be widely performed on the stage during Navarātri and in some cultural shows, where they offered a major avenue for articulation of Gujarati identity, especially in the context of the newly established Indian nation with linguistically demarcated states.[13] The 1970s and 1980s saw tremendous growth in men's participation in the newly emerging form of large-scale Navarātri *garbā* in the cities of Gujarat. The increase in male participation coincided with the beginning of organized events in which the traditional ritual elements were losing their centrality. Gradually, entry fees were also introduced.[14] Still, even in the late 1980s, *garbā* entrance fees were comparatively small. With India's economy opening up in the 1990s, the *garbā* scene began to change rapidly with higher entrance fees, demand for star singers, and large-scale sponsorship at popular venues. The contemporary *garbā* scene is embedded in this shift.

Contemporary Manifestations of *Garbā*

If innovations in *garbā* occurred within the framework of social reform and nationalism during the colonial period, they emerge in contemporary times within a framework where religion intersects with growing social acceptance of individual choice, globally thriving consumerism, politics, technology, and media. Today, Navarātri *garbā* in some contexts are grand in scale, complex in structure, and dazzling in ambiance. They engage multiple agents who introduce innovations in their form and add new layers to their meanings every year, some unimaginable earlier. A new style introduced in 2017, for example—salsa *garbā*, combining features of the Caribbean salsa, which has recently become popular in India, with *garbā*—would have been inconceivable in the preceding years.[15] Similarly, a few decades ago, people could not have expected to see billboards of sponsors at the entrances of *garbā* arenas and prizes for dancing and costumes given out by organizers and business ventures running in the thousands. *Garbā* at this scale need professional management. They apparently have extensive financial implications, but they also have unforeseen political and cultural implications, sometimes ironical.

Professionally Organized Garbā

After having left India many years ago, I first observed professionally organized *garbā* during my research trip to Gujarat in 2004, and I was astonished by their grand scale and financial implications. But what I witnessed in 2017 was enormously more complex and was driven by global consumer-market forces and media that have now effectively come to frame individual choices and societal processes. With coverage of all major festivals on national media and large-scale relocations of people for work and education within India, many people have become familiar and fascinated with *garbā*. Even though it is recognized as a distinctively Gujarati form, the dance has become popular across many regions and is performed during Navarātri not only in Gujarat but also hundreds of miles away, in cities such as Varanasi in the north and Gwalior in central India. During my research in 2017, even before Navarātri started, its fervor was apparent in Pune, Maharashtra, more than three hundred miles away from Vadodara and Ahmedabad, the well-known centers of contemporary *garbā*. On the eve of Navarātri, the Pune edition of the *Times of India* published the responses of several university students on questions regarding their *garbā* plans. Most responses were based on the students' experience of professionally organized *garbā*. Two questions that emerged for me were, What is the basis of this widespread appeal of *garbā* as a way to celebrate Navarātri? And how do organized *garbā* events engage this appeal?

According to the responses published in the *Times of India* and of several dancers in Gujarat, the most powerful appeal of *garbā* as a form of Navarātri celebration is its participatory spirit expressed through dance.[16] Professionally organized *garbā* strive to maximize this experience mostly as business. But, in the process, they also provide platforms that allow articulation of diverse cultural, financial, social, and political aspirations. Their prevalence rests on balancing acts between innovation and tradition, business and religion, by multiple actors. Within this framework, the goddess is paradoxically absent and present.

Business dimensions associated with sponsors and organizers of these *garbā* become clear starting with announcements in newspapers, on billboards, and on websites, where images of dancing men and women, photographs of singers and guest celebrities, and logos of sponsoring businesses appear (figure 2.5). The goddess is either conspicuously absent or relegated to a corner in most of these visually striking announcements. The same goes for entrance tickets for such venues. Except for the *garbā* organized by city or state governments, educational institutions, and nongovernmental organizations (NGOs), a majority of professionally organized *garbā* charge fees that range from INR 150 to 700 per night depending on the ambiance, the quality of music, and the security arrangements. In more-exclusive places, they can be even higher. Of the organized *garbā* events I attended in 2017—at Vardhman Lawns in Pune, United Way in Vadodara, the Aman Aakash plot and GMDC (Gujarat Mineral Development Corporation) grounds in Ahmedabad, and Modella Mill Compound in Thane—only the GMDC *garbā*, organized by the Gujarat Tourism Cor-

Figure 2.5. Tickets and a billboard for professionally organized *garbā* (2017). Photos by author.

poration, were completely free. United Way had season fees of INR 3,000 for men and INR 300 for women. Others charged INR 250 per night per person. Upon entering a venue of this type, after the security check, one is usually greeted by large billboards of sponsoring businesses. Except for the GMDC grounds, all organized *garbā* events I attended had such billboards. The GMDC grounds instead showcased Gujarat's cultural heritage and the achievements of the current government in an exhibit. In these grand displays, the goddess has little relevance.

The goddess is also absent as a festival image at the center of the dancing arena, where the largest edifice is the stage for the singers. A few venues have no image at all. At some, an image of the goddess may appear fleetingly on large television screens on the sides or at the back of the stage, which also project the dancing people via sophisticated video-recording devices such as drones. When asked about the absence of the image, a few participants gave an explanation that appears to have gained currency in recent times. They said that because no proper *pūjā* can be conducted in such venues and people often do not observe appropriate etiquette for being in the presence of a sacred image—such as taking off shoes or keeping off the grounds by menstruating women—it is more respectful not to have it in this space, which is meant for cultural expression and enjoyment. At most venues, the agents contributing to these *garbā*—the organizers, the sponsors, and the participants—seem to have agreed to circumvent any ritual by excluding the image. In a few venues, the goddess's image is kept in a corner and is offered some ritual worship. Yet her presence is not the center of activities in the dancing ground. These venues are similar to the Durgā Pūjā *paṇḍal*s (temporary structures) in the cities of Bengal today, where, as Kunal Ray, a Bengali living in Pune, pointed out, most happenings are nondevotional and related to the articulation of Bengali cultural identity.[17]

In the place of the light sieving through the *garbā* images at the center in traditional contexts, the sources of visual appeal inside the dancing grounds of professionally organized events comprise the colorful decorations arranged by the organizers and, importantly, the attire and the dancing of the performers. The decorations may cost the organizers many thousands of rupees. The dancers generally wear expensive traditional Gujarati dresses in a dazzling variety of colors and designs that are radically different from their Western daily wear, like pants and shirts. Considering that the performers would put on these clothes only during Navarātri, the amount of effort and money spent on them often seems astounding to their elders. Disha Thakkar, the owner of Disha'z, a designer traditional-Indian-dress store in Pune and a sponsor at the *garbā* event at Vardhman Lawn, indicated that, per season, they easily sell more than one thousand dresses custom-made in Gujarat, each costing anywhere between INR 1,500 and 8,000. Ankit Dani, a teacher at a *garbā* school in Ahmedabad, had an intricately embroidered dress that cost over INR 25,000. Because multiple sets of dresses are needed for the nine-night festival along with matching jewelry and makeup, the net financial transactions just around attire run into many millions of rupees in each city. While these expenses often create friction between young dancers and their parents, the former see them as a way to connect to their culture with an element of choice. The understanding of cultural heritage is reshaped through the mediation of individual-oriented consumerism.

The same trend can be seen in the dance form as well. Even though every year a majority of new dancers still learn *garbā* movements from their friends, a large number also train under teachers who choreograph innovative steps. Many of these steps are complex and can be mastered only with months of practice. Several *garbā* classes in cities, charging monthly fees of INR 1,500 to 4,000, are full by the end of May. Ankit Dani of Ahmedabad and his friends teach new steps to over one hundred students every year. Dancers trained at a *garbā* class often visit *garbā* venues in a group, wearing similar attire, and dance within a small circle of their own rather than as participants in the larger circle as in the traditional context. Groups compete with their rivals in fine moves and finesse to win various prizes. On each ground, one sees some impressive *garbā* dancing, which is full of innovations yet not disconnected from the tradition (figure 2.6). Even though the dancers do not see their performance as ritual, they cherish it as a Navarātri tradition. When I asked Rutwa, a medical student, if it wouldn't be more reasonable to have this type of nonritual dancing during schools' summer or Christmas breaks, she sharply protested. "Oh no," she said, "we would never let that happen. This is our distinctive Navarātri tradition." The layer of religious meaning has receded to the background for young dancers. But, as a cultural tradition, the association of the dance with the festival still has a strong hold on them. As I will discuss later, in some ways, this meaning is more inclusive.

The goddess's image is absent as the core visual object in the business framework of grand events, but she becomes present in the space through two audible aspects—the *ādyaśakti āratī* and the *garbā* songs. In traditional contexts, the *āratī* is sung generally at the end, just before the distribution of the food offering. In professionally organized *garbā*, it is usually sung at the beginning. A large majority of people sing this eighteen-stanza-long Gujarati hymn by heart along with professional singers on the stage, even as the dancers position themselves to start the dance. At these events, the *āratī* serves almost as what the folklore scholar Richard Bauman calls a "frame." In his seminal work *Verbal Art as Performance,* Bauman discusses

Figure 2.6. Young women dancing in *garbā* at a professionally managed venue, Ahmedabad. Courtesy: Darshana Jamindar, *Gujarat Headline*.

"frames" as comprising utterances around a verbal performance that give cues to understand it. "Invoked and shifted" to form a "culturally conventionalized metanarrative" (Bauman 1984, 12, 16), frames convey explicit or implicit instructions about interpreting a performance. They may contain special codes that are archaic and different from everyday language. Bauman's notion of frames is helpful in looking at the singing of the *ādyaśakti āratī* at organized *garbā* events. Invoked for its culturally defined role as the Navarātri hymn for the goddess but shifted from its usual place at the end of the dance, the *āratī* offers a frame for what is to follow. Even with all the innovations in the dancing arena, its singing suggests, the dances that follow must be seen as related to traditional *garbā*. As a frame, the *āratī* effectively creates an aura of authenticity for the commercially managed events.

Like *āratī*, *garbā* songs dedicated to the goddess remain a staple in professionally organized events and make her musically present. But they are situated at the juncture of tradition and business in a more complex manner. Unlike *āratī*, a stand-alone hymn, goddess-related *garbā* are a part of the larger repertoire that also includes nonreligious songs. In professionally organized contexts, they are not sung in a call-and-response manner as in traditional *garbā* but are sung exclusively by professional singers on the stage. In *garbā* events with internationally known singers, which have the feel of star-studded rock concerts, they are sung with heavy percussion and dancing on the stage by the star singer as well as television and film actors (who charge hundreds of thousands for a one-time appearance). The goddess is overshadowed by the attention given to the glamorous singers and actors. And yet, paradoxically, the singer demanding tremendous respect among *garbā* lovers around the globe, Atul Purohit, is a middle-aged man clad in simple everyday clothes who does not use heavy percussion or dancing on the stage in his shows. Purohit and his Rutambhara group have sung for United Way *garbā* in Vadodara for eighteen years, drawing thousands of dancers. This group does not depend on heavy orchestra or compromise the musical structure of *garbā* and sings numerous goddess-worship songs interspersed with other songs every night. Dancers who hear them year after year show special enthusiasm in their dancing for some goddess-related songs. The night I visited, dancing to the song *avi nav nav ratri re,* which describes the goddess's beauty as she dances, was extremely energetic, with thousands of dancers raising both hands on the refrain. The commitment to many traditional features of *garbā* has won United Way an emblematic status. *Garbā* from the venue are televised every night during Navarātri in Mumbai and other cities. United Way is an aspirational destination for even those performers who dance in *garbā* at rock-concert-like events. Rucha Vaishnav, from Vadodara, prided herself in dancing there, and several dancers in Mumbai asked me only to visit that venue if I wanted to see "real *garbā*" (figure 2.7). The success of both rock-concert-like *garbā* and Purohit's group presents another example of the paradox of enchantment for innovation but respect for tradition among the dance's contemporary enthusiasts.

Attracting millions of participants, professionally organized *garbā* are the most visible format of the dance within Gujarat and in other parts of India today. But they are not equally accessible for everyone. Entrance fees and age can be constraining factors for many. Entrance-fee-based *garbā* are out of reach for innumerable dancers, not just because of the ticket rates but also because of the associated expenses for suitable attire and makeup. As mentioned earlier, some venues are more expensive than others, making venues of *garbā* markers of economic class. It is not uncommon to hear mention of specific venues made to articulate class identity.[18] Rutwa Shah indicated she would only go to the venues that are affordable for her and not to others. Some people cannot afford any entry fees. An attractive alternative to such class barriers is offered by school- or NGO-run events and, notably, the government-run GMDC-ground *garbā* in Ahmedabad, where people from all economic classes come because the government invites reputed singers and the venue is well decorated as

Figure 2.7. United Way *garbā*, Navarātri 2017. Photo by Tapan Parikh, Vadodara.

well as safe. My taxi driver, who had declined to accompany me inside ticket-based venues, was delighted to join me there. In addition to money, age can also be a barrier for entry to these glamorous venues. A large majority of dancers here are under the age of thirty-five. Dancers over forty-five are seen only in small numbers.

Even with the widespread enthusiasm for professionally organized *garbā*, the changes they have been bringing about have met with substantial critique. During my recent visit, Veerbalaben Dani of Ahmedabad described these *garbā* as "mechanical" movements without voice and spirit. She missed *garbā* in the city in the 1950s, when everyone in the large circle sang. Years ago, Avinash Vyas had critiqued "the selling of *garbā*" as distorting its "personality" and hurting its dignity. He was also critical of glamor-ridden *garbā* that pushed older women out (Vyas 1983, 10–11). Sonal Shukla, the director of the Vacha ("voice") trust for women, also sharply criticized the emerging format in a 1987 article aptly titled "A Woman's Festival Taken Over." Shukla not only critiqued the loss of women's agency and the creation of class barriers, she also expressed concern over the increasingly forceful articulation of Hindu identity at large *garbā* venues. She termed it "communal chauvinism" (Shukla 1987, 10–13).

The legitimacy of Shukla's concerns became apparent in some incidents with political coloring in recent years, especially in 2014, when some Hindu-nationalist individuals and organizations issued diktats to ban Muslims from organized *garbā* venues. Some of them referred to *love jihad*, a term widely used in anti-Muslim rhetoric in India and elsewhere to suggest that Muslim men allure, marry, and convert non-Muslim women as a form of jihad. Some politicians, however, justified the diktats in terms of Islamic beliefs, stating that if Muslims are opposed to saying "Vande Mataram" (a popular slogan meaning "bow to Mother," here referring to India) because of its connection to the goddess in the slogan's source lyric, it would be against their religion to participate in *garbā*. The diktats received much media attention and were indeed temporarily followed at a few venues in some cities. But, overall, they proved inconsequential.

Muslims have been long associated with *garbā* as decorators, sound-system managers, drummers, and, importantly, as singers. Major singers like Osman Mir and Farida Mir still pull huge crowds. A Muslim *garbā* teacher in Vadodara, Muhammad Irshad Mansuri, is immensely popular. And now the professionally organized *garbā* without the conventional ritual format have opened space for Muslim dancers as well. The diktats received little support from organizers or dancers. On the contrary, young dancers across both Hindu and Muslim communities criticized them for generating fears around a prized and shared cultural tradition. Senior political leaders, including the prime minister, advised against such diktats, and the Gujarat state government issued orders for the police to prevent their implementation. Ironically, the diktats were welcomed by some Muslim clerics and leaders. One of them thanked the concerned Hindu nationalists for trying to stop Muslim youngsters from doing what is un-Islamic, something they themselves had been trying to do for years rather unsuccessfully. The positions taken by various groups and individuals turned the usual political equations topsy-turvy. The debate turned out to be more between conservative and liberal inclusive voices across two communities than between rival political groups that try to garner support for themselves by taking opposite positions around an issue.[19]

Organized Neighborhood Garbā

Away from the grandeur and business ethos of professionally organized *garbā*, one finds clusters of dance events organized by residential communities. Depending on the average income in the community, the leaders collect funds from each family for the season for DJs, lights, grounds, and possibly food. In these *garbā*, one often finds ritual components like *garbo* images and lamps at the center, spirited expression of comradery and revelry among dancers of all age groups, and music and attire maximally affordable for the community. Of the two community *garbā* I observed in Ahmedabad, one was in the middle-class Shanti Dayal Society in Memnagar, and other was in a slum community near Shreyas Crossing. There was, of course, a clear income-based difference between the two in terms of music, ambiance, and lighting. But with the presence of a sanctified image of the goddess at the center, the absence of competition, and people's familiarity with one another, there were the easy exchange of jokes and collective trying out of new *garbā* steps at both. The festival seemed to have truly come alive there. These *garbā* with DJs and light decorations, which are a recent and modified version of earlier neighborhood events, form a bridge between the traditional and commercialized *garbā* forms and offer a space for carefree enjoyment of Navarātri among people of a community. Yet the very notion of community demarcates a boundary that can, in some contexts, turn into ground for violence.

During Navarātri 2017, reports of attacks on three young boys from the Dalit communities came from three different villages in central and northern Gujarat, not far from Ahmedabad and Vadodara. Dalit communities, formerly called "untouchables," are viewed as the lowest in caste hierarchies. Per the reports, dominant-caste men in each case asked Dalit youths to leave *garbā* venues, and when the latter resisted, they were brutally attacked. The venues in question do not appear to be organized *garbā* venues. In the communities in the reported cases, Navarātri seems to have been seen by the involved dominant-caste men as an occasion to claim control over public space. In response to such media reports, one community redefined *garbā* for itself. A Dalit leader started a *garbā* tradition in his neighborhood where the image of the goddess was replaced by the iconic twentieth-century Dalit leader B. R. Ambedkar. The songs were also addressed to him. The new *garbā* provided a space to embrace Dalit pride.[20] But, on the account of violent human actions around caste-based inclusion and exclusion, the goddess was pushed out of a *garbā* arena.

Conclusion

An examination of *garbā* in various forms that prevail simultaneously during Navarātri in Gujarat and elsewhere draws attention to how, in contemporary times, nonreligious forces reshape structures of rituals in public contexts and reshuffle their layers of meaning. Paul Post and Arie Molendijk (2005, 280) specify "individualization," "deinstitutionalization," and "(de-/re-)sacralization" as processes linked to the changing dynamics of religion that impact the interaction between space and ritual in the postmodern Western world. In contemporary *garbā*, we find an example of a ritual in postmodern India in relation to which these processes operate in a slightly different way. As a popular participatory ritual in open space without priestly intervention, *garbo* always had a "deinstitutionalized" form, which gave it the potential for being transported to nonritual venues like professionally organized events with new meanings. In preindependence Gujarat, this potential was put to use by reformers and nationalists. What the postmodern era, energized by market forces and technological advances in media, has brought along is the powerful element of individualization, which leads to both de- and resacralization and plays a significant role in restructuring the form and reshuffling meanings of *garbā* in some contexts. The stress on individual choices, propelled by the consumer market and media, transports a worship dance from a ritual space to a mega dancing field in professionally organized *garbā*. The sponsors, organizers, dancers, singers, and celebrities all contribute to this transformation through incorporating components like billboards, exhibits, glitter, and tickets and through shifting elements like the *āratī* that give the events an aura of authenticity. In these grand and glamorous events within the framework of business, in which boundaries for inclusion and exclusion are influenced by the economic class and age of the dancers, the goddess is marginally present as needed. The restructured form redefines *garbā* as cultural heritage rather than religious ritual in these spaces. And yet this very "de-sacralization," provides a basis for revitalization of *garbo* in a secular democratic framework.

In responses to the diktats banning Muslims from the *garbā* arena, the most vital resistance came on the grounds that *garbā* form a cherished cultural heritage of Gujarat to which all its people have a claim. The Dalit community that organized *garbā* around Ambedkar's image rejected the traditional religious meaning but retained their claim to the dance as their cultural heritage. These responses signal a perspective much needed in order to turn religious diversity in the land into a pluralistic ethos of meaningful interactions. Understood as a cultural form, *garbo* allows participants to engage with diversity constructively. *Garbā*'s energetic prevalence in public spaces provides an example of Berger's observations regarding religion in the postmodern age. Berger has argued that pluralism is not only an external factor now but has emerged as an "internal psychological fact." He has also stressed that for religions to maintain their vitality in our times, when the grip of their conventional forms on individuals is weakening, they have to be reconciled to the secular forces of liberal democracy (Berger 1981, 32; 2001, 452–53). Delinked from the traditional contexts, large *garbā* venues provide platforms for articulation of new interpretations of cultural identity and aspirations of a wide range of groups, including politicians. They have, however, not led to the disappearance of traditional *garbā* where the goddess reigns at the center as the mother of the world and recipient of worship. I suggest that, along with the reconciliation of religion with secular democratic and market forces in professionally organized events, it is in these events' simultaneity with traditional as well as community-based *garbā* that the dance continues to thrive vibrantly. Furthermore, though varied in their orientations and all their outer aspects, they share the core of the kinetic experience—"total low intensity"—through which a dancer feels connected to all dancing bodies around. In the exhilarating energy generated in and around the multiple manifestations of *garbā*, the *ādyaśakti* (primordial energy) dances, even in the circles from which the goddess has been exiled.

Notes

I am deeply grateful to the families of Trupti Vaishnav, Priti Nanavati, and Pragna Dani for their generous help in arranging my visits to various *garbā* sites and interviews. I thank FLAME University in Pune, India, for their support during the research for this essay.

1. The chapter refers to terms and texts in Gujarati and Sanskrit. Both are Indo-Aryan languages; the former is derived from the latter. The chapter follows the standard diacritics for Indic languages: long vowels indicated by a horizontal bar on the top, etc.

2. See the discussion of Bhandas's lyric in this chapter.

3. For just two examples, see Swami Swatmananda, "Navratri 2017: Who Are the Three Devis You Worship during Navaratri and Why?," *Indian Express*, http://indianexpress.com/article/religion/navratri-2017-who-are-the-three-devis-you-worship-during-navratri-and-why-4856437/; and *Gujarat Samachar*, p. 4, http://www.gujaratsamachar.com/index.php/articles/display_article/ahmedabad/many-names-of-adivas-shakti-aparna-gana-kriya-ananta-muktakashi-chita-abhaya-; both dated September 23, 2017, and accessed October 3, 2017.

4. The interviews conducted in 2017 and cited in this chapter were as follows: Kajal Vakharia and Disha Thakkar, September 24, 2017; Rucha Vaishnav, September 26 and September 29, 2017; Rutwa Shah, September 28, 2017; Veerbala Dani, September 28, 2018; and Ankit Dani, September 28, 2018.

5. For a discussion of desecularization, see Berger (1999, 1–18). For a discussion of the factors that contribute to the resurgence of religion in the context of globalization, see Karner and Aldridge (2004, 5–32).

6. Pathak and Panchal's (1954) volume is the most extensive of these.

7. For a detailed discussion of the etymology of the term, see Hazrat (1981, 21–24).

8. Interview with Bhikhiben Oza and her daughter-in-law, October 15, 2004. For parallels to the efficacy attributed to the *kolu* display by non-Brahmin households adopting this practice in Kāñcipuram, see Ilkama's chapter in this volume.

9. The term *rās* is used synonymously here for *garbo,* even though it is a somewhat different genre of dance.

10. *Kasumbī* literally means "the color of safflower."

11. These include Veerbala Dani of Ahmedabad, whom I interviewed on September 28, 2017, and my mother, Usha Shukla, who still sings with gusto popular freedom songs of the time.

12. See Makrand Mehta's (2017) article on preindependence *garbā.*

13. Kallolini Hazrat (1981, 10–11, 36–38) describes her activities related to stage *garbā* in their respective compilations.

14. In an article in the *Economic Times,* D. P. Bhattacharya and Vasudha Venogopal (2014) cite Achuyt Yagnik for the information on the beginnings of large-scale *garbā* in 1970s.

15. For salsa *garbā* news, see Niyati Parikh, "Garba Gets a Salsa Twist This Navratri," *Times of India,* September 17, 2017, https://timesofindia.indiatimes.com/city/ahmedabad/garba-gets-a-salsa-twist-this-navratri/articleshow/60714723.cms.

16. "Aye Halo! Let's Play Dandia," *Times of India,* Pune edition, September 20, 2017, p. 2.

17. Conversation with Kunal Ray, September 25, 2017.

18. On the performance of class identity in Navarātri dances in Rajasthan, see Ortegren's chapter in this volume.

19. The debates surrounding the diktats have been widely covered in media since 2014, with reporters often taking strong positions. Balanced and well-rounded coverage of the topic is provided in an article by Zeeshan Ahmed for IndiaTomorrow.net, a nonprofit, independent journalist group: "Gujarat Govt. Orders Police to Defeat VHP Ban on Muslims at Garba Venues; Muslims Welcome Ban," September 25, 2014, http://www.indiatomorrow.net/eng/gujarat-govt-orders-police-to-defeat-vhp-ban-on-muslims-at-garba-venues;-muslims-welcome-ban. For the views of Muslim and Hindu youths, see the interviews in NDTV India's video coverage, "Muslim Garba Teacher in Gujarat Protests 'Love Jihad' Diktat," September 24, 2014, https://www.youtube.com/watch?v=1ppcN5IGGWs.

20. For more on the Dalit *garbā* in the village of Rampura, see "After Series of Attacks, Dalits in Gujarat Celebrate Navratri with 'Ambedakr Garba' " in the online newspaper *The Wire,* https://thewire.in/184578/gujarat-dalits-ambedkar-garba/ (accessed October 3, 2017).

References

Bauman, Richard. (1977) 1984. *Verbal Art as Performance*. Long Grove, IL: Waveland Press.

Berger, Peter. 1981. "The Pluralistic Situation and the Coming Dialogue between the World Religions." *Buddhist-Christian Studies* 1:31–41.

———, ed. 1999. *The Desecularization of the World: Resurgent Religion and World Politics*. Washington, DC: Ethics and Public Policy Center; Grand Rapids, MI: William B. Eerdmans.

———. 2001. "Reflections on the Sociology of Religion Today." *Sociology of Religion* 62 (4): 443–54.

Berger, Peter, Ross Douthat, and Kristen Lucken. 2015. "Why Hasn't Religion Died Out?" Discussion at the Veritas Forum, Harvard Divinity School, December 2, 2015. Veritas Forum video, December 5, 2015, http://www.veritas.org/why-hasnt-religion-died-out/.

Bhandas. 1998. "Ganganmaṇḍal nī gāgarḍī." Lyric in *Madhyayugīn Urmikāvyo* [Gujarati; Medieval Lyrics], edited by Chimanlal Trivedi, Balvant Jani, and Chinu Modi. New Delhi: Sahitya Akademi.

Bhattacharya, D. P., and Vasudha Venugopal. 2014. "Garba Becomes yet Another Excuse for Communal Chatter in Gujarat." *Economic Times*, September 24, 2014, Politics and Nation.

Chidester, David. 2005. *Authentic Fakes: Religion and American Popular Culture.* Berkeley: University of California Press.

Enthoven, R. E. 1914. *Folklore Notes: Vol. 1—Gujarat*. Bombay: British India Press.

Forbes, Alexander Kinloch. (1856) 1878. *Rās Mālā; or, Hindoo Annals of the Province of Goozerat, in Western India*. London: Richardson.

Hazrat, Kallolini. 1981. Introduction to *Maro Garbo Ghumyo* [Gujarati; My *Garbo* Swirled]. Edited by Kallolini Hazrat, 21–42. Mumbai: SNDT Women's University/Madhuri Shah Education Foundation.

Jani, Arunodaya. 1978. "Garbā ni vyutpatti, utpatti, ane rahasya" [Gujarati; *Garbo*'s etymology, origin, and meaning]. *Swādhyāya* 1:84–89.

Karner, Christian, and Alan Aldridge. 2004. "Theorizing Religion in a Globalizing World." *International Journal of Politics, Culture, and Society* 18 (1/2): 5–32.

Mehta, Makrand. 2017. "Polono Itihas" [The History of Lanes]. *Gujarat Samachar Plus*, September 28, 2017, Heritage, 2.

Pathak, Ramanarayan, and Govardhan Panchal. 1954. *Rās ane Garbā, ena Svarup and Vikās nī Ruparekhā* [Gujarati; *Rās* and *Garbā*, the History of Their Forms and Development]. Delhi: Indian National Theater.

Post, Paul, and Arie L. Molendijk. 2005. "Holy Ground: Reinventing Ritual Space in Modern Western Culture." *Material Religion* 3 (2): 279–82.

Schechner, Richard. 1985. *Between Theater and Anthropology*. Philadephia: University of Pennsylvania Press.

Shukla, Sonal. 1987. "A Woman's Festival Taken Over." *Manushi* 38:9–13.

Shukla-Bhatt, Neelima. 2016. "Celebrating Materiality: *Garbo*, a Festival Image of the Goddess in Gujarat." In *Sacred Matters: Material Religion in South Asian Traditions*, edited by Tracy Pintchman and Corinne G. Dempsey, 89–113. Albany: State University of New York Press.

Vyas, Avinash. 1983. *Vartul: A Collection of Garbā Songs*. Mumbai: N. M. Tripathi.

Propriety versus Creativity in Navarātri

3

Can Didi Truly Become Durgā?

The Riddle of the Two Goddesses

MOUMITA SEN

Introduction: Political Deification

The contemporary Durgā Pūjā of Kolkata is both an industry and a mass, media-driven, corporate-funded, politically patronized Hindu festival thriving on creativity and novelty. When compared to versions of Navarātri in Hindi-speaking parts of North India, particularly in the light of the resurgence of Hindutvā (Hindu nationalism) since the election of Narendra Modi in 2014, the popular discourse among elite *savarnā* (colloq. "upper caste") Bengalis suggests that Kolkata's Durgā Pūjā is almost a nonreligious festival with an ever-shrinking space for religiosity and a burgeoning space for revelry. While this is not true, as I will show in this chapter, one can understand that it is tempting to make this kind of argument in the face of the fluidity, malleability, and permissibility of this festival. The 2000s saw Durgā Pūjā productions excelling in aesthetic merit with zealous rivalry between different organizing committees. Since 2011, with the change in the government from the Communist Party of India (Marxist), or CPI(M), to the Trinamool Congress, or TMC, there have been many changes in the patronage and the style of the *pūjā* productions.

Since 2010, we have seen the chief minister of West Bengal, Mamata Banerjee,[1] making and consecrating Durgā *mūrtis*, inaugurating and speaking at dozens of *pūjā paṇḍals*, and even appearing as the theme of Durgā

Pūjās as a metaphor for *śakti*, where she was compared, as a powerful female minister, with the powerful demon-slaying goddess. Elsewhere, I have shown how the TMC has very effectively used the network of local clubs, the organizers of the Sārbajanin Durgā Pūjā in Bengal, to connect the idea of *śakti* as the feminine power of the Great Goddess and the charismatic persona of their female political leader, Mamata Banerjee (Sen 2018b). But this process of likening the goddess to the minister through the metaphor of *śakti* (divine feminine power) found its logical conclusion in a small *pūjā* in the Nadia district of Bengal, where the main *mūrti* (image) was a lifelike, fully colored statue of the goddess with ten arms behind her. Finally, Didi (as Banerjee is referred to in Bengal) had taken on the form of the Mā Durgā! This would not have been so striking if this image had appeared as political satire or propaganda during or following the election campaign. It was not political graffiti celebrating or deriding her on a nondescript city wall. It wasn't a satirical cartoon floating in social media, causing the anglophone elite Bengalis to shake their heads in disapproval at this connection between religion and politics. In this case, Didi appeared to replace Durgā as a spectacular devotional icon in the *paṇḍal* where the goddess is formally worshipped. In other words, Durgā and Didi were no longer loosely connected metaphors for *śakti*; they appeared to morph into each other.

It is, however, difficult to argue that this type of political deification is unique or exceptional. This is common practice in Indian democracy, despite the problems of analytical categories separating the political and the religious in Eurocentric scholarship, which identifies it as a deformity in the political system, which should be "equal, disinterested and impersonal" along the lines of the classical European understanding of democracy (Piliavsky 2014, 5). Yet it would be a mistake to assume that the separation of religion and politics is a purely analytical problem among anglophone elites and in Eurocentric political thought; political practice in postcolonial India is similarly informed by the question of such separations. Even among political actors at the grassroots level in India, political deification is not easily avoidable, nor is it easily acceptable. This leads to a process of conscious mobilization of religious affects toward electoral gains on the one hand and public disavowals of the same on the other. Let me clarify with some examples. A year after his landslide victory in the election of 2014, a village in the state of Uttar Pradesh built a temple to the prime minister of India, Narendra Modi (Jain 2015). A model of him was the deity worshipped by local farmers in this small village. When Modi formally rejected such deification, they simply placed another deity in the *garbhagṛha* (sanctum sanctorum), a *mūrti* of Śiva, and turned Modi's idol toward Śiva, as if in an act of worship. Technically, Prime Minister

Figure 3.1. Photograph of a poster of a Bhārat Mātā Pūjā, which has been taking place in Kolkata during the Durgā Pūjā since at least the 1990s. The poster mentions TMC ministers Partha Chattopadhyay and Debabrata Majumdar as the chairmen of the club and other ministers in important positions in the club organization at the helm of the *pūjā*. Photo by author.

Modi was now a devotee of Śiva, not just a deity. Similarly, Mahatma Gandhi was seen as a miracle-performing *Gandhi-bābā* by the peasants of Uttar Pradesh in the 1920s (see Amin 1984). *Dhorai Charitmanas*, a great novel by Satinath Bhaduri, points out how voting was understood as a ritual act of delivering a message to the god-man *Gandhi bāwā* (see P. Chatterjee 2004, 11). Later, Indira Gandhi, ostensibly against her wishes, was portrayed as Durgā by the great modernist M. F. Husain.

Not so long ago, Indira Gandhi's daughter-in-law, Sonia Gandhi, was portrayed as the goddess Lakṣmī in the form of a "public statue" to mark the contribution of the Indian National Congress party during the separation of the state of Telengana (Sengar 2017). The erstwhile chief minister of Tamil Nadu, Jayalalitha, is known to have embraced this kind of political deification, appearing dressed as the goddess Durgā, Kālī, and the Virgin Mary in public. This type of deification, however striking in the context of Western understanding of democracy, is rather commonplace in India. I argue that this is related to the relevance of ideals of kingly models (Price 1989), patrimony (Price and Srinivas 2016), and the charismatic leadership of "big men" (Mines and Gourishankar 1990) in the electoral politics of India. However, despite this alterity of Indian democratic practices, the case of West Bengal is somewhat exceptional because of the long regime of the CPI(M) and their ideological disavowal of all forms of religious practice in public and political institutions.

Had it not been for the political ideology put in place by the thirty-three-year-long Communist government in West Bengal, it would not have been surprising that Mamata Banerjee has actively engaged with the Durgā Pūjā festival of Kolkata. The CPI(M) was deeply opposed to any kind of formal ties with religious institutions and festivals, relenting only toward the very end of their regime, when they began to identify the bustling Durgā Pūjā festival of Kolkata not as a religious festival but as a cultural event filled with fun and nostalgia for the Bengalis. Their main political opponent, Mamata Banerjee, was, however, using the Durgā Pūjā platform for what she called *janasanyōga* (mass communication) as early as 2009. In 2011, when she formally became the chief minister of West Bengal, she revised what the preceding Communist government understood to be *secularism*: the separation of the state from all religious institutions and activities. Instead, she understood *secularism* to mean equal state support of all religious festivals of majority and minority groups in the state (Sen 2018b).

Since the election of the TMC and their increased involvement in the Durgā Pūjā, a common refrain among the elites of the city has been "eṭā tō ār Durgā pujo naẏa; eṭā tō TMC pujo" (This festival is no longer about worshipping Durgā; this is about worshipping the TMC). Ostensibly, this is correct, in light of this transformation of the chief minister into the city's patron goddess. As Anastasia Piliavsky (2014) has argued, this is a common practice in South Asia because of the politics of patronage in the Indian democracy. However, this identification of the goddess with the minister is never truly complete, even though it appears to be so. Political patronage is understood as a bad thing in scholarly literature; politics in general is considered dirty by common people in most parts of India. Therefore, even as local clubs try to associate these two icons, they try to dissociate them just as consistently. In this chapter, I want to look at the series of disavowals that accompany such acts of political deification. First, I will discuss the issue of political patronage in the context of the Durgā Pūjā of Kolkata. Second, I will provide two examples of such political deification. Following this, I will look at the problem of the two goddesses. Finally, I will focus on the question of disavowals, the fault lines along which the morphing of the bodies of the minister and the goddess remains crucially and necessarily incomplete.

Durgā Pūjā and the Network of Political Patronage

By way of introducing this issue in her volume *Patronage as Politics in South Asia*, Anastasia Piliavsky (2014, 2) shows us a poster where the politician Vasundhara Raje is portrayed as the goddess Annapurna. While Raje's allied ministers' faces appear superimposed on the bodies of Annapurna's attendant gods, the potential voters are shown as suppliant *bhakts* prostrated at the feet of the goddess. Piliavsky rightly points out that this image of the political leader vis-à-vis her potential voters goes against the grain of liberal Western political thought. Democracy in a liberal Western context cannot function in a situation of such blatant and absolute inequality between the voter and the representative. Nor can democracy function with *bhakti* instead of rational choice as the basis of voting behavior. Yet Indian democracy is a vibrant, thriving structure, which demands that, instead of conforming to Eurocentric conceptions of democracy, we redefine it.

Political patronage, although it has been widely studied by village ethnographers and South Asianists, is a dubious term in political science and in current anthropology. One of the reasons that political patronage has been abandoned in recent years as an analytical category is that it is symptomatic of a "desperate" political system where transaction replaces accountability (Piliavsky 2014, 15). Piliavsky argues that political patronage is a coconstitutive system where the clients are not simply oppressed; they are empowered and brought into political agency in these systems. Even in the *jajmānī* system, which village anthropologists have repeatedly written about, the roles of the patron and client are coconstitutive (Mines and Gourishankar 1990). While different *jātis* provide their services to the patron and derive their identity from him, the patron's place is also determined by this clientele and their loyalty. However, while I agree with Piliavsky's impassioned critique of the canons of Eurocentric disciplines, I posit that her argument remains limited within the framework of disciplinary Eurocentrism and fails to take into account the complaints of middle-class and working-class Indian people without formal political affiliation who regularly make the same complaints about Indian democracy. If patronage ties were only an analytical problem in disciplinary frameworks alone and not in the field as well, there would be no need for political actors to publicly disavow formal ties with organized politics to avoid allegations as I show in this chapter. In what follows, I will illustrate the problem of disavowals with two distinct case studies.

Let me now focus on the relationship between the Durgā Pūjā and political patronage. The relationship of the patron, or *zamindar*, to the festival in the *jajmānī* system is clear from the descriptions of the role of the image makers, painters, and priests in the Durgā Pūjā of nineteenth-century Bengal (see Ghosha 1871, 2–5). The *Sārbajanin* Durgā Pūjā[2] of the twentieth century democratized this structure, creating other forms of ownership and patronage (see Guha-Thakurta 2015; McDermott 2011). The local youth clubs, civic organizations of mostly male members representing a neighborhood, became the organizers of this event. As the festival grew, it became more artistic instead of spectacular (Guha-Thakurta 2004); it also became highly commoditized. Around the 2000s, local clubs were competing with each other for status, visibility, corporate sponsorship, and what they call "footfall" of the masses. The patrons of the *pūjā* were roughly the local residents, the club organization, and their corporate sponsors; there were no political leaders involved directly in the patronage of the *pūjās*. The crowds gathered to see the work of high-profile artists or designers who were the stars of the festival in the 2000s. But once the TMC came into power in 2011, they took over the role of patronage and overshadowed the stardom of the *pūjā* artists and designers. Civic funds support the *pūjā* productions in addition to corporate sponsorship. Arguably, TMC's current hegemony over the Durgā Pūjā industry is closer to the nineteenth-century *jajmānī* system. And, like the *jajmānī* system, it is a symbiotic, if not equal, relationship that is shared by the patron and the client.

I have shown elsewhere that the local clubs place a TMC minister as their chairman or chief patron in the interest of obtaining more advertising revenue from networks of crony capitalism (Sen 2018b). In addition to being funded by the state government, they also come under the favorable gaze of the ruling party. But how does the party stand to benefit from funding these massive *pūjās*? The formal strategy of the TMC behind patronizing the *pūjās* has been *janasanyōga* (mass communication). Being civic organizations open to all men of a neighborhood, the local youth clubs are supposed to be politically neutral organizations formally. But in practice the neighborhood club functions as an intermediary organization between individual ministers and local councilors and the residents of the neighborhood. "Each club," I was told at a South Kolkata club, "has two hundred to three hundred families attached to it. The club influences their political opinion in a major way. When a party patronizes that club, they stand to win over their loyalties and their votes" (interview with club member, Bhabanipur Durgotsav Samity Club, October 2016). Funding Durgā Pūjās is another way of extending the network of political patronage to new groups of clients.

But how is this related to political deification? As we know from the literature around the "big man," the show of loyalty and devotion to the political leader leads to grants of largesse from him. In other words, the giving of adoration leads to the receiving of gifts. This mechanism of both flattering and publicly displaying one's loyalty to the minister has led to the political deification of Mamata Banerjee in Bengal. Organizers

Figure 3.2. Photograph of a portrait of Mamata Banerjee. Photo by author.

from local clubs put her image in the Durgā Pūjā *paṇḍal* as a means to get into her good books, and this kind of deification is also used by her cabinet ministers to rise in rank within the political party. Since 2013, there have been reports in local newspapers about TMC ministers rivaling each other to please the chief minister. For instance, over the last four to five years, a prominent minister in TMC called Madan Mitra has been patronizing several *pūjās* in South Kolkata, where his name appears in signs and posters as "Chief Patron." But in 2014, in the throes of a notorious financial scam, he turned up in the role of designer and artist for Bhabanipur Shadhin Sangha, his own neighborhood club. The theme of the *pūjā* was a poem written by the chief minister herself. Since then, each year, this club has been creating *paṇḍals* as elaborate illustrations of poems penned by Mamata Banerjee. Mitra's rival minister Firhad ("Bobby") Hakim, who is a Muslim man, is also a major patron of the Durgā Pūjās of South Kolkata. Since Banerjee funded the Mother's Wax Museum in Kolkata, wax and silicone statues have captured the popular imagination.

Hakim wanted so-called wax statues of Mamata Banerjee at all the *pūjās* he was patronizing. One of the artists reported that Bobby Hakim repeatedly rejected several statues due to their lack of likeness until he was sure that Banerjee would not find the portraits offensive in any way. For the ministers in different ranks of the TMC, the Durgā Pūjā has become a platform for complimenting Mamata Banerjee, through which they can rise in rank within the party by gaining her grace.

While the portrayal of Banerjee as Durgā is unabashed in the visual field, the local clubs are rather evasive about this in the discursive field. When speaking about these images, they clearly state that they have not turned our chief minister into a deity. Typically, they point to a smaller image that receives the ritual treatment while the spectacular image of Mamata and/as Durgā is merely for show. This is where we arrive at the problem of two goddesses in the same ritual space, placed next to each other, ostensibly serving very different functions. However, the two goddesses appear all over Bengal in all kinds of Hindu festivals, such as Kārtik Pūjā in Bansberiya, Sarasvatī Pūjā in Magra, and Kālī Pūjā in Barasat. In cases where the spectacular or novel image of the goddess is deemed ritually inappropriate, the Brahmin priests refuse to worship it (Sen 2018a, 90–91). In such cases, a smaller image is brought so that the goddess can serve a dual function: In her spectacular avatar, she can be a crowd puller. And in her humble, clay form she can fulfill the Brahmin priest's demand of ritual propriety.

While this practice of staging two goddesses is not particular to cases of political deification, it is crucial to how such a practice is legitimized in discourse. In the following sections, I will cite two such examples of the minister's image being intertwined with that of the goddess. In both cases, the clubs appear to be seeking political patronage or proving their loyalty to the party. And in both cases, despite the obvious presence of the minister's image and her ideology all over the *paṇḍal*, the clubs repeatedly disavow any relationship with politics. While questions of political patronage are raised by one goddess in the *paṇḍal*, the other goddess is used to answer those questions. Let us first look closely at one such case in South Kolkata, the home constituency of Mamata Banerjee, before we look at another such case in a census town in another part of Bengal.

The Case of the Communist *Asura*

In 2016, the Bhabanipur Durgotsav Samity Club of South Kolkata created a theme called "inspiration." Since the inspiration was the life of Mamata Banerjee, the *paṇḍal* was based on her biography. The main sponsorship of the *paṇḍal* came from Biswa Bangla (lit. global Bengal), an industry launched by Banerjee to commoditize the "handcrafted heritage" of Bengal and the face of the government-owned handicrafts industry of Bengal. While the money came from advertising the Biswa Bangla label, the main patrons of the *paṇḍal* (as their banner stated) were two politicians of the TMC, both of whom are also local councilors for the Kolkata Municipal Corporation. When asked about the rampant political patronage of Durgā Pūjās in the TMC regime, the club secretary observed the following:

> The leaders of the CPI(M) were anti-religion as per their party constitution. They had to change their attitude to religious festivals when they came to hold public offices. The TMC has no such ideological position against religion. In addition, the present TMC ministers were all involved in the organization of Durgā Pūjās as young men. Now that they are ministers, they are using the platform of the *pūjā* to make themselves and their party more visible in the public space. The goal of the party's involvement in Durgā Pūjā, even according to the minister's speeches, is *janasanyōga*, or mass communication. (Interview with club secretary, Bhabanipur Durgotsav Samity, 2016)

A group of students from the local art academy painted a series of naturalistic images showing the watershed moments in Banerjee's political career and abstract expressionist images showing her contribution to the development of Bengal. They recreated photographs from newspapers to mark some of the iconic moments of Banerjee's life, such as the time she stood on top of an Ambassador car and pretended to strangle herself to death. But other moments—such as the time she was dragged out of the main administrative building of Kolkata by the hair—were never photographed. So, they had to imagine these. These paintings were lined in three rows on the four walls of the *paṇḍal*. Each image bore the face of the political leader in many moods.

At center stage was the image of Durgā, like in any other *paṇḍal*. But at the feet of Durgā was a slightly larger-than-life-size model of Banerjee praying to the goddess. The model wore a white-and-blue sari and Hawai *chappals* (flip-flops), which is the iconography of the leader repeated across the country in all her images. Mamata Banerjee's self-fashioning has a lot to do with her political persona as a female activist from humble roots who, unlike the bourgeois male CPI(M) leaders, can truly empathize with the poor millions she governs.[3] The similarity between her blue-and-white sari and that of Mother Teresa has never been explicitly stated by the party but is implicit in the clear visual mirroring. The combination of the colors blue and white has been laboriously established as the party colors of the TMC to override the red hues of the erstwhile Communist government (see Sen 2018b). There were several Banerjee statues in the 2016 *pūjās*. But no one integrated her image into the Durgā image complex, which typically consists of the goddess; her so-called children Gaṇeś, Kartik, Lakṣmī, and Sarasvatī; the demon Mahiṣāsura, whom she slayed; and her lion. This act of integrating a living political leader into the goddess image was shocking enough to make it into the newspaper as a must-see oddity of the year. In addition, there was another scandal that almost threatened to cover up the image and stop the *pūjā*.

The media reported that the *asura* figure in the Durgā image complex (see figure 3.3) bore an uncanny likeness to Surjakanta Misra, the head of the CPI(M) and the main political opposition to Banerjee. In the market of the so-called theme *pūjās* and designer Durgās, there are no prescriptive guidelines for any of the figures in the Durgā image complex. Compared to many designer Durgās, this was a relatively conventional image. It was a combination of what the clay modelers call *putula mūrti* (naturalistic image) and Oriental *mūrti* (stylized and twisted in the manner of Ajanta and Ellora cave art). The *asura* in these images also has a particular stylistic repertoire: dark skin, curly hair, thick eyebrows, rippling muscles, and an anguished face (see figure 3.4).

This *asura* image was truly unconventional by those standards. The *asura* here was shown as a fair-skinned man who appears unfazed despite being pierced by the raging goddess's trident. The media read this image as a thinly veiled political allegory: Mamata Banerjee is offering her devotion to the goddess, who is in turn blessing her with her right hand. With one of her other arms, she is slaying Banerjee's main political rival in West Bengal.

Figure 3.3. The Durgā *mūrti* at Bhabanipur Dursotsav Samity (Kolkata, 2016). Photo by author.

Figure 3.4. A typical *asura* with dark, curly hair and an enraged or anguished expression (Kolkata, 2013). Photo by author.

But even though the media reported on this political allegory, the organizers claimed no relationship to *rājanīti* (politics) whatsoever. According to them, the theme of the *pūjā* was inspiration under the aegis of Biswa Bangla. Could we see Didi as the icon of the new confident, global Bengali? the organizers asked through this production. Banerjee's early life was a harsh struggle against the patriarchal, upper-caste, upper-class Communist government. The youth of the city are completely unaware of the struggles this woman had to endure in order to become the chief minister of the state. The organizers involved young artists from the art academy to illustrate these moments of struggle for the "young generation who are not interested in politics" (interview with club member, Bhabanipur Durgotsav Samity, 2016).

The club denied the allegation of working with a political agenda. As for the scandal regarding the image of Misra, the secretary told me that these are just jealous residents of the adjoining neighborhood who cannot stand the rising prosperity of their club *pūjā*. "People are mean and conniving; they are trying to ruin our reputation," he said. When I asked him how it was possible to have no political agenda while involving the image of Banerjee in their Durgā *mūrti,* he asked me, "Who said this is Mamata Banerjee? It is a woman wearing a blue-and-white sari. It could be Sister Nivedita or Mother Teresa . . . it could be any woman wearing a white-and-blue sari!" The remarkable likeness of the model to Banerjee was a matter of coincidence, according to the club secretary.

One little fact that disrupted the narrative about the image of the woman being "anyone in a sari" was that this image was not ritually treated. When I asked the organizers why the priest had worshipped a smaller image placed in front of the large tableau, I was told that that it is not permissible to worship an image of a living person in the "Vedic way." A humble, smaller *mūrti* was placed at the feet of the large goddess image. The priest worshipped this *mūrti* instead of the large one. Therefore, while the devotees and *paṇḍal* hoppers were seeking *darśan* from the main goddess image, the ritual offerings from the Brahmin priest were limited only to the smaller image.

On one hand, there is a great need to deny any form of political patronage. Even in a situation where the banner of the club shows politicians as "chief patrons" and the goddess image has the chief minister's model in it, repeated attempts are made to deny any form of political patronage. On the other hand, this image was considered ritually inappropriate. Despite such disavowals, these politically motivated *pūjās* are burgeoning in Bengal. Let me look at another example from a marginal club in a small town far away from Kolkata.

The Case of the Minister Goddess

Prantik Club in Chakdaha, in the Nadia district, created a social media spectacle—a scandal to some, and a joke to others—by portraying Mamata Banerjee as Durgā in their *paṇḍal*. A lifelike, fully colored public statue of Mamata Banerjee stood with her hands folded while ten arms radiated out behind her, each holding a successful project Banerjee has initiated during her tenure as chief minister of West Bengal. The projects were represented in a visual form typical of Nadia: with lifelike miniature clay models in a painted backdrop. For example, Kanyasree, a project working toward the education and empowerment of girls in Bengal, was represented as two schoolgirls in school uniforms riding bicycles near a school building. At the base of the image was the representation of the peasant uprising at Singur and Nandigram, an event that overturned the leftist regime of thirty-three years. Miniature figures of rebelling farmers were shown protesting against the left-wing government under the large, looming figure of the minister-goddess.

Formally, the theme of the Prantik Club was "cēnā mukha, natuna

Figure 3.5. Mamata Banerjee with ten arms behind her, each holding a visual representation of one of her projects in Bengal (Chakdah, October 2016). Photo by author.

Figure 3.6. A close-up of the image showing the representation of Kanyasree, a project initiated by the TMC to subsidize and encourage the education of girls in Bengal. Photo by author.

Figure 3.7. A close-up of the scene showing protesting peasants as miniature figures holding posters of Mamata Banerjee at the feet of the large *mūrti*. Photo by author.

rupa" (known faces, new avatars). Speaking about the idea behind the theme, the secretary of the club said that they were inspired by *unnaẏana* (development), which also happens to be the main agendum of the TMC in Bengal. "We think about *unnaẏana;* we do *unnaẏana;* we stand in support of *unnaẏana*—this is the motto of our club," he said. "We wanted to welcome the efforts of our chief minister, who has been waging a great struggle alongside the common people towards the development of Bengal, having been inspired by the great persons of our past such as Rabindranath Tagore, Kazi Nazrul Islam, Sister Nivedita, and Mother Teresa." He added that since Mā Durgā is a form of female *śakti,* they thought of Mamata Banerjee to represent her. "During the great battle against Mahiṣāsura, there were many gods and goddesses, yet none were strong enough to kill the *asura.* But Mā Durgā used her infinite, mysterious power to kill him." This analogy, translated to political terms, can only mean that if Durgā is a metaphor for Banerjee, then the erstwhile CPI(M) chief minister is likened to Mahiṣāsura. It was a natural assumption that this club has ties with the TMC.

Yet, when asked about the club's relationship to the TMC, the secretary vehemently denied any kind of political association: "This is a local club, *Didi* [Sister]; how can a local club be patronized by one political party? It's a politically neutral organization!" The secretary went on to say that the members of the local administration—the district chairman, subchairman, local members of the Legislative Assembly, the chairman of Chakdaha, the chairman of the adjoining Kalyani, and a noted member of the Legislative Assembly from the TMC—were very pleased with their efforts.

The network of political patronage extends beyond the ministers and the organizers of the *pūjā.* Subir Pal, a National Award–winning clay modeler from nearby Krishnanagar (Nadia), created this spectacular image. Speaking of Subir Pal's work, the secretary of the club said, "We have involved only those people who like *unnaẏana* in this project. Subir Pal likes *unnaẏana,* so we chose him to make this *mūrti.*" Having worked with Subir Pal and his family extensively as part of my research, I asked him, "But Subir Pal's cousin Tarit Pal is also a National Award–winning clay modeler. Does he not like *unnaẏana*? Why didn't you approach him?" At this point, the club secretary truly revealed what he meant by "liking development" or "in support of development." He replied, "Because Subir Pal likes development, he took very little money for this image!" Similarly, the other professionals involved with this production, such as the *paṇḍal* decorators, painters, electricians, light artists, and so on, were all "in support of *unnaẏana,*" which meant that they provided their services either for free or for very little money. Presumably, every artist, craftsman, decorator, flower seller, and other professional attached to this *pūjā* came to be acquainted with the ministers due to this *pūjā*. Even though they did not profit financially from this production, the acquaintance with the minister is often a lot more lucrative than money. In other words, when one becomes acquainted with a minister, begins to refer to him as *Dādā* (Older Brother) or *Māmā* (Maternal Uncle), and carries his personal phone number in their mobile telephone, they come into the informal patronage network of the minister and, by extension, that of the party. In the future, for instance, if the *paṇḍal* decorator buys a piece of land and gets into a thorny legal dispute with his real estate *dālāl* (broker), they will call the minister whom they now refer to as *Dādā* or *Māmā*. One phone call from the local minister or someone higher up in the ranks of the party, depending on the seriousness of the problem, can very easily solve the legal dispute for the *paṇḍal* decorator.

I could not help asking the organizers whether the Communist Party members were offended at the portrayal of Mamata Banerjee as Durgā. The secretary explained,

> Madam, you are just not understanding what I am saying. We have *not* shown Mamata Banerjee as Durgā at all! Our Durgā *mūrti* is in front of the *paṇḍal* . . . behind her, we have done an installation showing *unnaẏana* in Bengal, the many projects of our chief minister that has led to this development! Yes, thousands of people are coming to seek *darśan* at the *paṇḍal*, and they are folding hands and doing *praṇāma* in front of the installation at the back, but the goddess that is being worshipped is in the front! Look at all these women offering sweets and flowers to the *real* goddess during the hour of *Sandhya ārati* [evening prayer].

The "real goddess" was a small, traditional, and delicately made unfired clay image in a secluded shed in the middle of the *paṇḍal* (see figure 3.8). And, as the secretary pointed out, the crowd in the *paṇḍal* was divided in two. Married women waited in a long queue to offer boxes of sweets and flowers to the priest, who in turn offered these to the goddess. Once the sweets were blessed by the goddess, they were returned to the women as *prasāda*. Right behind these women, a crowd had gathered in front of the minister-goddess. Some did *praṇāma*, some just stared in absolute awe, some took photographs with phone cameras or large DSLR cameras, and some took selfies with this spectacular image behind them.

"So people are offering *praṇāma* to your installation as if she were Goddess Durgā?" I asked. At this point, it was clear that that I was trying the secretary's patience. "This is such a common matter . . . Don't you

Figure 3.8. Two goddesses and their devotees. Photo by author.

know our culture at all? Many people touch my mother's feet every day; they do *praṇāma*. If I go to your house and meet your mother, you'll see that I will also touch her feet and do *praṇāma*. We respect our elders as if they were gods and goddesses. We don't know our gods and goddesses in any direct manner! But we accept our elders and parents like *dbitīẏa bhagabāna* (lit. "second only to the gods"). Don't you know this?" In other words, according to the secretary, the minister-as-goddess was not Durgā at all; she is merely an installation showing the work of development in Bengal. When it comes to *darśan*, or ritual gazing, it is not clear what the act of folding hands and offering *praṇāma* to this image means to lay Hindus standing in front of this so-called installation. The organizers argue that when people do offer their devotion to her, it is not because she is portrayed in the form of Durgā but in the way that Hindus worship their parents and ancestors and other "special persons" (see Taves 2012).

Nevertheless, is this act of bowing to the minister-as-goddess in a *paṇḍal* in the context of Durgā Pūjā comparable to touching an older person's feet in a social context? In Bengal, *pujo* (colloq. for *pūjā*, or worship) is a polyvalent term that popularly refers to rituals performed by priests or lay devotees, dedicated to a deity embodied by an image or a *ghat* (pot), on a particular day in the ritual calendar or during the larger festival period including the festivities around the worship of the deity. In the context of Durgā Pūjā, which is special to the city, for example, Bengalis are likely to refer to the entire proceedings around Durgā Pūjā under the brief and ubiquitously intelligible shorthand *pujo*.[4] The buying of new clothes around this time will be called *pujo shopping*, the crawling traffic meandering around massive *paṇḍals* on streets will be called *pujo traffic*, haircuts and beauty treatments will be called *pujora style* by the media and young people of the city, and even the season will be called *pujo time*.

In common parlance, touching someone's feet as an act of respect is not readily called *pujo*. It is called *praṇāma*, which, despite being an act of offering respect, is not seen as an act of formal worship or festivity, which *pujo* popularly means. However, returning to the idea of attribution of sacral qualities to "special persons" from the perspective of the study of religion (Taves 2012), it is clear that these boundaries between deities, religious leaders, celebrities, and highly respectable persons are somewhat fuzzy. From the anthropology of South Asian religions, we know that the larger definition of *pūjā* cannot be conflated with that of *karmakāṇḍa*, or the ritual services provided by Brahmin ritual practitioners in exchange for offerings and money, known as *dakṣiṇā*, to worship a supernatural deity. *Pūjā*, at its core, is simply "an act of respectful honoring" (Fuller 1992, 62) directed toward anyone higher than oneself in a social, familial, or cosmic hierarchy. The act of folding hands, or *praṇāma* (which has also been called *añjali*), is the basic performative act that accompanies *pūjā*. Therefore, the way one is socially trained to perform the act of *praṇāma* when meeting a stranger is the same as when one meets a strange god, even when the strange god is a living person portrayed as a goddess. The Prantik Club effectively uses the fluidity of Bengali Hindu religiosity to disavow any allegations about creating a situation where potential voters are devoutly bowing their heads in front of their looming goddess-like political representative.

Like the Bhabanipur Durgotsav Samity club secretary, who said that the model bearing a clear likeness of the chief minister could be any woman in a white-and-blue sari, the Prantik club organizers asserted that they had not shown Mamata Banerjee as Durgā, even though they had portrayed the minister with ten arms behind her. Here too, this minister-goddess was not ritually worshipped by the Brahmin priest. For the ritual purposes, they had a smaller traditional image in front of the spectacular installation. This second, smaller *mūrti*—traditional and ritually appropriate—stands as a token of Brahminical religiosity while the festival embraces a neoliberal economy of pleasures, spectacles, commodities, and novelties.

Twin Goddesses of Bengal

One way of understanding this fluid and border-crossing nature of popular Hindu religiosity—in this case, that of Bengali Hindus—is by turning to the concept of polytropy. As Michael Carrithers (2000, 835) defines it, "Polytropy is a wholly and thoroughly social concept, denoting that the consumers of religion actively turn to persons, not to impersonal or natural powers. Such persons may be straightforwardly divine, such as gods and goddesses, or living divine persons such as gurus, or even living persons such as priests or mediums who may intercede with a divine person on your behalf." In this sense, one can understand the fluidity of Bengali Hindu religiosity, which has allowed Durgā's face to be modeled after the popular Bollywood heroines of the 1960s despite the popular assumption that living women should not serve as models for the goddess.[5] Mahiṣāsura has been shown variously as a nude self-portrait of the artist or as Osama bin Laden right after 9/11 (McDermott 2011, 145). Durgā has been repeatedly shown in the context of contemporaneous political events, whether in the Bengal famine, a change in political regime, a local train accident, or a global situation such as the demolition of the Bamiyan Buddha (see Agnihotri 2001). Both Durgā and Kālī have been shown in wildly popular *paṇḍal*s based on popular Western films such as *Titanic*, *Avatar*, and *Harry Potter*. As part of a highly commoditized festival, the icon of Durgā now has an inextricable bond with advertising products ranging from women's clothing, makeup, and jewelry to paint, shoes, mobile phones, computers, car tires, and even alcohol.

Over the years, the theme *pūjās* of Kolkata have wholeheartedly embraced all the features of the postliberalization economy in India. The contemporary Durgā Pūjā is characterized above all by the libidinal energy of a large mass of consumer-spectators, in addition to all forms of media, fetishization of commodities, and the obsessive visual consumption and recording of the city turned into both a museum and a carnival. Novelty, spectacle, and advertising revenue are the driving forces behind this festival. In both popular and academic literature, one finds the idea that the Durgā Pūjā is secularizing into a mass festival. For some, the argument is based on the shift away from religiosity to festivity (Rodrigues 2018). For others, the argument is based on how piety and strict adherence to ritual propriety gave way to a mass festival driven first by spectacles and then by a growing discourse around art and design (Guha-Thakurta 2004). Mamata Banerjee's patronage style in the festival, I have argued elsewhere, has introduced a new phase in the festival involving the overt visibility of the political party in the festival-culture arena all over Bengal (Sen 2018b). It is rather tempting to understand this politicization in light of the larger secularization of the Durgā Pūjā festival, whether it is around the decline in expressions of piety or in the secular discourse around the aesthetic merit of Durgā Pūjā art. What stands in the way of this argument is the second small *mūrti*.

The secularization thesis in this context refers to the diminishing control of the Brahminical hegemony over the Durgā Pūjā. While the Durgā Pūjā, or indeed any other mass festival in Bengal, does not have an easy relationship with contemporary forms of Brahminical hegemony that characterize the religiosity of North India under the Bharatiya Janata Party,[6] it is not free from the demands of Brahminical Hinduism either. These festive spaces are colored by rampant commodification, revelry, partying, and the consumption of meat, alcohol, and other items forbidden to pious North Indian Hindus. Yet the *karmakāṇḍa* still forms a major part of the festival for lay Hindus in any neighborhood, particularly for the married women. For example, on *aṣṭamī*, or the eighth day of the *pūjā*, most middle-class Bengali Hindu families gather at the *paṇḍal* to offer *puṣpāñjali*, while some families do the same on the seventh or the ninth day, according to their familial tradition. On *bijaẏā daśamī*, or the final day of Navarātri, when the goddess is immersed, the married women of the neighborhood gather to ritually bid farewell to the goddess, following which they engage in *sindura khēlā* (the play among married women with vermillion powder, a mark of their marital status, symbolically celebrating their wish to die as *sadhabā* [married], i.e., before their husbands). The affective aspects of Durgā Pūjā as it is played out in the life of the community are inextricably tied to the ritual calendar, the Brahminical ritual activity, and the mediation of an authorized Brahmin priest. The second Durgā image is both a necessity and a symbol of this aspect in the so-called secularizing Durgā Pūjā (cf. Guha-Thakurta 2004; Rodrigues 2018).

So, what does this second image of the goddess look like? So far, I have only spoken about the images of Durgā that appear in the public spaces of the city. There is also a parallel domestic worship that is modest in scale and marked by a higher adherence to what Brahmins prescribe as ritually correct. Any caste-based cluster of image makers or clay modelers in Bengal caters to all patrons, ranging from the rich TMC-patronized clubs to a lower-middle-class family with a shoestring budget for a domestic *pūjā*. While some clay modelers work for months on one image that can cost up to INR 100,000, others provide small mass-produced, hollow images made from molds in unfired clay. Typically, these small, inexpensive *mūrtis* are made by the apprentices or women of the workshop. The faces are generic; in technical terms, this face of the goddess is referred to as *putula murti*, or a human-like goddess.[7] Unfired clay, a mixture of earth and water, is said to contain life (Bean 2011, 607). According to Brahminical textual sources and the opinion of clay modelers, it is the first among the materials considered ritually appropriate for the *mūrti* of a Hindu deity (Bean 2011, 607).

Even though the crowds enjoy a Durgā image that looks like a popular Bollywood heroine, or one that is made entirely of dried chilies, or one that is made of silicon and mechanically moves around a *paṇḍal*, some Brahmin priests often refuse to worship these unconventional images, although this is not always the case (Sen 2018a).[8] In some cases, the priests refuse to worship these images because they are not made of unfired clay; in other cases, they find the style too outlandish to inspire any serious devotion. In such situations, a smaller *mūrti* is brought in in the interest of ritual propriety. The thousands of visitors to the *paṇḍal* engage in *darśan* with the larger, more spectacular image, barely even noticing the small one. But it is the small one that is the focus of the ritual practitioner and the devotees (mostly women), for whom the priest turns sweets into *prasāda*. In many cases, this space of *karmakāṇḍa* (priestly worship) is sometimes banished out of the *paṇḍal* in the interest of unencumbered display, as at the Talbagan Club in 2013, where the rituals and the priest were exiled to a small area behind the *paṇḍal*, out of the way of the visitors. It is increasingly common in the Sarasvatī Pūjā of Magra, where the *paṇḍal* houses the spectacular goddess, whereas the *karmakāṇḍa* takes place away from the *paṇḍal* in the clubhouse, where the smaller *mūrti* is placed. Irrespective of how far or how small the space for *karmakāṇḍa*, to the best of my knowledge, there is not a single example where the *karmakāṇḍa* is completely absent.

In cases of political deification, the smaller *mūrti* is a way of fulfilling the political goal without flouting Brahminical principles because, as I have already shown, it is against the "rules," as I was told repeatedly, to worship an image of a living person "in the Vedic way." The smaller *mūrti*, I argue, shows us the place of Bengali Hindu religiosity and the shrinking-yet-inviolable presence of Brahminical hegemony in a festival that several Bengalis identify as "almost nonreligious." Had Durgā Pūjā been a secular festival, there would have been at least one *paṇḍal* that had no space for *karmakāṇḍa*. If the Durgā Pūjā of Bengal was truly a secular space for a show of art, design, and creativity, this smaller *mūrti* would have become redundant. But a Durgā Pūjā is not one or the other; it is a remarkable cohabitation of all these impulses (see also Sen 2018b). As the festival morphs into an industry catering to uncontrolled pleasures and consumption, it is nonetheless marked by Brahminical rituals around which the affective, emotional ties of a community to this festival are played out.

Conclusion: Necessary Disavowals

At the time of writing this article, the religiosity (or the lack of it) among Bengali Hindus came under attack from Hindu nationalists. This is yet another attempt on the part of the ruling right-wing party to create a totalitarian regime of "Hindi-Hindu-Hindustan," which seeks to standardize the religiosity and language of all of India by erasing other religions, other languages, and all other regional versions of Hindu piety in favor of the North Indian forms of Hinduism. They condemn the fact that part of the revelry of the Bengali Durgā Pūjā is the consumption of nonvegetarian food while North Indians fast and refrain from eating even onion or garlic during Navarātri. In addition, they vandalized and forced an apology from a popular hair-salon chain run by a Muslim entrepreneur, Javed Habib, for issuing an advertisement that shows the goddess and her four children getting haircuts, facials, and other beauty treatments at the salon (Dasgupta 2017). The right-wing activists thought of this advertisement as maligning the great glory of the goddess; they also condemned Bengali Hindus as bad Hindus for allowing such behavior. However, the fact remains that Kolkata has seen more than fifty years of such creative advertising, which has always been received in good humor. In the face of the allegations from North Indian Hindu fundamentalists, the permissiveness of middle-class Bengali Hindu religiosity appears remarkable. In popular and academic writing, now more than ever, there is an idea of the Durgā Pūjā as a secular festival. Yet there are limits to its permissiveness. The creative drive of the Durgā Pūjā constantly pushes against what is ritually appropriate. The fact that Brahmin priests can decide that certain images will not be treated ritually shows their relevance in the festival. In this context, the contradiction between what patrons want to show, people want to see, and priests want to worship is precisely why there are two images. Some of these impulses are contradictory, such as the space of ritual propriety in a Brahminical sense and the space of creative and ludic transgression. While there is a tremendous pull toward the ludic, the novel, and the spectacular, the small *mūrti* acts as a mark of disavowal of that very impulse. I have argued that the two *mūrtis* seen in the festivals of Bengal signify the contradictory impulses, however unequal in their force, that bolster the development of this festival culture together.

The other contradiction that is the heart of this discussion is the disavowal of any form of political patronage in the face of obvious connections with a political party. How do we explain this contradiction? The answer might lie in why Piliavsky (2014) thinks patronage studies have fallen out of favor in the last few decades. She believes that this kind of academic disavowal "issues from deep-seated prejudices and from two beliefs about patronage to which we hold fast, if often unwittingly. We believe that we already know what patronage is, and we believe that it must be a bad thing" (5). While her volume correctly argues for the fact that, despite the unequal power relation, political patronage is also empowering for the clients, this notion of political patronage as a "bad thing" is by no means a prejudice held by academics alone. I argue that the reason behind the disavowal of any political connection among the men of the organizing clubs is the popular perception that politics is dirty. The dirty nature of politics is part of popular idioms in Bengal (Ruud 2001). While Ruud argues for the *artha / dharma* (material / spiritual) dichotomy in the Bengali psyche, which renders all politics and business essentially amoral and "dirty," I will veer away from this essentializing attribution and instead ascribe this perception of dirtiness to the nature of Indian democracy, wherein parties have little accountability, criminals play a major role, and corruption is ubiquitous. But, as Ruud points out, these corrupt politicians are the only options that the voters have. Political patronage is one way they negotiate their agency in informal networks with the powerful. While these networks are desirable, people continue to disavow any public admission of desiring these networks, for fear of being accused of taking unfair advantage of political ties, being dishonest, or simply being part of dirty politics.

To conclude, I have shown the elaborate network of power, patronage, and political interest among actors such as club organizers and TMC ministers, which leads to the deification of the minister in various forms. I have also pointed out that, just as there is an unrestrainable process of entwining the image of the goddess and that of the minister, simultaneously, there exists an undeniable process of disavowals and dissociations. I have shown what these disavowals are and why they are necessary, no matter how close the icons of Durgā and Mamata Banerjee may come to each other; even if they are infinitely repeated and juxtaposed on flex posters in every alley and on every street corner, they never truly become indistinguishable in the contemporary Durgā Pūjā of Kolkata. For as long as there are two goddesses in the *paṇḍals* of Kolkata, the two icons of Durgā and Didi will venture very close but never fuse together.

Notes

1. In the election of 2011, following some major turning points in the political history of West Bengal, Mamata Banerjee was elected as chief minister of West Bengal after thirty-three years of the communist party regime in the state.

2. *Sārbajanin pūjā* refers to a particular organizational structure that we still see in Bengal. In the twentieth century, the goddess in the *Sārbajanin pūjā* traveled from the courtyards of aristocratic homes to the streets. The *Sārbajanin pūjās* of the early twentieth century introduced a new structure wherein *paras*, or neighborhoods, were represented by youth clubs raising communal subscriptions from the citizens.

3. Mamata Banerjee's self-fashioning as a female political leader (Nielsen 2016) and as an artist (Sen 2018b) have been discussed widely in the Bengali media over the years.

4. For example, when a woman in the house says "pujo debo" (I will give *pujo*), she could mean *anhik*, or the daily ritual offering to the deities in her domestic shrine, or she could mean going to the local temple and offering sweets and *pranami* (most commonly money) to the priest, who in turn offers it to the deity. When a young boy, eagerly waiting to play a lively game of kite flying with his young local rivals, excitedly says "Biswakarma pujo aschhe" (The *pujo* of Biswakarma is coming up), in this context he means the assigned day of the worship of Biswakarma is coming up.

5. Despite some condescension from the celebrated master clay modelers of Kolkata and Krishnanagar, the images of Durgā modeled after Hema Malini and Sridevi were popular in the 1980s and 1990s (Agnihotri 2001, 84). For decades now, the popular program *Mahalaya* on Bengali television channels has seen heroines from Bollywood, such as Hema Malini, play Durgā. To this day, heroines from the Bengali film industry play Durgā on screen for the *Mahalaya* program.

6. The consumption of mutton (goat meat) and even alcohol are permitted, if not necessary, on the ninth night of Durgā Pūjā. However, a large media controversy broke out on this issue when a blogger posted a recipe for a Bengali-style egg roll on social media, earning the ire of pious Hindus from the Hindi Belt (Chakraborty 2017). This was followed by a social media conflict and vandalism of the premises of a salon chain run by a Muslim man who, following the long tradition of such advertisement, had published an image showing Durgā and her children at a beauty parlor getting different kinds of beauty treatments (Dasgupta 2017). In the face of the condescension of upper-caste North Indian Hindus who were ashamed and outraged at the practices of Bengalis, who according to them were not real Hindus, the Kolkata Bengalis argued back by saying that the North Indians do not understand their religiosity (J. Chatterjee 2017) and should, at the least, leave it alone.

7. Elsewhere, I have shown how the face of the traditional Durgā has changed over time to naturalize this representation (Sen 2018a).

8. In some cases, ambitious artists who want their piece to be become part of an art collection want to avoid the possibility of the *mūrti* getting soiled by to the application of *sindur*, flowers, and other ritual offerings (see Sen 2018a).

References

Agnihotri, Anita. 2001. *Kolkatar Pratimashilpira*. Kolkata: Ananda.

Amin, Shahid. 1984. "Gandhi as Mahatma: Gorakhpur District, Eastern UP, 1921–2." *Subaltern Studies* 3:1–61.

Bean, Susan S. 2011. "The Unfired Clay Sculpture of Bengal in the Artscape of Modern South Asia." In *A Companion to Asian Art and Architecture*, edited by Rebecca M. Brown and Deborah S. Hutton, 604–28. Chichester, UK: Wiley-Blackwell.

Carrithers, Michael. 2000. "On Polytropy: Or the Natural Condition of Spiritual Cosmopolitanism in India: The Digambar Jain Case." *Modern Asian Studies* 34 (4): 831–61.

Chakraborty, Saptarshi. 2017. "Why Was a Bengali Trolled for a Video about Eating Egg Rolls during Durga Pujo?" *Scroll.in*, September 15, 2017. https://scroll.in/article/850448/why-was-a-bengali-trolled-for-a-video-about-eating-egg-rolls-during-durga-pujo.

Chatterjee, Joyjayanti. 2017. "Leave Durga Maa Alone: An Angry Bengali Woman Hits Out at Hatemongers." *DailyO*, September 23, 2017. https://www.dailyo.in/voices/durga-puja-controversy-egg-roll-video-jawed-habib-muharram-mamata-bjp-rss/story/1/19675.html.

Chatterjee, Partha. 2004. *The Politics of the Governed: Reflections on Popular Politics in Most of the World*. New York: Columbia University Press.

Dasgupta, Piyasree. 2017. "Those Ranting against Jawed Habib's Durga Ad Know Nothing about Bengal's Puja Traditions." *HuffPost India*, September 7, 2017. https://www.huffingtonpost.in/2017/09/07/those-ranting-against-jawed-habibs-durga-ad-know-nothing-about-bengals-secular-puja-traditions_a_23198947/.

Fuller, Chris. 1992. *The Camphor Flame: Popular Religion and Society in India*. Princeton, NJ: Princeton University Press.

Ghosha, Pratapachandra. 1871. *Durga Puja*. Calcutta: Hindoo Patriot.

Guha-Thakurta, Tapati. 2004. "From Spectacle to 'Art': The Changing Aesthetics of Durgā Pūjā in Contemporary Calcutta." *Art India* 9, no. 3 (quarter 3): 34–56.

———. 2015. *In the Name of the Goddess: The Durga Pujas of Contemporary Kolkata*. Kolkata: Primus Books.

Jain, Mayank. 2015. "Gujarat's Modi Temple Isn't the First Shrine to the PM: UP Village Already Has One." *Scroll.in*, February 12, 2015. https://scroll.in/article/695974/gujarats-modi-temple-isnt-the-first-shrine-to-the-pm-up-village-already-has-one.

McDermott, Rachel Fell. 2011. *Revelry, Rivalry, and Longing for the Goddesses of Bengal: The Fortunes of Hindu Festivals*. New York: Columbia University Press.

Mines, Mattison, and Vijayalakshmi Gourishankar. 1990. "Leadership and Individuality in South Asia: The Case of the South Indian Big-Man." *Journal of Asian Studies*, 49 (4), 761–86.

Nielsen, Kenneth Bo. 2016. "Mamata Banerjee: Redefining Female Leadership in India's Democracy." In Ruud and Heierstad 2016, 101–34.

Piliavsky, Anastasia. 2014. Introduction to *Patronage as Politics in South Asia*. Edited by Anastasia Piliavsky, 1–35. Cambridge: Cambridge University Press.

Price, Pamela. 1989. "Kingly Models in Indian Political Behavior: Culture as a Medium of History." *Asian Survey* 29 (6): 559–72.

Price, Pamela, and Dusi Srinivas. 2016. "Patrimonial and Programmatic Talking about Democracy in a South Indian Village." In Ruud and Heierstad 2016, 79–100.

Rodrigues, Hillary. 2018. Conclusion to *Nine Nights of the Goddess*, Simmons, Sen, and Rodrigues 2018, 317–30.

Ruud, Arild Engelsen. 2001. "Talking Dirty about Politics: A View from a Bengali Village." In *The Everyday State and Society in Modern India*, edited by Chris Fuller, 115–36. London: Hurst.

Ruud, Arild Engelsen, and Geir Heierstad, eds. 2016. *India's Democracies: Diversity, Co-optation, Resistance*. Oslo: Universiteitsforlaget.

Sen, Moumita. 2018a. "From the Great Goddess to Everywoman: Western Naturalism and the Durga *murti* in West Bengal." In *Religion and Technology in India: Spaces, Practices and Authorities*, edited by Knut A. Jacobsen and Kristina Myrvold, 75–94. London: Routledge.

———. 2018b. "Politics, Religion, and Art in the Durgā Pūjā of West Bengal." In Simmons, Sen, and Rodrigues 2018, 105–20. Albany: State University of New York Press.

Simmons, Caleb, Moumita Sen, and Hillary Rodrigues, eds. 2018. *Nine Nights of the Goddess: The Navarātri Festival in South Asia*. Albany: State University of New York Press.

Sengar, Resham. 2017. "Sonia Gandhi Temple in Telangana Has an Idol of Her Posing Like a Goddess." *Times of India*, November 22, 2017. https://timesofindia.indiatimes.com/travel/destinations/sonia-gandhi-temple-in-telangana-has-an-idol-of-her-posing-like-a-goddess/as61750414.cms.

Taves, Ann. 2012. "Special Things as Building Blocks of Religions." In *The Cambridge Companion to Religious Studies*, edited by Robert A. Orsi, 58–83. Cambridge: Cambridge University Press.

4

Limits of Creativity

Kolu in Brahmin Vaiṣṇava Households in Kāñcipuram

UTE HÜSKEN

Some scholars claim that festivals encompass a variety of genres of activities, such as play, ritual, and spectacle, nested in one another (MacAloon 1984); others focus instead on the different modes of activity observable during celebrations, such as ludic, expressive, dramatic, or aesthetic modes (Grimes 2013, 204). Festivals like Navarātri are time and space set apart from everyday activities and, as such, provide occasion for creativity. But how creative can one be within the frame of a joyful and ludic yet religiously significant festival? In this chapter, I explore an instance of ritual creativity occasioned by Navarātri that—in the eyes of some festival participants—borders on transgression. I will thus focus on the limits of creativity. When and why is ritual creativity acceptable, even welcomed as innovation, and when and why is creativity perceived as inappropriate?

Navarātri in Brahmin Vaiṣṇava Settings

Kāñcipuram, a town circa 70 km west of Chennai in Tamil Nadu, is an old religious center of South India. This rather small temple town[1] has long been well known as the southernmost of the "seven holy cities of Hinduism," promising liberation (*mokṣa*) from the cycle of rebirths and deaths.[2] While, historically, many religious traditions have played an important role in Kāñcipuram,[3] today the Hindu traditions of Vaiṣṇavism, Śaivism, and Śāktism dominate the religious landscape of the city. Inhabitants of the town often speak of it as being divided into two sections, Viṣṇukāñci in the southeast and Śivakāñci in the northwest, which encompasses also the largest temple of a goddess in town (figure 4.1). This perception is based on the distribution of the biggest and many of the oldest temples in town, since the northwestern center of the town is dominated by the huge Ekāmranātha temple (a form of Śiva) and also houses the temple of the goddess Kāmākṣī, who is often represented as Ekāmranātha's wife (Schier 2018). The southeast is characterized by many of the older Viṣṇu temples, with the huge Varadarāja temple at its easternmost end. Most of the Brahmin Vaiṣṇava communities cluster in this part of the town. Many of the local Vaiṣṇavas[4] live either in the streets directly adjacent to the Varadarāja temple or nearby. In this contribution, I am looking at Navarātri practices of a range of participants from this rather orthodox Brahmin Vaiṣṇava milieu in Kāñcipuram.[5] Some are priests (*arcaka*) in the Varadarāja temple, but the main protagonist in this chapter, Sundararajan, is connected to the temple through other ritual services that he inherited from his ancestors.

As explained in detail elsewhere (Hüsken 2018), Navarātri is celebrated in the temple setting, but the temple celebrations in the Varadarāja temple differ significantly from those in temples of goddesses: in contrast to the Kāmākṣī temple in Kāñcipuram, where the goddess is the main actress during the entire celebration, in the Varadarāja temple we find very little emphasis on the goddess. Yet, importantly, while the temple

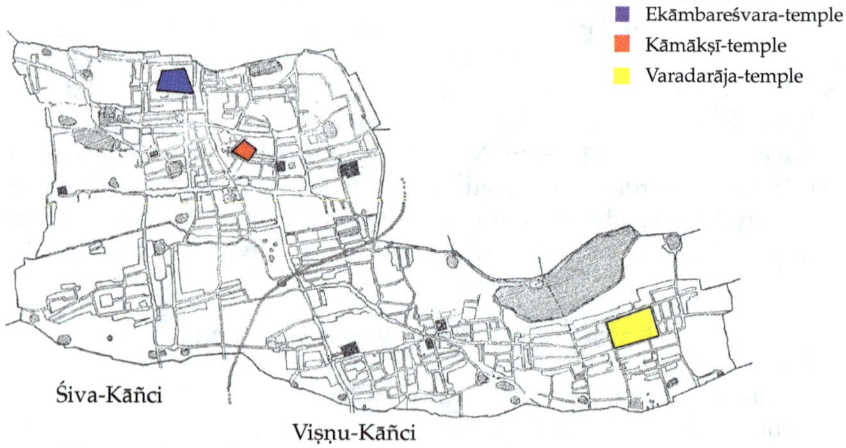

Figure 4.1. Map of Kāñcipuram showing Śivakāñci and Viṣṇukāñci. © Ute Hüsken, adapted from the map given in Porcher (1984, 27).

celebrations differ—even if they complement each other—the domestic celebrations of Navarātri are surprisingly similar, irrespective of the sectarian affiliation of the household. Significantly, this also holds true for the households of the priests serving in the different temples.

Kolu and Brahmin Temple Priests

Thus, the major Navarātri ritual in Brahmin households in Kāñcipuram is *kolu*, the display and veneration of dolls on a multitiered stage resembling steps (for details, see Ilkama, this volume). This *kolu* setup in many of the priests' households[6] is, in its sheer physical presence, very prominent: often the *kolu* dominates the space in the priestly families' living rooms, where guests are received (figure 4.2).[7] The *kolu* is also ritually prominent, as the ritual activities and visits connected to *kolu* are a major part of each evening and night of the nine-day-long festival. Mostly, female guests are received, honored, and entertained, and the women and girls of the households themselves spend a lot of time visiting other *kolus* in the neighborhood.

While one can find hardly any difference between the *kolu* setup in households and the rituals connected to it of the priests of a Viṣṇu temple, of a Śiva temple, or of a temple of the goddess,[8] there are, in fact, sectarian ritual differences during Navarātri. In the households of the Varadarāja-temple priests, no worship of girls (*kanyāpūjā*) or worship of auspiciously married women (*sumaṅgalīpūjā*) will be performed, whereas, for example, the priests of the Kāmākṣī temple would arrange for such *pūjās* every day. Moreover, in the Śaiva and Kāmākṣī settings, during the last ten to fifteen years a spillover of *kolu* into the temple has begun: people who do not maintain *kolu* in their own homes often donate *kolu* sets to the temple in order to fulfill a certain vow (*vrata*), which might, for example, be connected to the wish for a good marriage partner for the daughter. Accordingly, the Kāmākṣī temple, for instance, now maintains stairs with *kolu* dolls in the Navarātri *maṇḍapa* during the Navarātri festivities (see Ilkama, this volume; Narayanan 2018; Sivakumar 2018). In contrast, no *kolu* is set up in the Varadarāja temple. Both ritual differences—the lack of *kanyāpūjā* in Vaiṣṇava households and of *kolu* in the Varadarāja temple—are closely connected to the rather strict separation in terms of ritual practices and rules between the temple and the domestic setting in this specific Vaiṣṇava context. Yet even in the much more conservative Varadarāja temple, one finds performative echoes of the domestic *kolu* setting: the toddlers and younger children of the Vaiṣṇava families connected to the Varadarāja temple are, during Navarātri, often dressed up as deities of the Sanskritic Hindu pantheon or as Vaiṣṇava saints and

Figure 4.2. *Kolu* dominates the space in the priestly families' living room, where guests are received (October 11, 2005). Photo by author.

taken to the temple in the evenings (figure 4.3). Āṇṭāḷ, Kṛṣṇa, Sarasvatī, and Lakṣmī then chase each other through the temple courtyard, while Varadarāja and Lakṣmī are admired in the thousand-pillar *maṇḍapa*.[9] The dressed-up children can be seen as resembling the dolls in the domestic *kolu* setting, which in this way spills over into the temple, albeit only for the time of their temple visit.[10]

Figure 4.3. Children during Navarātri in the courtyard of the Varadarāja temple, dressed up as deities and mythological figures (October 14, 2007). Photo by author.

Apart from being the seat of the goddess who is venerated in the *kolu*, the *kolu* setup is also an important playful educational device, both in terms of religious education and of family history. The dolls are explained especially to children—but also to inquisitive foreigners—and, at that time, the mythology behind a scene is explained as well as the personal history of each doll and how it was acquired. For example, Kṛṣṇa lifting a mountain refers to the Govardhana story but also might remind the family of the great-grandfather's trip to Varanasi, where he bought this specific doll.[11]

A distinctive feature of *kolu* as practiced in the homes of temple priests deserves mention. In contrast to other Brahmin households, where women are in charge of the *kolu* setup (Ilkama 2018), in the Bhaṭṭars' (the Vaiṣṇava-temple priests') houses, usually the men set up the *kolu*.[12] Here, aesthetics and the kind of creativity connected to *kolu* are seen as areas of the male priests' expertise, as they are in charge of the deity's decoration (*alaṃkāra*) in the temple, which is an important source of pride for the priests and is the domain they put their hearts into.[13]

At the same time, one can easily see that most *kolus* set up in the households of the Bhaṭṭars are rather traditional in character. In these *kolus*, we mainly find deities, scenes from Purāṇic mythology, or rural scenes. While new themes clearly have been integrated at some point in time, these processes seem to take place much more slowly than in other domestic settings. Thus, a Mickey Mouse greets the onlooker enthusiastically from amidst the mythological themes (figure 4.4), and a village scene shows people sitting in front of a television set. At the beginning of the twenty-first century, though, neither Mickey Mouse nor a television set can be considered innovative.[14]

Not innovation but adherence to tradition is valued in the Bhaṭṭars' *kolus*. However, within these confines there is still much room for creativity and individual expression. The *kolu* of Kṛṣṇasvāmi Bhaṭṭar is exemplary in this regard. Not content with using prefabricated clay-doll sets, he consistently makes efforts to replicate scenes from Vaiṣṇava mythology in creative ways by working on a perfect setup for these scenes. First, he dug a hole in his living-room floor, which serves as a temple tank during Navarātri. Ten years later, this temple tank displays both the Gajendramokṣa myth and the floating festival (Tamil: *teppoccavam*) of the Varadarāja temple (figure 4.5). This household's *kolu* stands out through its size and attention to detail (see figure 4.2), not through innovative themes. In short, the Bhaṭṭars' *kolus* typically are neither extremely innovative nor creative in

Figure 4.4. *Kolu* of a priestly family in Kāñcipuram displays mythological scenes along with a figure of Mickey Mouse (September 24, 2006). Photo by author.

Figure 4.5. The replica of a temple tank displays the Gajendramokṣa myth along with the floating festival of Viṣṇu and Lakṣmī (October 3, 2011). Photo by author.

their content, though a high degree of professionalism and love of detail is certainly visible in their execution. However, the display of traditional themes, attention to detail, and care in execution are not enough for the success of a *kolu*, as we shall see soon. In one specific setting, innovation and inventiveness, coupled with the attempt to propagate ecological awareness, are taken too far.

Life-Sized Dolls

Mr. Surasika Sundararajan is part of the conservative Vaiṣṇava milieu connected to the Varadarāja temple. He is—on his mother's side—a descendant of the Tātācārya families[15] and is even able to trace his ancestry back to Lakṣmīkumāra Tātācārya, a famed benefactor of the temple, who was spiritual advisor to the Vijayanagara kings and whose statue is enshrined and worshipped in the temple's Vedānta Deśika shrine.[16] Sundararajan lives with his wife in a recently constructed house on West

Maṭa Street, facing the western temple wall, on the grounds of the house where Lakṣmīkumāra Tātācārya lived.

Sundararajan's family had for a long time been deeply involved in the temple affairs, including the right to sponsor certain rituals every year. His great-grandfather was a trustee of the temple for sixty years, until 1908,[17] and his grandfather, R. Kumāra Tātācārya, was trustee of the temple in 1918 and again from 1935 to 1941. Accordingly, Sundararajan preserves a number of otherwise little-known stories about the temple. Thus, he told me that "in olden days" there was a tunnel from Lakṣmīkumāra Tātācārya's house (that is now his) to the Tāyār (Lakṣmī) shrine inside the temple, to enable orthodox Vaiṣṇava women to visit this shrine without being seen.[18] He also reports that at that time there was a separate entrance to the temple tank for the women of the Tātācārya families.[19] Sundararajan's wife, Dr. Nirmala Sundararajan, did her PhD in Indian music on the topic "Compositional Diversities in Carnatic Music." She is an internationally recognized performer of Carnatic music who regularly performs in India, Europe, and the United States. Both Sundararajan and his wife are very cosmopolitan and traditional at the same time. They both have traveled a lot, and both are perfectly fluent in and happy to speak English. At the same time, the couple observes a number of ritual rules, which might be considered outdated by other Vaiṣṇavas in town. For example, they are fully aware that in earlier times during the Brahmotsava celebrations (Brahmotsava is the biggest annual festival of the Varadarāja temple) no private function was conducted in town, and nobody was supposed to cross the town limits. Accordingly, Nirmala Sundararajan told me that in 2006 she, along with a number of others, went to the Toll Gate east of the temple for the duration of the hoisting of the flag (*dhvajārohaṇa;* on this ritual, see Hüsken 2013b). The Toll Gate is considered the border of Varadarāja's terrain, and by going there she made sure that she was not "in town" during the beginning of this festival (marked by the hoisting of the flag), since she knew that she would have to leave the town during the festival.

Her husband, Sundararajan, had visited the United States in the 1960s and brought back a camera with him, with which he took many pictures. In spite of the resistance and objections of many dignitaries in the temple against taking pictures even of the festival statue (*utsavabera*),[20] Sundararajan—through his authority as Tātācārya—continued to take pictures until people got used to it and even asked him for prints of his photographs. From his narration about the specific history of photography at the Varadarāja temple, it is evident that Sundararajan admires and promotes creativity. It was certainly his experience with photography, which he managed to introduce as an innovation in temple life in the 1960s, that made him also more adventurous with *kolu,* as we shall see.

Sundararajan's Family Tradition

When discussing Navarātri practices, Sundararajan suggests that Navarātri *kolu* is a "special *pūjā* by ladies" and "a social event . . . during which unmarried girls visit each other" to display their "wifely" skills such as musicality, dance, and making *kolams* (all interviews quoted from in this section were conducted on October 3, 2017).[21] As a ritual sequence of importance mainly for unmarried girls, he seems to imply that it is—at least for Vaiṣṇavas—not a strictly religious event. He also sees the *kolu* doll collections as very similar to a stamp or coin collection, as a hobby that one pursues. This attitude reflects a prevalent view among male Brahmin Vaiṣṇavas on vernacular and performative ritual traditions that are not codified in (Sanskrit) texts.[22]

This attitude might also explain why he, as a rather conservative Brahmin Vaiṣṇava, does not hesitate to experiment with *kolu* the way he does. He takes this hobby rather far in that he actually makes the dolls he displays on his annual *kolu*. By doing so, he continues a family tradition. Both his father's mother and his mother's mother made dolls. After them, his mother's brother made dolls, too. His mother then also started to make dolls, with the important restriction that she did not spend any money on the material she used.[23] Sundararajan recollects, "She used to collect waste-cloth pieces from the tailor's shop and make stuffed dolls. She used to make bodies stiff by using the steel wire from the crackers thrown away . . . nothing was bought and no money was spent." In spite of this restriction, Sundararajan's mother, Padma, was able to create an impressive number of dolls within only two or three years.

While traditionally the first *kolu* dolls in a Brahmin household are presented to a woman in her first year after marriage, and this initial stock of dolls usually is supplemented with annual purchases of dolls thereafter, this evidently did not happen in Sundararajan's family. According to Sundararajan's recollection, in his home, *kolu* was not set up until he moved out to attend college.[24] Until then, rather than setting up *kolu*, his mother had been a self-taught maker of dolls—a clear indication of her determination and creativity. Although her doll-making skills were not appreciated much in the village in which he grew up, his mother's passion came into the limelight after his parents moved in with him and his family in their Chennai home. Sundararajan explains, "Chennai was a metropolitan city, and we used to have a lot of contacts. It was a good place for display of my mother's *kolu*." When Padma lived with her son in Chennai, she emphasized the educational purpose of her doll making: "She hit upon the idea of making complete sets of dolls, for showing Ramayana, story of Krishna, etc., and she used to arrange the *kolu* in such a manner that schoolchildren could see well. So she used to display them on low tables rather than usual traditional Navarātri steps." At this point, Sundararajan started to help his mother with small carpentry jobs. In this way he involved himself in *kolu* making.[25] Another factor was the growing public interest in his mother's *kolu*: "We used to have a big hall in our house in Chennai, and that attracted a lot of visitors. My mother became very famous." Since there was also some media attention to his mother's *kolu* (she was soon known as Kolu Mami), they also started to hand out printed invitations. Over time, the preparations for Navarātri became more elaborate and time consuming, and the *kolu* was not removed at the end of Navarātri but stayed on display for one or two months. Until Padma's death in 1999, they maintained this Navarātri *kolu* tradition in their Chennai house.

Thus, in this family the *kolu* tradition, and especially the act of making dolls, connected and continues to connect the generations. With his own retirement, Sundararajan and his wife moved to Kāñcipuram, and, as he had more time on his hands, Sundararajan started his own *kolu* by displaying his mother's arrangements in his house. I first encountered this *kolu* in 2006. Unlike the *kolu* I had seen in other houses, his was not displayed on a specifically erected construction resembling stairs; the doll ensembles with various themes were spread over the entire house, including on the staircase leading up to the first floor. Importantly, all the themes were and continue to be local, directly referring to the rituals, mythology, and festivals celebrated in the Varadarāja Perumāḷ temple. Upstairs was a scene from the Varadarāja-temple myth *Hastigirimāhātmya*, in which Viṣṇu prevented Goddess Sarasvatī (who took the form of the river Vegavatī) from destroying Brahmā's sacrifice by blocking her way with his body. Here, Sundararajan also displayed the sacrificial fire from which Viṣṇu later appeared as Varadarāja (figure 4.6).

Over the years, Sundararajan became even more creative. He started to make life-size dolls that replicate the statues in the Varadarāja temple (figures 4.7 and 4.8). Year by year, encouraged by his friends from Chennai, Sundararajan became more ambitious. He started to create the main deity Varadarāja every year, mounted on one of the huge wooden animal vehicles (*vāhana*) that carry him through town during the processions of the annual Brahmotsava festival. In 2010 he prepared a huge *siṃhavāhana* (lion vehicle) for Navarātri in his house, intending to convey a rendering as close as possible (in size and appearance) to the original statue in the temple.[26] In later years, he even re-created the priests and the umbrellas that accompany the deity during these processions (figures 4.9 and 4.10). He displays all these creations in his house during Navarātri, at a time when other houses display *kolu*. Sundararajan says, "Since I don't have

Figure 4.6. Sundararajan's replica of the central scene in the text *Hastigirimāhātmya* (September 25, 2006). Photo by author.

enough space and I use the same size as the temple, I display only one *vahanam* every year. This is my *kolu*."

At the same time, Sundararajan acknowledges that "the specialty of the *kolu* is not very well recognized by the women of Kāñcipuram . . . it is not about liking; they cannot enjoy it." And in fact, while he often showed me around proudly, I rarely encountered his local peers visiting to attend his *kolu* display. Though he asks his neighbors to come, he realizes that they mainly come out of politeness, if at all. Yet they avoid commenting on the *kolu* and do not sit and sing in front of his arrangements. His wife, Nirmala, observed in 2017, "They [i.e., their female neighbors] don't appreciate it at all. Nowadays they do not even come when they are invited." This is, in fact, extraordinary. As emphasized by a number of authors of the Navarātri working group (Ilkama, this volume and 2018; Narayanan, this volume and 2018; Wilson 2018; Sivakumar 2018), *kolu* during Navarātri is a major occasion for women and girls to visit each other's houses and to look at and appreciate the *kolu* set up there, and it is considered an insult if the neighbors do not pay a visit during this time.

Figure 4.7. The adorned festival images of Varadarāja and Tāyār along with Varadarāja's further consorts Śrīdevī and Bhūdevī during Navarātri (October 12, 2005). Photo by author.

Figure 4.8. Sundararajan's replica of the festival images of Varadarāja and Tāyār along with Varadarāja's further consorts Śrīdevī, Bhūdevī, Āṇṭāḷ, and Malayāla Nācciyār (April 1, 2010). Photo by author.

Figure 4.9. Varadarāja on Yāḷi *vāhana* during the festival Brāhmotsava (June 8, 2009). Photo by author.

Figure 4.10. Sundararajan's replica of Varadarāja on Yāḷi *vāhana* (October 15, 2015). Photo by author.

Yet, clearly, Sundararajan and his wife Nirmala are also fully aware of why the *kolu* in their house does not attract many local visitors. The theme of Sundararajan's *kolu* is not unusual. Replications of the religious and ritual activities in town can also be found in the regular miniature *kolu* of his neighbors. There, one finds processions of the deities and often special features of the temple, such as the gold and silver lizards. But Sundararajan's display differs from the display of the Brahmotsava processions in the normal *kolus* in the size of his dolls and in the material he uses to construct these. Like his mother, he uses mostly throwaway household material, such as plastic bags, tubes, old pipes, and so on, to create his dolls (figure 4.11). He does so because he wants to demonstrate and propagate ecological awareness. While this choice of material follows the example set by his mother, who also used rags and discarded wires, from a conservative religious point of view, waste material is considered impure and thus an entirely inappropriate material for even a replica of a god. The conventional *kolu* dolls, at least the important and old ones, are made from clay, wood, or plaster.

The close resemblance of Sundararajan's creation with the Varadarāja statues in the temple might even be one major factor preventing his neighbors from coming. The two *pratimās* (reflections) might be too similar to each other—the one made according to āgamic injunctions from a mixture of metals called *pañcaloha,* and the other made of used material that has been thrown away. This inbuilt ritual impurity is not countered but rather emphasized by the excellent artistic execution of the replicas. How can someone make the beloved deity Varadarāja Perumāḷ out of waste? This seems to be too much of a stretch for the conservative Brahmin Vaiṣṇava audience connected to the Varadarāja temple, Sundararajan's peers. Accordingly, the Brahmin neighbors avoid Sundararajan's house during Navarātri. Sundararajan reports that, in contrast, his non-Brahmin neighbors tend to appreciate and respect his skills, as do his friends from Chennai when they come for a visit.[27] Sundararajan thinks that they are exposed to more experimental art and therefore can appreciate his work.

Conclusion

On the one hand, while Sundararajan's creativity is appreciated by an art crowd and by an audience that is less concerned with ritual purity (a non-Brahmin audience), as a *kolu* that serves this specific ritual purpose, his creations have failed. In this sense, his ritual creativity has gone too far. The dolls created by him are, in this conservative setting, not ritually acceptable, and they are even perceived as a transgression by Sundararajan's peers, orthodox Brahmin Vaiṣṇavas of Kāñcipuram. On the other hand, the acceptance by the non-Brahmin audience shows that the permissible degree

Figure 4.11. Armature serving as the base for Sundararajan's replicas of Varadarāja's *vāhanas* (August 1, 2016). Photo by author.

of inventiveness and creativity always depends on the specific context. Yet it remains to be explored whether those who admire Sundararajan's creations see them as ritually efficacious. In contrast to the conservative Vaiṣṇava Bramin setting, where Sundararajan's creations are not seen as ritually efficacious, Ilkama (this volume), in her research on other *kolu* settings in Kāñcipuram, shows that in non-Brahmin families who have rather recently adopted the practice of setting up *kolu*, creativity and change is a precondition for the efficacy of *kolu*. Here, even meat and alcohol might be the appropriate offerings to the goddess installed in the *kolu*, and the goddess might manifest her presence in the hostess, possessing her and speaking through her to the visitors. Both practices would be unthinkable in the context of the *kolu* of the local Vaiṣṇava Brahmins.[28] The different assessment of creativity and innovation in *kolu* is thus connected to different categories: notions of ritual purity on the one hand and ritual efficacy on the other. Importantly, even within the same setting (i.e., the same ritual, location, and time), the concrete context decides what works and what does not work, urging us to pay attention to every detail.

Notes

1. In the 2011 Census of India, Kāñcipuram had a population of 164,384; see 2011 Census Data, Primary Census Abstract Data, accessed May 25, 2018, http://www.censusindia.gov.in/pca/SearchDetails.aspx?Id=721293.

2. *Brahmāṇḍapurāṇa* 3,40.91. Mentioned already in texts from about the second century BCE, Kāñcipuram can boast of having "a proven history of urban habitation dating back at least 2,000 years, making it one of the oldest continuously settled cities in southern India, and indeed in South Asia" (Heitzman and Rajagopal 2004, 239).

3. Kāñcipuram is also called the "city of the thousand temples," as it is characterized by innumerable sacred buildings and spaces, from small roadside shrines to monumental temples housing many gods, goddesses, and saints. On the history of Kāñcipuram, see Mahalingam (1963); Srinivasan (1979).

4. The local Brahmin Vaiṣṇavas are subdivided into numerous groups, but these subdivisions are of no relevance for this chapter.

5. This chapter is based on my work on the Varadarāja temple in Kāñcipuram; I attended Navarātri there in 2003, 2005, 2006, 2007, 2008, 2009, 2011, 2015, and 2017.

6. In general, all priests' households would keep *kolu* during Navarātri. However, if the household is affected by impurity—for example, due to a death or birth—*kolu* is usually skipped for one year.

7. There are, however, a few priests who establish their *kolu* in the *pūjā* room of their house, which then necessarily restricts the size of a *kolu* and access to it.

8. However, in the Varadarāja-temple priests' households, the mythological scenes displayed on their *kolu* might rather be from the Vaiṣṇava mythology.

9. Interestingly, during that time, small boys are often dressed as girls, and girls as boys. While the small children pose for photographs, adolescent girls of marriageable age are presented in their best clothes, often dressed in a sari for the first time. The girls are displayed and judged, and occasionally first steps toward marriage arrangements are taken.

10. This practice also reminds one of the live tableaux in which children pose as deities, customary in some areas of northern India (Luchesi 2014).

11. As I have argued elsewhere (Hüsken 2012), *kolu* shows that "religious play" is not limited to the world of children. *Kolu* is mainly practiced by both

children and adults, often in a very passionate manner. The educational aspect of *kolu* sustains this strong link between the world of children and the world of adults, between play and ritual.

12. Yet, importantly, in the priests' houses as in other Brahmin households, the daily ritual practices connected to *kolu* are enacted mainly for and by women.

13. While working on temple rituals, I realized that a well-done *alaṃkāra* is widely admired and that the priests are especially proud of their achievements in this regard. Interestingly, the making of *alaṃkāras* pertaining to the deity is not regulated by the ritual texts (e.g., Pāñcarātrasaṃhitā, Vaikhānasāgama) and thus does not follow any written norm.

14. Both the television set and Mickey Mouse were also produced by the traditional doll makers (Tamil: *pommaikkāraṉ*), who live and work not far from the Varadarāja temple.

15. These families trace their lineage back to religious leaders who were closely connected to the rulers of the Vijayanagara kingdom (Appadurai 1981, 97ff.) and play an important role in the management and ritual procedures of the Varadarāja temple.

16. The details of Sundararajan's family's practice of *kolu* were the topic of several interviews over the years, the latest taking place in 2017. According to Sundararajan's documents, his genealogical line from Lakṣmīkumāra Tātācārya runs as follows: (1) Tirumalai Ettoor Immidi Kotikannikadanam Lakshmikumara Tatadesikan, (2) Venkatavarada Tatdesikan, (3) Veeraraga Tatadesikan, (4) Sudarsana Tatachariar, (5) Tirumalai Tatachariar, (6) Rajadurkam Kumaratatachariar, (7) Rajadurgam Krishnaswamy Tatachariar, (9) Padma (Varadachariar), (10) Sundararajan (Nirmala), (11) Subhashini (Parthasarathy), (12) Surasika (i.e., Sundararajan) and his brother Suhrith.

17. Sundararajan's grandfather also introduced the VIP ticket for Garudaseva in 1935.

18. However, Sundararajan also admits that neither has he seen this tunnel nor does he know of anyone who has seen it. He also heard of a tunnel from the Vāhana Maṇḍapa to the place where Pavitrotsava is performed today, near the Mirror Hall. He heard that his grandfather, R. Kumāra Tātācārya, had once ventured into this tunnel with the help of many others. There, they found many elephant tusks—presumably from deceased temple elephants—and also a second metal festival statue of Varadarāja. Presumably this is the *utsavabera* that is now kept in the jewel room (Hüsken 2017). In this context, Sundararajan stated that at the time of Lakṣmīkumāra Tātācārya tunnels as escape routes were common.

19. Sundararajan is indirectly involved in some temple affairs through his son, who serves as advocate for the Tātācāryas in some lawsuits pertaining to temple affairs.

20. Today, in the Varadarāja temple, as in many of the big South Indian temples, photography of the main statue in the inner cella (*mūlabera*) is generally prohibited, while the movable statues may be photographed. This is changing rapidly, however, with the ubiquitous use of cell phones in all areas of peoples' lives, including in the temple, and with the increasing quality of cell-phone cameras.

21. A *kolam* is a white, often intricate pattern of rice powder strewn on the floor. This is a widespread art of women in Tamil Nadu, corresponding to the North Indian *rangoli*.

22. However, as shown in Hüsken (2013a), women's rituals during pregnancy seem to be generally acknowledged as important yet beyond the competence of male Brahmins.

23. From our conversation, it remained unclear whether Sundararajan's mother could not or did not have the means to purchase material to make dolls or whether not using money was considered a virtue. However, later in the interview, it seemed as if *kolu* might not have been set up in Sundararajan's family because of the lack of means to do so.

24. Sundararajan suspects that the fact that *kolu* started in his home only when he left has to do with the fact that his mother then had more time. Clearly, keeping and maintaining *kolu* requires a great investment of money, time, and effort. Moreover, as Sundararajan added, *kolu* would mainly be set up in houses with daughters.

25. Not only did Sundararajan assist his mother in her elaborate *kolu* arrangements, but they also together made a stuffed elephant for his grandson as a toy. In addition, Sundararajan and his mother made a toy chariot (Tamil: *tēr*), resembling the one at the Varadarāja temple.

26. In that year, Sundararajan asked me to provide him with my video coverage of the *siṃhavāhana* procession music so he could play it in his house while the *kolu* was on display.

27. Furthermore, Nirmala and Sundararajan say that foreign tourists enjoy the replicas, especially when they are not allowed to enter the temple building to see the original statues (non-Hindus cannot enter beyond the *dhavajstambha* in this temple).

28. Similar restrictions pertain to the creativity in the temple during Navarātri. While the decoration (*alaṃkāra*) of the deities is an important factor in both the Brahmin and the non-Brahmin temples, there seem to be hardly any limits to the inventiveness in the temple of Paṭavēṭṭammaṉ, for example, where Ilkama (this volume) has witnessed the full transformation of the entire temple. This is not unlike the *paṇḍals* in Kolkata, where creativity and artistic execution are major factors in their evaluation. Sen, in her contribution to this volume, even calls the Kolkata Durgā Pūjā a "Hindu festival thriving on creativity and novelty" (67).

References

Appadurai, Arjun. 1981. *Worship and Conflict under Colonial Rule: A South Indian Case*. Cambridge: Cambridge University Press.

Brahmāṇḍapurāṇa. 1984. Edited by Ganesh Vasudeo Tagare. *Brahmāṇḍapurāṇa: Part IV and V*. 2 vols. Delhi: Motilal Banarsidass.

Grimes, Ronald L. 2013. *The Craft of Ritual Studies*. Oxford: Oxford University Press.

Heitzman, James, and S. Rajagopal. 2004. "Urban Geography and Land Measurement in the Twelfth Century: The Case of Kanchipuram." *Indian Economic Social History Review* 41 (3): 237–68.

Hüsken, Ute. 2012. "Training, Play, and Blurred Distinctions: On Imitation and 'Real' Ritual." In *Religions in Play: Games, Rituals, and Virtual Worlds*, edited by Maya Burger and Philippe Bornet, 177–96. Zürich: Pano Verlag.

———. 2013a. "Denial as Silencing: On Women's Ritual Agency in a South Indian Brahmin Tradition." *Journal of Ritual Studies* 27 (1): 21–34.

———. 2013b. "Flag and Drum: Managing Conflicts in a South Indian Temple." In *South Asian Festivals on the Move*, edited by Ute Hüsken and Axel Michaels, 99–135. Wiesbaden, Germany: Harrassowitz.

———. 2017. "Gods and Goddesses in the Ritual Landscape of Seventeenth and Eighteenth-Century Kāñcipuram." In *Layered Landscapes: Early Modern Religious Space across Faiths and Cultures*, edited by Eric Nelson and Jonathan Wright, 63–81. New York: Routledge.

———. 2018. "Ritual Complementarity and Difference: Navarātri and Vijayadaśamī in Kāñcipuram." In Simmons, Sen, and Rodrigues 2018, 179–94.

Ilkama, Ina Marie Lunde. 2018. "Dolls and Demons: The Materiality of Navarātri." In Simmons, Sen, and Rodrigues 2018, 157–77.

Luchesi, Brigitte. 2014. "Jhāṅkīs: 'Living' Images as Objects of Worship in Himachal Pradesh." In *Objects of Worship in South Asians Religions: Forms, Practices, and Meanings*, edited by Knut A. Jacobsen, Mikael Aktor, and Kristina Myrvold, 35–50. London: Routledge.

MacAloon, John J. 1984. "Introduction: Cultural Performances, Culture Theory." In *Rite, Drama, Festival, Spectacle: Rehearsals toward a Theory of Cultural Performance*, edited by John J. MacAloon, 1–15. Philadelphia: Institute for the Study of Human Issues.

Mahalingam, Teralundur V. 1963. *Kāñcīpuram in Early South Indian History*. Bombay: Asia Publishing House.

Narayanan, Vasudha. 2018. "Royal *Darbār* and Domestic *Kolus*: Social Order, Creation, Procreation, and Re-Creation." In Simmons, Sen, and Rodrigues 2018, 275–97.

Porcher, Marie-Claude. 1985. "La représentation de l'espace sacré dans le *Kāñcīmāhātmya*." In *L'espace du temple: Espaces, itinéraires, médiations*, edited by Jean-Claude Galey, 23–52. Paris: Éditions de l'École des hautes études en sciences sociales.

Schier, Kerstin. 2018. *The Goddess's Embrace: Multifaceted Relations at the Ekāmranātha Temple Festival, Kanchipuram*. Wiesbaden, Germany: Harrassowitz.

Simmons, Caleb, Moumita Sen, and Hillary Rodrigues, eds. 2018. *Nine Nights of the Goddess: The Navarātri Festival in South Asia*. Albany: State University of New York Press.

Sivakumar, Deeksha. 2018. "Display Shows, Display Tells: The Aesthetics of Memory during Pommai Kolu." In Simmons, Sen, and Rodrigues 2018, 257–73.

Srinivasan, C. R. 1979. *Kanchipuram through the Ages*. Delhi: Agam Kala Prakashan.

Wilson, Nicole A. 2018. "*Kolus*, Caste, and Class: Navarātri as a Site for Ritual and Social Change in Urban South India." In Simmons, Sen, and Rodrigues 2018, 237–56.

Gendered Identities in Navarātri

5

Navarātri as a Festival of Hanumān and Male Asceticism

R. JEREMY SAUL

Gendering a Hanumān-Centric Navarātri

It is commonly observed that in recent decades the monkey god Hanumān has become significantly more prominent in Indian public life as a symbol of resurgent Hinduism and public morality.[1] At the same time, by virtue of his superlative powers, exemplified in his chaste devotion to his divine lord, Rāma, he has been embraced, now more than ever, as a provider of miracles to his many devotees. Consequently, particularly in northwestern India, the area of my fieldwork, many new temples have been erected since the 1990s in which Hanumān himself is the primary deity to be worshipped.[2] Inevitably, then, we may ask how Hanumān's increasing celebrity maps onto the performance of Navarātri, the ritual reenactment of Rāma's victory over demonic chaos, in which Hanumān played such a crucial role. Has Hanumān assumed a greater role in Navarātri in line with this enhanced public image? In this chapter I will discuss two cases where Navarātri has indeed evolved into a festival where the worship of Hanumān himself is paramount. Moreover, as I will discuss, Hanumān's centrality in these instances of Navarātri models male asceticism as a moral way of being to be emulated among young men, in particular, and revered in society at large.

As many devotees say, we live in a dark era, the Kali Yuga, variously characterized as a time of human degeneracy or as the age of machines (likened to industrialized modernity), which threatens the integrity of ancient Indic dharma. At present, humanity has only one hope: to seek devotional refuge with an accessible and incorruptible god who can serve as a moral guide. For many, Hanumān reflects these qualities and is therefore well suited as a god of our times. At the time of Navarātri, when many all over the country recall Rāma's triumph, the indispensability of Hanumān in that effort easily morphs into a celebration of the monkey god himself.[3] This is not to say that Hanumān has become an overwhelming presence in every celebration of Navarātri; India remains too diverse for that. Instead, I bring to light how specific local societal conditions spurred the centrality of the monkey god in this festival. In both case studies, young male devotees are at the heart of the ritual activity, performing as ideal followers or as Hanumān himself, while women and nonperforming men compose a devotional audience. In this study, drawn from ethnographic fieldwork at the sites discussed, I therefore apply a gendered perspective, with an eye toward discerning how masculinity is socially constructed in line with a cultural ideology privileging the male body as a ritualized portal to the divine.[4]

The first of the two cases to be discussed is an annual pilgrimage at the time of Navarātri to the temple of Bālājī, a local version of Hanumān in the village of Sālāsar in northern Rajasthan (figure 5.1). The most vibrant aspect of that festival is the arrival on foot of thousands of young men from villages and towns around northwestern India. Their presence signals a widespread conviction that the god is unmatched as a provider of miracles. The second case is the embodiment of Hanumān's *śakti*, or divine power, in young men of the city of Pānīpat, Haryana, also at the time of Navarātri (figure 5.2). These embodied Hanumāns, the highlight of the festival, are each referred to as *Hanumān Svarūp*, meaning "Hanumān in his own physical presence (not just impersonation)." During festival time, these embodied Hanumāns often participate in Pānīpat's Rāmlīlā performances, the reenactments of Rāma's battles against the demon king Rāvaṇa that take place nightly during Navarātri. Key to this analysis, in both case studies, young men, whether on pilgrimage in fulfillment of a vow for a miracle or embodying the divinity of Hanumān, demonstrate their devotion in ways that involve asceticism.

Hanumān's prominence in Navarātri may prompt us to wonder what has become of the goddess Durgā, who is often noted in scholarship as playing a central role in this festival, at least in certain regions (most famously in Bengal and Nepal). On the whole, she is not much represented in either case of Navarātri discussed here. There is a small Durgā

Figure 5.1. Bālājī (Hanumān), from a poster in the vicinity of the Sālāsar Bālājī temple. Photo by author.

Figure 5.2. A cloth merchant worshipping two Hanumān Svarūps in Pānīpat during Navarātri. Photo by author.

temple at the edge of Sālāsar, but it is merely one of many folk-deity shrines, and it gets no special attention during Navarātri, when all the public activity is centered on Bālājī. Traditionally, goddesses in Rajasthan were the protectors of Rājpūt kings. These days, in the absence of royal authority, Sālāsar Bālājī's Brahmin priests, some of whom claim that the god's name derives from a local word for "king," effectively serve as the local ruling elite. Meanwhile, in Pānīpat I observed the ritual worship of prepubescent neighborhood girls (and even a few boys) invited into homes on the morning of *aṣṭamī*, the eighth day of Navarātri, which is traditionally reserved throughout India for honoring the goddess. And that night I attended a vigorous *jāgraṇ*, or devotional song performance, for the goddess. Some Hanumān Svarūps were present, too, as honored guests on each side of the stage. Their presence signaled the importance of Hanumān in his own right and also of the neighborhood Hanumān Svarūp clubs that generally organize public activities during Navarātri.

Restoring Hindu Masculinity

One could conclude that Hanumān's enhanced significance in Navarātri today, as in Indian popular culture overall, is evidence of pervasive Vaishnavization. This development entails the nationwide glorification of Rāma as an avatar of Viṣṇu, along with the promotion of vegetarianism as a core *vaiṣṇava* value and the co-opting of goddesses into a *vaiṣṇava* framework. Seemingly alluding to this shift, Sālāsar's Brahmin priests disclosed that they have been active in stamping out traditional animal sacrifice and offerings of alcohol at local goddess shrines. Without naming Bālājī, Ann Gold (2008, 176n24) has mentioned the phenomenon of Hanumān images recently being installed in replacement of the goddess in some shrines of Rajasthan in order to make these places more respectable by current standards (hence no more sacrifice). This nationwide trend certainly boosts Hanumān, but I would argue that in order to understand the significance of worshipping Hanumān we also need to recognize his singular appeal as an antidote for the troubles of modern life. As Hanumān's devotees overwhelmingly confirm, he is deservedly popular because he relieves the suffering of life in the modern era, so he is popularly known as Saṅkaṭ Mocan, the "Reliever of Suffering." Hence, Navarātri, when Hanumān's divine efficacy is celebrated, is potentially a time of heightened public devotional activity.

I suggest that asceticism has particular resonance in these Hanumān-centric festivals because the ontology of the god himself provides a model of masculinized asceticism that appeals in the local cultural setting, where male space is a protected, even sanctified domain.[5] This practice simultaneously provides a strategy to win the god's beneficial favor. Ascetic devotion for Hanumān, as I am describing it, is an extension of the general Hindu practice of *vrat*, or ritual fasting and prayers. *Vrat* is not restricted to one gender or age and indeed may be more common among women, inasmuch as it often is a domestic practice for making everyday wishes. But the asceticism that I discuss in regard to Navarātri is characteristically performed as a public spectacle and is cultivated in the young male body, while a female would face some inhibition because of the god's emphatic masculinity and chastity, which precludes female contact. I argue that this masculinized asceticism fulfills a broader societal discourse of reconstructing Hindu men in the mold of Hanumān.

To many, especially older Indians (perhaps looking back to the days of selfless nationalist commitment to Gandhian or Nehruvian ideals), this moral integrity is now lacking in society due to the corrupting impact of globalized socioeconomic modernity. Moreover, bringing the monkey god into the sanctified male body through ascetic practice actualizes Hanumān's masculinized morality as a physical reality, thereby rendering his supernatural potency immanent and accessible to everyday worshippers. This is evident in both instances discussed here. At Sālāsar, prostrating devotees who have walked from afar are understood to be fulfilling an intimate personal pact with the god, and they are allowed to immediately enter Bālājī's temple without waiting in line like the others in recognition of their extreme, sanctifying devotion. Meanwhile, in Pānīpat the Hanumān Svarūps are accepted as true emanations of the god due to the performers' austerities in preparation, and so these Hanumāns bestow truly efficacious blessings.

The notion that modern Hindu men might need to reclaim primordial moral vigor has an intellectual genealogy going back to colonial days, when nationalist discourse advocated reconstituting the honorable Indian male, long subdued by Muslim and colonial rule. For instance, in analyzing the British colonial discourse of the Hindu male as "effeminate," Mrinalini Sinha (1999) saw the early seeds of a subsequent nationalist reaction of remasculinizing Hindu men, to save them from creeping Westernization.[6] Flipping this gender narrative to the other side, Tanika Sarkar (2001) observes a nineteenth-century policy among the indigenous population in Bengal of keeping women in the home as resistance to gender-emancipatory colonial hegemony. This domesticity put a burden on women to stay traditional while men, who engage in the outer world, needed to conform to changing times.[7] But nowadays, I suggest, Hanumān is providing a way for men to reclaim that lost integrity. Furthermore, on a more regional level, Prem Chowdhry has investigated in numerous publications how

Punjab-Haryana society, and particularly the Jāṭ caste—which I have situated at the center of devotion to Bālājī—valorizes heroic masculinity as a core societal ethic.[8] From this standpoint, it is entirely understandable that Hanumān's role has expanded in this region, as demonstrated in this study. I approach Navarātri through this lens, analyzing masculinized Hanumān as representing personal and cultural scripts about what it means to be a man in this age and how to cultivate the ideal male for the broader sake of society.[9]

Cultures of Masculinized Devotion

In the Navarātri festivals of Sālāsar and Pānīpat, ideologies of masculine asceticism arguably serve ethnic-caste cultural interests in affirming group identity through the performance of an ideal type of male as a positive representation of the community. In postindependence life, both of these communities have been challenged with forging identities in changing sociopolitical circumstances. For instance, Jāṭs, the dominant community of the Punjab-Haryana-Rajasthan tristate border region, have been deeply embroiled in caste politics because of their struggle for inclusion in the government's caste-based reservation program (affirmative action), not to mention efforts to revise negative perceptions of this community as made up of unruly scoundrels (a view that has its origins in British times).[10] Jāṭ society cherishes a discourse of masculine independence that emphasizes martial or athletic prowess as well as agricultural mastery.[11] I suggest, then, that the Jāṭ worship of Hanumān, including in his local form as Bālājī, is illustrative of how Jāṭs would like to represent themselves. Indeed, many Jāṭ devotees assert that Hanumān, a paragon of masculinized military leadership in the *Rāmāyaṇa* and of loyalty to the male hierarchy (personified in Rāma), is essentially a Jāṭ.[12]

On the other hand, Pānīpat's largely Sikh-Hindu community, originating in pre-Partition West Punjab, has its own imperatives in embracing the monkey god. Many of their forebears, predominantly weavers, had to leave behind their large handlooms in the migration of 1947, but it is said that one of them managed to bring a Hanumān mask that had been used in Rāmlīlā performances. In the decades since its relocation to Pānīpat, this pre-Partition folk practice has been revived and has expanded to the point that it is now a symbol of the city's own post-Partition integrity as a unified society, albeit with added significance for the migrant community. As with most Indians who originated in what is now Pakistan, their social networks reflect ancestral ties, but nowadays they can maintain only a nostalgic link to their ancestral homeland. These days, at the time of

Navarātri, many Hanumān performers, accompanied by cohorts of young male followers, stride through the market area, stopping especially at the migrant-community-run shops to give blessings, in a process confirming community continuity. As in Sālāsar, this devotion has undoubtedly been spurred by Hanumān's popularization throughout Indian society in the last few decades.

In investigating how masculinity is socially produced in devotional asceticism, I draw from the work of Joseph Alter on Indian asceticism, which typically involves chastity as a cultural technique for building male spiritual and physical power. This is not only seen in holy men, who develop powers through their ascetic lifestyle, but also in indigenous sports culture, particularly wrestling, at least in its traditional terms (dedicating oneself to wrestling to the exclusion of worldly pursuits). As Alter (1992, 325) has noted, the retention of semen in celibacy has long been regarded as a foundation for accumulating inner power (and even muscularity, if part of a physical regimen). It is no coincidence, then, that Hanumān, the symbol of masculine chastity, is now commonly depicted as a kind of bodybuilder in posters and even installed as an image of worship in many wrestling or bodybuilding establishments. It is understood that his superlative strength, which he dedicates to the service of Rāma, is bolstered by his asceticism in giving up any aspiration for household life. Similarly, the pilgrimage to Sālāsar Bālājī on foot (the ideal mode for those keeping a vow to the deity) and the embodiment of Hanumān, both requiring much stamina, effectively assign to physically fit young men the role of performing in the model of the monkey god.

Putting these elements of masculinity and asceticism together, I find a useful model for theorizing a masculinized, ascetic Navarātri in Filippo Osella and Caroline Osella's (2003) study of the male-only Sabarimala pilgrimage of Kerala in southern India.[13] This mountain shrine is interesting because it is the abode of Ayyappan, a deity who, like Hanumān, is an ascetic male. Ayyappan acquired his superlative power through devout celibacy, so women of childbearing age have traditionally been forbidden to visit the shrine. But for men the physically arduous journey to the shrine on foot, in conjunction with *vrat* to purify their bodies, is seen as a process of remasculinizing their core selves after the spiritual-physical depletions of everyday family and business life (Osella and Osella 2003, 733). Here we can see a corollary with the way I have theorized male devotion to Hanumān at the time of Navarātri. While *vrat* and austerities are desirable for all people, I suggest that for men uncertain about their future, particularly for younger men, performing as an exemplary devotee of Hanumān is a strategy that gives them an edge in competitive adult life. Indeed, a common benefit that male devotees cite from worship of

Hanumān is not simply miracles but also self-confidence (*ātmaviśvās*), which they see as a boon for attaining one's aims in life, all the more so in these days of neoliberal-era careerism.[14] Both pilgrimage to Sālāsar and the practice of austerities to embody Hanumān are masculinized ascetic undertakings that help to ensure such success—in effect, a rationalist equivalent to a miracle.[15]

Navarātri in Sālāsar: Hanumān Celebrated as an Ascetic

Although pilgrims steadily come to Bālājī's temple in Sālāsar throughout the year (especially on the full moon), it is only during the ten days of Navarātri that this small village truly overflows with visitors. This is the time when Hanumān's power to grant wishes is believed to be at its strongest, due to the festival's association with the monkey god's feats in service to Rāma. Therefore, this is the best occasion to see how devotion to the god is performed in public. Although understood to be a manifestation of Hanumān, the idol of Bālājī represents him as a bearded hermit, or *sant* (essentially a sadhu), which not only underscores the god's ascetic associations but also is pivotal to understanding Bālājī's history. According to local lore, now replicated in pilgrim handbooks and readily recited by the temple's priests, in 1754 a Jāṭ farmer came across Bālājī's image in a field, and at the same time Hanumān bestowed the boon on a local hermit devoted to him that henceforth his descendants, counted through his sister's line, would have the sole right to perform rituals for this deity at his temple in Sālāsar.[16] Moreover, Hanumān declared, he would always appear to the world here in the guise of this faithful hermit rather than in his familiar monkey form. The narrative thus both explains the hereditary right of the priests to represent Bālājī and highlights his ascetic qualities.

Bālājī's history of the last several decades is anecdotal, as the devotional handbooks only discuss the founding of the temple. It is locally said that the Mārvāḍīs, merchants tracing their ancestry to northern Rajasthan but now living in cities throughout India, were the first to acclaim the god's miraculous powers by the late 1980s.[17] This development is coeval with rising nationwide interest in Hanumān, which came to a head in the political movement to restore a Rāma-centered Hindu polity, as seen in L. K. Advani's controversial Hindu-nationalist cross-country *yātrā*, or procession, in 1990.[18] Later in that decade, after Mārvāḍī patronage had enabled the construction of numerous rest houses in Sālāsar, Jāṭs and others started coming in increasing numbers, having become convinced from stories of Bālājī's miracles that he was the most powerful manifestation of this god on earth.[19] The long-standing Jāṭ-caste narrative of manly heroism easily incorporated Hanumān and Bālājī into Jāṭ male-centric culture, with its emphasis on demonstrating physical vigor. Jāṭs like to say that they win far more athletic medals and contribute more recruits for the armed forces than any other group in India. For many young men in the Jāṭ-dominant hinterland, then, pilgrimage during Navarātri is an opportunity to demonstrate their fitness as Jāṭs through publicly conforming to Hanumān's regime of moral-physical strength.

Bālājī's ascetic nature is undeniable since he not only looks like a sadhu-hermit but is one temperamentally as well. One can discern this in contrasting him with another Bālājī in Rajasthan, perhaps even more famous, who is worshipped as a manifestation of Hanumān in the village of Mehandipur (around 225 kilometers to the southeast) and is famous for presiding over exorcisms. Devotees typically point out that Sālāsar Bālājī is Hanumān as a bearded young adult (*javān*), whereas Mehandipur Bālājī is regarded as a child (*bālak*) and is therefore depicted in a nonbearded simian form. Thus Sālāsar Bālājī is said to also be a more mature, cool Hanumān, who only grants the kinds of boons that could be associated with canonical, Sanskrit-centric aspirations (such as opportunities in education, career, and family). On the other hand, Mehandipur Bālājī is a hot, untamed, juvenile Hanumān who is energetically suited to fighting demons, which entails a more Tantric, nonscriptural mode of devotion.

This temperamental distinction helps us to situate these two Hanumāns in terms of an encompassing gender ideology. That is, both are celibate males, but because of their different ages they are imagined as behaving in different ways in relation to women. As a devotee at Mehandipur once told me, since Mehandipur Bālājī is a child, he is not affected by the gender segregation expected of adults; therefore, this child-god can freely enter into women's bodies to expel unwanted spirits. This is a consequential capacity, since most afflicted people brought to Mehandipur (and probably all shrines where exorcism is carried out) are indeed women. Since Sālāsar Bālājī is a postpubertal hermit and the charge of a lineage of Sanskrit-educated Brahmins, he is not surprisingly understood to prefer the kind of scriptural authority that privileges Brahmin men and, by extension, exemplary male devotees who can replicate him in devotional practice. Of course, women come to Sālāsar in great numbers too, albeit always in family groups, but their presence during Navarātri itself is somewhat muted because the presence of so many groups of men, especially of the younger generation, dominates the picture of public devotion.

While many devotees come to Sālāsar by vehicle, many groups of young men arrive on foot, often from distances of two hundred kilometers or more. These foot pilgrims, many of whom originate in villages or

Figure 5.3. Pilgrims prostrating in the street on the way to Bālājī's temple in Sālāsar during Navarātri. Photo by author.

small cities in the Jāṭ-dominant region to the north of Sālāsar, contribute a sensibility of masculine asceticism in performing the arduous journey. Surmounting this physical challenge is the means of winning the god's favor, as it is commonly said that one needs to go without modern conveniences in order to truly gain the attention of Bālājī, the personification of ancient virtues. In demonstrating chaste vigor, young devotees emulate the monkey god's service to Rāma, a relationship that is nowadays idealized throughout India as the ultimate act of devotion and as a dharmic model of male-male relations. Furthermore, after walking from afar, those making wishes or repaying a vow for a fulfilled wish will be publicly seen as representing this relationship by covering the last kilometer up to the temple in repetitions of prostrations (known in Hindi as *daṇḍavat*; figure 5.3). For the common devotee arriving in Sālāsar, this final stretch constitutes the emotional-spiritual climax of the festival.

Ascetic Masculinity on the Road

In the villages of southern Haryana, it is said that during Navarātri much of the population is on the road to Sālāsar, so the villages become especially quiet. While young men commonly walk in their own groups, families are more likely to arrive in trucks hired for transportation. Often a group of youths on pilgrimage may be accompanied by locals hired to drive a tractor laden with food supplies for the journey, funded by village devotional clubs. These young men may even sleep at rudimentary roadside tent shelters set up by local devotional committees during Navarātri, where free meals may also be available. I have been told that before twenty years ago few came on this walk, as there were no facilities, so it was regarded as truly risky. Alongside the development of supportive infrastructure, Rajasthan has been reified in northern Indian society as the ultimate land of asceticism—the holy land of *sants*—by virtue of its arid landscape, which seems amenable to those who wish to escape modern householder life. Bālājī's popularity as a god of miracles and as an ascetic himself, not to mention Hanumān as a deity of masculine fortitude, is thus fully supported by perceptions about this locale.

Since educational institutions are closed for the duration of Navarātri, students, in addition to farmers and others, are more likely to go on a long-distance pilgrimage at this time. But lest others regard this as just seeking adventure on the road, young men have devised various ways of upping the perceived value of their physical exertion. For instance, reminiscent of pilgrimage to certain other religious sites in the northwest, such as the goddess shrines of the Himalayan foothills, some come together on long-distance bicycle pilgrimages. When they arrive, they leave a commemorative plate on a sanctified tree outside the temple stating their names, places of origin, and dates arrived. Others take turns running the whole way while carrying Hanumān's red flag. Some groups even come on motorcycle pilgrimages, which transmutes the physical asceticism of walking into a public statement of masculine freedom, equipped with decals and flags honoring Bālājī-Hanumān. In this arena of young male performance, the ability to independently organize a walk with one's cohort is thus an assertion of autonomous youth culture in the rubric of northwestern Indian male society.

In more extreme cases of vow keeping, one may walk the entire length barefoot. During Navarātri I met an eighteen-year-old male who was keeping such a vow, in the company of his entourage. He stated that he had come in repayment for having successfully entered the air force. As I witnessed, before each meal, with the red flag of Hanumān propped up nearby, he recited the *Hanumān Cālīsā*, the invocation of the monkey god (around fifteen minutes in length), which is probably the most popular sacred recitation in northern India today and to which miracles in countless times of peril have been attributed (figure 5.4). Following his recitation, the youth then broke off a bit of flatbread and some lentils and lifted it twice to a small picture of Sālāsar Bālājī. Only after this ritual each day would this young man eat. His male gender culturally privileged him to perform this kind of intimacy with the god; it is unlikely that a woman could ever perform in this way toward Bālājī due to the injunction against physical contact. And so, we are reminded that while all devotees may pray for miracles from the monkey god, those who are male are better enabled to set up such a close relationship.

I have noted that the ascetic highlight of a pilgrimage to Bālājī takes place in the final kilometer extending through a narrow street of Sālāsar from the temple (at the edge of town) of Añjanī Mātā, Hanumān's mother, to Bālājī's own temple. During Navarātri this street is jammed with improvised stalls selling ritual paraphernalia, including devotional CDs and DVDs, which are constantly played at full blast. During Navarātri, countless male youths, and even an occasional woman or older man, often at the point of near physical exhaustion, make the final series of prostrations. We can say that the male-dominant setting emanates from the god himself. In contrast, at a famous temple for a local representation of Kṛṣṇa around one hundred kilometers to the south, known as Khāṭu Śyām, I saw significantly more prostrating women, many of them quite young, during its main annual festival around the time of Holi (in

Figure 5.4. Two pilgrims praying to a makeshift shrine for Bālājī in their rest-house room in Sālāsar during Navarātri. Photo by author.

March). Upon asking about this situation, I was told that this is because Kṛṣṇa is a "lady's god," being famous for his flirtations with women, while Bālājī-Hanumān is of course more accessible to men. Hence, we can theorize a correlation between Bālājī's ascetic masculinity and the inclinations of his devotional public.

Only those repaying a vow or intending to present a wish will perform prostrations while companions supportively cheer them on. At a minimum, each prostrating devotee necessarily relies on a spotter for protection from the throngs of pedestrians and vehicles, such as motorcycles and camel carts, all pushing ahead in a dusty, chaotic mass. The spotter carries a bag of *sindūr*, the sacred red powder that coats most Hanumān images, and uses it to draw a line on the asphalt road in front of the devotee, who then extends an arm to that line when performing the prostration, as if marking progress towards Bālājī's temple one step at a time. Depending on the devotee's level of physical strength, the prostrations may be a solemn act of lowering and lifting oneself or a more vigorously performed kind of athleticism. In the latter form, typical of young men wishing to show their physical match with Hanumān, they thrust their head and shoulders up while the pelvis is pressed to the ground, the same motion seen in gymnasium exercise routines over which Hanumān presides as a patron deity. For these devotees, the physical regimen at a local gym is a kind of training for this ultimate test of devotional stamina.

Navarātri in Pānīpat: Hanumān as the Ideal Modern Man

Navarātri in Pānīpat is quite different from what we have seen so far. Unlike Sālāsar, a village situated in a semidesert rural region, Pānīpat is a city straddling a major road that has historically linked commerce between urban centers from Kolkata to Lahore. And Navarātri is celebrated as an event entirely within Pānīpat's society, so, unlike at Sālāsar, pilgrimage does not come into play. Also different from Sālāsar, devotion to Hanumān in Pānīpat is not centered on a single temple. Rather, it is diffused among numerous male-only neighborhood Hanumān Svarūp clubs, each of which independently organizes around one or more local men (most often in their twenties or older, combined with younger apprentice Hanumāns) who publicly embody Hanumān in the Navarātri celebration. The same people may continue to perform in this way each year as desired. These men embody Hanumān's *śakti*, or divine power, after undergoing ritual austerities for forty days before they perform on some or all of the days of Navarātri. It is clear that preparing for performing as Hanumān in this festival upholds a gendered ideology of ascetic, chaste masculinity.

Based on locals' testimony, it appears that the performance of Hanumān Svarūp has been associated with Rāmlīlā, the ritual reenactment of the *Rāmāyaṇa,* from its earliest days, but only a handful of the oldest people today can say much about its early history. In the Rāmlīlā of pre-Partition West Punjab, perhaps no other divine character but Hanumān was represented with a mask, and this has continued to be the core feature of the Rāmlīlā of Pānīpat. However, whether the performer was truly regarded as embodying Hanumān in the way he is now is not yet clear. In current practice, performers of other characters in Rāmlīlā do not seem to be expected to undergo the regimen of ritual austerities that is reserved for Hanumān, who doubly performs as a walking object of worship far beyond the other divinities. I theorize that Hanumān's singular role in Pānīpat is indicative of how he has been locally transformed in line with the growing nationwide perception that he has a special moral message to impart to modern humanity. He is, after all, a model of what men—especially younger men in need of cultural guidance—should aspire to be.

Notwithstanding a lack of textual history, Pānīpat's Hanumān devotees readily say that Rāmlīlā performances with Hanumān masks were known in several villages of what is now Pakistani Punjab, predominantly Siraiki-speaking areas north of Multan, and also in Jhang District and were especially favored among the weaving castes. Partition endangered this practice's socioeconomic continuity, as refugees could take few objects such as masks with them. However, those coming to Pānīpat appropriated the looms left behind by the substantial Muslim weaver population that had gone to Pakistan at the same time, enabling them to reconstitute their livelihood. Having settled near each other in cities of northwestern India, the migrants have maintained Siraiki-Punjabi identity, reflected in a distinctive dialect that many still speak. In the new setting of Pānīpat, the Hanumān Svarūp practice was revived, perhaps initially with just the one mask as an attraction among those who were nostalgic for their ancestral land. But locals say that this practice "very gradually" (Hindi: *dhīre dhīre*) expanded beyond its original migrant population to its present citywide extent, albeit still centered on the diasporic cloth-industry community. Despite this narrative of gradual growth, I am inclined to think that Hanumān's growing stature as a heroic deity throughout India, especially since the 1990s, has supercharged the god's local appeal through his symbolism in national discourse as a representation of the honorable Indian man.

When I asked for details about how the practice of Hanumān Svarūp had expanded over the years, I was told that a main reason was competition among men wanting to perform as Hanumān, which was seen as an enviable way to demonstrate physical and spiritual strength. I interpret this to mean that performing as Hanumān is an opportunity for a youth to step into the spotlight and be seen among peers and neighbors as a powerful, divinized adult male in line with their cultural model of masculinity; this is not unlike what is going on in the very physically demonstrative pilgrimage of young men that one sees at Sālāsar (and even at other shrines). As it was related to me, over the years this competition compelled an increasing number of young men, ensconced in neighborhood clubs, to order their own masks from one or more of the local craftsmen so as not to be left behind. There are no restrictions on joining these devotional clubs, but, when the time comes, an older member will have the prerogative to decide which boys can wear any of the masks.

At least some locals in Pānīpat regard the act of performing as Hanumān to be part of a cultural project of reconstituting men as morally upstanding citizens. Respondents pointed to the ascetic process of prayer, chastity, and remembrance of dharmic values and subsequent embodiment of the monkey god as producing a male public that is more impervious to the negative, selfish influences of modernity. When I asked them to specify what bad behaviors Hanumān performance would alleviate, they immediately cited rape as an example, perhaps recalling the nationwide furor over a notorious gang rape on a bus in Delhi in 2012.[20] Obviously, the practice of ascetic chastity with a sense of purpose would counteract unrestrained sexuality and other worldly desires. Devotees frequently note Hanumān's exceptional relevance to solving today's social problems. As is well known, he is a deity that uniquely continues to live close to earth in each era and therefore remains accessible to humanity in times of need.[21] A telling illustration of this perception is seen in the common statement that Hanumān temples generally stay open throughout the day, whereas Rāma temples close down in the middle of the day because he is less attached to everyday devotional needs. So the viewpoint that following Hanumān's moral regimen would inculcate good morality, particularly in young men in need of direction, is consistent with the popular perception of Hanumān's special role in modernity.

When a member of a Hanumān club hoping to embody the god during Navarātri undergoes purificatory withdrawal for forty days, he should optimally sleep in a neighborhood temple each night and avoid any contact with women. Sometimes this ritual space might even be the neighborhood's Hanumān Svarūp clubhouse, which may be part of a club leader's home. Being married does not bar a man from undergoing this process, but he should remove himself from family life for the duration of his preparation, although it appears that in some instances a performer may quietly stay at home, albeit with reduced contact with women. Performers are likely to sleep in proximity to the masks so as to gain the approval of their divine charisma; if a performer happens to keep a mask in his own home, then that will become his ritualized living space. Hanumān performers are also expected to spend their days up to Navarātri reciting popular scriptures. And, throughout this period, they must eat only certain *sātvik*, or spiritually pure, foods, such as fruit, milk, and white rice, and not smoke or drink alcohol.

It is fair to say that there is leeway for individual variation in the ascetic preparation phase, since the club members are the main ones who evaluate whether adepts are appropriately following the protocol, although if local temples provide the setting for the activity, then elders in the neighborhood may also have a say. As is normal in Indian public life, the Hanumān Svarūp process is a community effort, especially for young men; there are no solitary performers. Despite the expectation of asceticism, I was told that nowadays many youths are merely attracted to the idea of becoming Hanumān for the sake of thrill or prestige without having properly cultivated the requisite moral disposition. This is actually a common complaint also made about youthful pilgrims going to Sālāsar; they want to show off the manly qualities of Hanumān, but they have supposedly forgotten the need to develop genuine piety. Still, there are supernatural consequences for improper preparation. I was told that a youth who did not stop smoking while preparing for Navarātri became violently ill in retribution when he tried to put the Hanumān mask on.

During Navarātri, I was able to observe potential performers in retreat in the upstairs room of a joint Sikh-Hindu temple under the gaze of a panel of Hanumān masks. This setting illustrates how the culture of Hanumān Svarūp performance has transcended sectarian boundaries in an era when Hanumān has been embraced as a national superhero. From morning to evening each day, around eighteen young men sat reciting the *Rāmcaritmānas*, the Hindi version of the *Rāmāyaṇa* (figure 5.5). Occasionally, they stopped to listen to a group leader exhort them to embrace Hanumān as our moral savior in this era of the Kali Yuga.[22] Some of the men might not have intended to perform as Hanumān but joined the retreat so as to cultivate a pure state of mind for the festival. Downstairs, the Sikh scripture known as the *Gurū Granth Sāhib* occupied the central space, as in any *gurudvāra*, but on the left side was a large Hanumān statue covered in *sindūr*.

During the nights of Navarātri, men and women of the neighborhood congregated in this *gurudvāra*-temple with the two genders sitting on opposite sides, as is usual in Indian devotional events. The men were all obligated to wear a scarf over their heads, as in any *gurudvāra*, and upon entering each devotee would bow before the Sikh altar and then

Figure 5.5. Hanumān Svarūp performers reciting the *Rāmcaritmānas* in a joint Hindu-Sikh temple in Pānīpat in the days preceding Navarātri. Photo by author.

face a temple official who led the whole congregation in devotional songs for Navarātri. In this era, when newspapers frequently report communal tensions across India, locals see this combined worship as proof of social harmony that affirms their common heritage as descendants of refugees from West Punjab. Indeed, my primary respondent, the most senior Hanumān Svarūp performer known to me (just over forty years old), was born a Sikh in a refugee-descended family but later embraced Hanumān as a personal savior. Now he cuts his hair and follows mainstream Hindu conventions but raises his sons with uncut hair in the Khālsā tradition.

Hanumān Embodied in Rāmlīlā

An important distinction between Pānīpat and Sālāsar during Navarātri is that in Pānīpat the performance of Rāmlīlā, the traditional dramatic reenactment of the *Rāmāyaṇa* that is associated with this festival, is quite prominent, whereas it seems to be absent in Sālāsar (as the ritual focus is entirely on Bālājī's temple). Particularly when Rāmlīlā in Pānīpat is performed outdoors in a field, a suitably spacious setting, Hanumān Svarūp performers regularly participate in the drama. Along with the other characters, Rāma and his brother Lakṣmaṇa will also be present. These two gods are of course highly revered but preside as regal onlookers rather than active agents in the performance. Conversely, Hanumān, as embodied by a performer, brings divine immediacy into the event due to many prior days of ritual sanctification. Once the crowd has assembled at dusk, several Hanumāns and their cohorts start arriving, with an earsplitting drumroll, from adjacent neighborhoods. Organizers of the event, who live nearby, already know the clubs and so call on them to participate. Only one Hanumān performer will actually join in the drama on any one night, while the others watch from the sidelines. However, at the end of the night's performance, all the Hanumāns pay obeisance to Rāma and Lakṣmaṇa, one by one, after which they may offer blessings to individuals in the crowd.

The most visually impressive aspect of a Hanumān Svarūp performer is his mask, which is essential for embodying the deity and therefore should only be worn once the performer has undergone austerities. Of course, since the mask is the repository of the god's masculinized divinity, no woman may touch it. I was told that currently there are approximately 1,100 Hanumān Svarūp masks in use in Pānīpat, representing hundreds of clubs. Clubs commission masks made of a shellacked composite material and painted orange from a few families of craftspeople. The style of the masks is reminiscent of folk images of Hanumān worshipped in countless Indian villages. A critical element of each mask is a high, tower-like crown that is elaborately decorated with colorful glass and other fixtures, and perhaps even representations of other deities such as Śiva or Rāma.[23] Once acquired, the masks may be richly embellished in accord with the individual tastes of those who look after them in clubs or temples throughout the year. The masks serve as objects of worship when performers are not wearing them, and they may also be worn in certain other festivals, such as Hanumān Jayantī.

I visited the home of an elderly man in Pānīpat whose father was said to have brought the original Hanumān Svarūp mask from his home village to India in 1947. Seeing the original mask, still kept in this man's home, it appears that its basic form has not appreciably changed over the years. After acquiring a mask, a group will call Brahmins to perform rituals to invest it with Hanumān's power. Although many masks may appear generic, they are regarded as having individualized charisma accrued from the worship they receive or where they are stored. Generally, whoever has responsibility for looking after a mask will assess whether a boy in the club who wants to perform is well matched with the divine energy of a particular mask before assigning it to him. If a boy feels ill or faint when trying on the mask, the guardian will decide that the *śakti* of that mask is not right for him, but he may provide another mask.

I observed the procedure of dressing performers as Hanumān in a club on the afternoon of Vijayadaśamī, the final day of Navarātri, when all the Hanumān Svarūp performers and their attendants make their final public appearance in the festival as participants in the ritual burning of Rāvaṇa and his warriors in effigy. As is typical with large public religious events in Indian cities, the local government and police, in cooperation with neighborhood committees, supervise this event. Before embarking for the burning ground, each neighborhood club will come together to dress one or more performers as Hanumān. This entails first stripping each performer down to some version of the *laṅgoṭiyā,* or loincloth, of the sort that Hanumān and wrestlers wear. Then the attendants affix the tall headpiece onto him, stabilizing it with a pole that is kept close to the body by means of a cummerbund-like wraparound. Next, they place the mask on the performer, and then all the members apply orange *sindūr* to him. They will then recite a brief prayer to Hanumān; at this point, the performer has become the god. Finally, the club members will perform *āratī* for the embodied Hanumān and set off to join the crowds heading to any one of four designated grounds, depending on proximity to their neighborhood.

Along the way to the ground, as in Hanumān Svarūp street processions on previous days, the deity may sometimes stop to receive prayers, especially in front of cloth businesses of West Punjab heritage. When a shop-front prayer takes place, the male employees are likely to take turns performing *āratī* before the Svarūp, who will typically lay a hand on the shoulder of each to give a blessing. Women may pray from a distance but will not come into contact with the deity. Throughout this time, I have been told, the performer who has become Hanumān retains some self-awareness, but it is likened to a dream state. If a performer is particularly esteemed from having carried out notable ascetic-devotional acts in past years, he will be especially called upon to stop and receive prayers, since the god is surely powerful in him. For instance, my own main respondent is locally famous for having made long barefoot journeys in full Hanumān Svarūp garb to certain well-known sacred sites hundreds of kilometers away, such as Mehandipur and Hardwar (to obtain Gaṅgā water). Thus, the ascetic qualifications of the performer are a factor in assessing his capacity to embody the god.

As they reach the ground, perhaps two hundred or more Hanumān Svarūps and their entourages are allowed by police to enter a barren ground of perhaps one hundred meters in diameter set aside for the burning of the effigies while great crowds of local onlookers press against the fence on the perimeter. Although the customary immolation of the effigies is formally the highlight, the Hanumān Svarūp groups have the privilege of being the only ones who can come close to the ritual burning,

Figure 5.6. Hanumān Svarūps shortly after arriving for the ritual immolation of Rāvaṇa in Pānīpat during Navarātri. Photo by author.

owing to the perception that they are collectively representing Hanumān's moral authority and his indispensable role in the *Rāmāyaṇa*, just as they show up for Rāmlīlā each evening. Some club members carry younger boys dressed as Rāma and Lakṣmaṇa on their shoulders to witness the event, but Sītā never appears, since this inner ground is a resolutely male space. All watch the effigies burn to the ground at the moment of sundown (figure 5.6) and then head home in a boisterous mood. And so, as in Sālāsar, the ritual setting of Navarātri permits young men, sanctified through physical challenges in emulation of Hanumān, to ritually occupy the center of the devotional event.

Conclusion

In this chapter I have presented two cases of Navarātri in which Hanumān has effectively become the main deity of worship. This development has taken place within the setting of the current nationwide enthusiasm for Hanumān as an exemplary devotee of Rāma and as a moral savior for our time. In both Sālāsar and Pānīpat, Navarātri, the symbolic triumph of Rāma over evil, has become the festival best suited for publicly performing devotion to the monkey god. There is a popular saying in Hindi, which is known throughout northern India, that Rāma could not have saved the world without Hanumān. This conviction underscores the widespread belief that Hanumān is the one deity who can truly help people in times of need. Navarātri is the public occasion when all those aspirations, and the austerities required to actualize them, are put on display. Certain other folk deities have acquired similar followings, but Hanumān's masculinized, martial identity has made him a model for the kind of man that modern society needs.

Although Hanumān has long been known in connection with the *Rāmāyaṇa,* I have suggested that the 1990s was a pivotal time for his development in localized practices of worship, as exemplified in Navarātri. Certainly, the festival existed before then, but it gained more resonance in this new era of Hanumān as a major deity in his own right. We can see a correlation with Hanumān's rise in northwestern India, not to mention elsewhere, in the visible rush to construct or significantly upgrade Hanumān temples throughout the region during the last two decades. Thus, although the case studies presented here are very locale-specific, they are consistent with the broader devotional direction of Indian society.

From a more local standpoint, I have argued that in Sālāsar and Pānīpat socioeconomic conditions have had a lot to do with the way core devotees have interpreted Navarātri. Jāṭs, Mārvāḍīs, and Brahmins have affirmed Bālājī as a superlative manifestation of Hanumān and as a local divine protector, while at the same time the diasporic Siraiki-Punjabi community of Pānīpat has acclaimed Hanumān Svarūp as an ultimate marker of solidarity that transcends sectarian background. In both cases, because of the current nationwide devotional climate, this community-specific worship of Hanumān has grown into a larger regional following. But although devotees are not restricted by gender or age, I have documented the formation of a privileged category of devotee that claims a special relationship with the monkey god—young adult males—who perform with a sense of emulating the god that goes beyond simply showing devotion.

Young male devotees strive to conform to what they perceive as Hanumān's own moral, masculinized rules, traditionally followed in sports, in which strength, endurance, chastity, and periodic ascetic withdrawal are vital. In effect, demonstrating chaste physical fitness, a domain that favors those who happen to be young and male, is a privileged status in Hanumān's realm. The reward for this endeavor, drawn from the classical Indic model of the ascetic who gains supernatural boons from deities in reward for his efforts, is entry to a successful modern life, as interpreted in Indian society. We can see parallel instances for this kind of appropriation of ascetic tradition in contemporary terms. I would point to the relatively new enthusiasm for groups of youths to make the long journey of many days on foot to obtain sacred water from the river Gaṅgā. Formerly, this was essentially the work of sadhus, but now it is embraced in youth culture, and it is a demonstration of young men performing for the sake of their communities at home.

I have suggested that in both Sālāsar and Pānīpat cultural gender ideologies foregrounding maleness in the practice of asceticism have allowed young male devotees who are willing to become like Hanumān for the occasion to also perform as a representation of the larger devotional community, who play the role of an active, supportive audience. In the devotional regimen discussed here, young adult males thus take center stage as the social group that publicly receives divine power, not only for themselves but on behalf of all. As I have noted, these sons are in effect the public face of a community's discourse about itself. On a more prosaic level, the festival may of course mark an opportunity for these devotees to demonstrate personal autonomy and solidarity among their peers, to personally ensure their future, and to be witnessed as empowered adults. One could no doubt bring youth psychology into this discussion as well; however, I have analyzed the performance of Navarātri primarily through the lens of gender. This is because, as a focal point of devotion, Hanumān himself, the presiding divine authority, represents a male-centered prescription for the concerns of contemporary life.

Notes

In this chapter, I have adopted the Sanskrit form of deities' names (with the final *a*), hence *Rāma* rather than *Rām* (as in Hindi). However, when I refer to a specialized Hindi term incorporating such a name, such as *Rāmlīlā*, I write *Rām* without the Sanskrit final *a*.

1. We can witness this shift in the monkey god's popularity in the proliferation of new Hanumān temples since the 1990s, which mark an upgrade from the traditional folk shrines for him that were more typical of earlier times. In scholarship, some of Philip Lutgendorf's many publications relating to Hanumān also address this phenomenon. For instance, in "My Hanuman Is Bigger Than Yours" (Lutgendorf 1994), he discusses the recent trend to build colossal Hanumān statues. More broadly, in his book *Hanuman's Tale: The Messages of a Divine Monkey* (Lutgendorf 2007), he explores the various forms in popular culture that devotion to Hanumān has taken in recent decades.

2. The information for this chapter was gathered in multiple visits to India, starting with fieldwork there under a Fulbright-Hays fellowship in 2010–11 and followed up by various later visits through 2017.

3. Nanda (2009), in writings such as *The God Market: How Globalization Is Making India More Hindu*, argues that a rise in public religiosity in India can be

linked to political and economic transformations in the era of neoliberal reform, among other factors, from the early 1990s on.

4. Within the broad literature on the construction of masculinity, I would point to Whannel (2002), especially pp. 17–29, for a summary of some of the main currents of masculinity studies and also his linking of male identity to physical culture, such as sports. Male pilgrimage to Sālāsar, as an act of physical endurance, could be theorized as an extension of team-sports culture in the agrarian society of southern Haryana.

5. Chowdhry (2014; accessed as an abstract), describes the reproduction of gender identities in Haryana society through the maintenance of social space for men only.

6. Sinha (1999, 447 and elsewhere) refers to a British colonial discourse of Hindu male effeminacy.

7. Sarkar (2001, 23–52). Especially note p. 32 for a reference to the notion of the Hindu *bābū* (clerks in the colonial bureaucracy) as "degenerate" due to loss of indigenous agency and p. 36 for a discussion of domesticity as a site of resistance.

8. Chowdhry (2013, 714ff.) discusses the colonial-era formation of a regional cultural ideology of manliness, particularly involving martial castes, such as the Jāṭs and Rājpūts.

9. Narratives of the imperfectly masculinized Indian male have persisted even in postcolonial times, at least in disciplines that claim a universal objectivity (not subject to Hindu-nationalist revisionism). Hence, psychologist Sudhir Kakar (1981, 111) writes that Indian boys are trained toward acceptance of "the passive feminine aspects of identity." Interestingly, he finds a cultural model for this disposition in the god Krishna, an androgynous youth. Inasmuch as Kakar never mentions Hanumān, it is worth keeping in mind that he wrote these views years before Hanumān's documented rise in public esteem in the late 1980s and onward.

10. Datta (1999, 23ff.) discusses negative perceptions of Jāṭs from Mughal and British colonial times.

11. Jaffrelot (2010, 430ff.) identifies three basic identities that have been popularly associated with Jāṭs at various times in their history (and often simultaneously): warriors, farmers, and backward caste.

12. I have often heard it said while in the field that Hanumān "was" a Jāṭ (in past tense, in reference to his feats in the *Rāmāyaṇa* of ancient days). Chowdhry (2013, 734) confirms this sentiment.

13. As outlined at the start of their article, Osella and Osella (2003, 732) argue that Ayyapan enables "constructing male identities" while "acting as a signifier of superior masculine purity." This argument parallels what I am theorizing about the process of male ascetic devotion to Hanumān.

14. Female devotees that I interviewed stated that women are ideally supposed to wish for the well-being of their husbands as opposed to gains for themselves, whereas men are expected to seek their own advantage. This testimony points to a gendering of wish-making practices.

15. Gill (2012) writes of an Indian film culture that exalts Jāṭ masculinity, a subject that has a bearing on my discussion of the Jāṭ emulation of Hanumān's masculinity.

16. Several Hindi devotional handbooks containing this story are usually available in Sālāsar's market adjacent to the temple. Among them, I highlight Subhash Bhedrak's (ca. 2010) *Sālāsar Bālājī Itihās* (History of Sālāsar Bālājī). Babb (1999, 3–8) provides the only scholarly discussion of Sālāsar Bālājī known to me. However, he focuses only on its foundational text in connection with his broader study on late premodern relations between the warrior and mercantile castes in Rajasthan, without addressing Sālāsar's subsequent history.

17. Hardgrove (2004), especially pp. 247–84, provides a useful analysis of the dynamics in the Mārvāḍī reification of their ancestral homeland in Rajasthan. Although she never mentions Sālāsar Bālājī, she does nonetheless discuss a similar kind of devotion from afar for Rani Sati, a goddess whose main temple is in Jhunjhunu, somewhat to the north of Sālāsar.

18. Advani's *yātrā* was not a stand-alone event but part of an ongoing effort over the years to frame national politics as a struggle to restore classical Indian values, as represented in the worship of Hanumān and Rāma. Among many possible references, see, for example, "Yatra Politics: How Advani Has Always Resorted to Yatras," *Firstpost*, October 11, 2011, https://www.firstpost.com/politics/yatra-politics-how-advani-has-always-resorted-to-yatras-104375.html.

19. Among numerous possible instances of this sentiment, I would point to Bhedrak's (ca. 2010, 3) introduction, where he states that Bālājī is an avatar, indeed just one of various manifestations that God (in the broadest sense, including Viṣṇu) takes in every era when demons threaten to undermine world order.

20. Among innumerable reports pertaining to this incident and its aftermath, see an overview by Sonali Pimputkar in "Nirbhaya Gang Rape Case: Complete Timeline of Events in 2012 Delhi Gang-Rape Case and How the Case Unfolded," *Free Express Journal*, July 9, 2018, https://www.freepressjournal.in/headlines/nirbhaya-gang-rape-case-complete-timeline-of-events-in-2012-delhi-gang-rape-case-and-how-the-case-unfolded/1312824.

21. Hanumān is regarded in Hindu tradition as one of the *cirañjīvīs*, or immortal beings, due to the boon he received from Rāma and Sītā in recognition of his unmatched faith in them. However, the average devotee is not necessarily aware of this rather scriptural-literary term and simply knows that the *Rāmāyaṇa* reveals that Hanumān was blessed with immortality.

22. Devotees commonly say that Bālājī, not to mention Hanumān, is especially suited for this darkened era. This view also registers in Hindi devotional literature. For example, in *Jai Śrī Bālājī*, a journal published in Rajasthan devoted to Bālājī, the editor Prashant Kumar Swami (2005) starts off on page 4 with a reference to Bālājī's special role in the Kali Yuga.

23. Only very rarely, one might see a performer wearing a Hanumān mask without such a crown.

References

Alter, Joseph. 1992. "'The Sannyasi' and the Indian Wrestler: The Anatomy of a Relationship." *American Ethnologist* 19 (2): 317–36.

Babb, Lawrence. 1999. "Mirrored Warriors: On the Cultural Identity of Rajasthani Traders." *International Journal of Hindu Studies* 3 (1): 1–25.

Bhedrak, Subhash. ca. 2010. *Sālāsar Bālājī Itihas* [*History of Sālāsar Bālājī*]. Chaumoon, Jaipur, Rajasthan: Roormal Bookseller.

Chowdhry, Prem. 2013. "Militarized Masculinities: Shaped and Reshaped in Colonial South-East Punjab." *Modern Asian Studies* 47 (3): 713–50.

———. 2014. "Masculine Spaces: Rural Male Culture in North India." Abstract. *Economic and Political Weekly* 49, no. 47 (November 22, 2014): 41–49.

Datta, Nonica. 1999. *Forming an Identity: A Social History of the Jats*. New Delhi: Oxford University Press.

Gill, Harjant. 2012. "Masculinity, Mobility and Transformation in Punjabi Cinema: From Putt Jattan De (Sons of Jat Farmers) to Munde UK De (Boys of UK)." *South Asian Popular Culture* 10 (2): 109–22.

Gold, Ann Grodzins. 2008. "Deep Beauty: Rajasthani Goddess Shrines above and below the Surface." *International Journal of Hindu Studies* 12 (2): 153–79.

Hardgrove, Anne. 2004. *Community and Public Culture: The Marwaris in Calcutta*. New Delhi: Oxford University Press.

Jaffrelot, Christophe. 2010. *Religion, Caste and Politics in India*. Delhi: Primus Books.

Kakar, Sudhir. 1981. *The Inner World: A Psycho-analytic Study of Childhood and Society in India*. New Delhi: Oxford University Press.

Lutgendorf, Philip. 1994. "My Hanuman Is Bigger Than Yours." *History of Religions* 33 (3): 211–45.

———. 2007. *Hanuman's Tale: The Messages of a Divine Monkey*. New York: Oxford University Press.

Nanda, Meera. 2009. *The God Market: How Globalization Is Making India More Hindu*. Noida, Uttar Pradesh: Random House India.

Osella, Filippo, and Caroline Osella. 2003. "'Ayyappan Saranam': Masculinity and the Sabarimala Pilgrimage in Kerala." *Journal of the Royal Anthropological Institute* 9 (4): 729–53.

Sarkar, Tanika. 2001. *Hindu Wife, Hindu Nation: Community, Religion, and Cultural Nationalism*. London: Hurst.

Sinha, Mrinalini. 1999. "Giving Masculinity a History: Some Contributions from the Historiography of Colonial India." *Gender and History* 11 (3): 445–60.

Swami, Prashant Kumar. 2005. "Sampadakiya" [Editorial]. *Jai Shri Bālājī* 1 (1): 4.

Whannel, Garry. 2002. *Media Sport Stars: Masculinities and Moralities*. London: Routledge.

6

Going Home for Navarātri

Negotiating Caste, Class, and Gender between Rural and Urban Rajasthan

JENNIFER D. ORTEGREN

On the sixth night of Navarātri in October 2013, my teenaged host sisters, Arthi and Deepti, stopped in the doorway of the bedroom I rented from their parents in Pulan, an emerging middle-class neighborhood of Udaipur, Rajasthan. "Are you coming?" they asked. They were dressed in cotton *salvār kamīz* (baggy pants and a long tunic) and carrying painted sticks for *ḍaṇḍiyā*, a dance of choreographed steps performed between partners who keep rhythm by tapping their sticks together that is central to Navarātri performances in Rajasthan. "We're going to dance!" Arthi said. I was surprised by the invitation because their older sister, Kavita, had once told me that their parents never allowed her to dance in Pulan, and I had assumed the same would be true for Arthi and Deepti. When I confessed this, Arthi explained that she and Deepti could dance as long as they only danced with each other. Deepti chided me to hurry up, and we headed toward a makeshift dance area set up in front of a large plaster-of-paris *mūrti* (image) of the goddess in her form as Durgā Mātā that had been installed along the main road that runs the length of the neighborhood.

When we arrived, a small crowd had already gathered around the ropes demarcating the dance area in the street. A group of young women and men were dancing to a Bollywood song blaring through speakers set up by a hired DJ. Deepti and Arthi joined the circle of dancers, and I sat watching with other neighbors. I waited expectantly for someone to coax me into dancing, as had happened at other celebrations, but the invitation never came. When the music stopped and the final *ārtī* (flame offering) of *pūjā* (worship) to the goddess had been performed, Arthi inquired as to why I had not danced. "You didn't ask," I said, "I didn't have a partner." "Oh," she replied sheepishly, "It's no problem. We'll dance in Rām Nagar [her father's village]. There, we can dance comfortably because everyone is from the same caste [*vahāṃ ham ārām se nāc saktī hai kyoṃki ek hī samāj hai*]." Their sister Kavita had made this same claim, and the next morning, when I explained to their older brother Krishna why I had not danced, he repeated the trope. Indeed, many women in Pulan had told me that they felt more comfortable in the village for various reasons, including the fact that they could dress more casually, had fewer responsibilities and more mobility, or simply that the weather was nicer. But almost invariably, when women made claims about feeling more comfortable in the village, they noted the significance of caste homogeneity.

In this chapter, I examine this claim to comfort among upwardly mobile families like those in Pulan who are members of what I call the emerging middle classes. Most of these families migrated to the city from rural areas in the past twenty to thirty years and consider themselves to be newly middle class. Yet they maintain strong ties to their rural homes and communities and must negotiate between overlapping, and sometimes contrasting, values and expectations. As a communal festival that includes both emerging-middle-class, pan-Indian traditions centered around Durgā and devotional practices dedicated to the *kuldevī* (family goddess) who is specific to local castes and/or villages, Navarātri is a time when these negotiations—and the boundaries of class, caste, and gender propriety therein—become public in distinct ways. By comparing Deepti's and Arthi's—and my own—experiences celebrating Navarātri in both Pulan and Rām Nagar, I analyze this claim to comfort in rural areas and show how Navarātri celebrations help to maintain caste identity, albeit in modified forms, in middle-class settings among young women.

Class, Caste, and Religion

In recent years, scholars have paid increasing attention to what they call India's new middle class, which began to emerge following economic liberalization in the early 1990s (see Donner 2011). The *new* of *new middle class* refers not only to the fact that their acquisition of wealth and middle-class status is relatively recent but also to the fact that the neoliberal middle class is defined in new ways related to consumerism. Leela Fernandes (2006, 30) notes that the "Gandhian ideals of austerity" and production-based identities that marked the postindependence middle class have given way to extravagant displays of wealth and middle-class identities rooted in the capacity to participate in a globalized marketplace. Scholars have emphasized practices related to leisure and space (Brosius 2010; Nisbett 2006; Srivastava 2012); fashion and youth (Lukose 2009; Nisbett 2009; on Nepal, see Liechty 2003); television, film, and advertising (Dwyer 2014; Mankekar 1999; Rajagopal 1999); and work (Atmavilas 2008; Radhakrishnan 2011) as sites for developing and displaying these identities. The number of Indians who self-identify as middle class is growing as the products, institutions, and performances associated with middle-class lifestyles become increasingly accessible—and important—across a wide demographic of communities.[1]

Shifting middle-class sensibilities both shape and are shaped by religious practices. At the most basic level, taking up new public religious practices helps to display middle-class economic standing, aesthetic sensibilities, and cultural competencies. Mary Hancock (1999) shows how the movement of domestic altars to central locations in the home helps to display familial wealth and aesthetic values within the home. Christiane Brosius (2010) and Joanne Waghorne (2004) have shown how the introduction of new architecture, Sanskritized texts, and worship practices in temples can help to raise the status of practitioners and even local goddesses.[2] New media, including comic books, ritual pamphlets, and television serials about Hindu gods, help to promote pan-Indian narratives and aesthetics that inform understandings of middle-class religiosity. Minna Säävalä (2001), in her discussion of lower-caste communities taking up the historically upper-caste ritual of *śrīsatyanārāyaṇa vrat*, suggests that adopting practices that have traditionally been performed by higher-class and higher-caste communities can be a strategy of upward mobility. That is, which rituals or festivals one celebrates, where and with whom one celebrates, and how one dresses and decorates ritual spaces are important indicators of relative wealth and cultural competencies to conform to middle-class sensibilities.

Yet, as Mark Liechty (2003, 72) contends, based on his work with middle-class communities in contemporary Nepal, "middle-class notions of propriety are typically rooted in a sense of community: the middle class is a moral community that 'restrains' its members in a sphere of 'suitable' behaviors." The behaviors that are deemed "suitable" are determined in connection, and contention, with other predominant social hierarchies in

South Asia such as caste and gender. Religious festivals, such as Navarātri, become critical testing grounds for experimenting with and negotiating shifting sets of suitable behaviors and middle-class moralities therein. Yet Navarātri is different from many other festivals such as Gaṇeśa Caturthī because it emphasizes practices, aesthetics, and forms of devotion to the goddess in both her pan-Indian, middle-class forms and her local, caste-specific forms, and therefore the different forms of suitability in each. Thus, celebrations of Navarātri reveal the tensions and resolutions that may exist between caste and class as moral identities.

Class, Caste, and Gender in Pulan

Located three miles northeast of the Old City at the center of Udaipur, the neighborhood of Pulan consists of twenty-four numbered *galīs* (small lanes) stretching back from a main road that serves as the central marketplace. Each of the *galīs* is approximately eight feet wide and lined on both sides by (mostly) multistory homes built with adjoining walls. The majority of the oldest residents in Pulan migrated from rural areas in search of opportunities for upward mobility and come from a wide range of castes, although almost all are listed by the Rajasthani government as Other Backward Classes, Scheduled Castes, or Scheduled Tribes. Yet, almost universally, families in Pulan self-identify as middle class, which they frame as being in-between (*bīc meṃ*). This in-betweenness is both an economic and moral marker. While families in Pulan cannot afford freestanding homes or automobiles like their wealthier counterparts, they have secure housing and basic amenities, such as televisions, motorbikes, and washing machines, unlike the urban poor. Also, unlike wealthy people (*paisevāle log*), who are thought to only care about themselves, and poor people (*garīb log*), who do not have the time or money to care about others, in-between people are distinct because they take care of their neighbors. Thus, this in-between position is the morally superior and ideal position.

While residents of Pulan self-identify as being middle class, I locate them as members of the emerging middle classes to mark that they are just now, in this generation, beginning to call themselves middle class and to experiment with middle-class lifestyles and aesthetics, although in limited ways. The Mali family epitomizes the experience of emerging into the middle class. Arthi and Deepti's parents, whom I only called Auntie-jī and Uncle-jī, moved to Pulan from Rām Nagar following their marriage thirty years ago. While they initially lived in a single-story, two-bedroom home, they saved up money from Uncle-jī's salary working at the city-run water plant to build a three-story home, the largest in their *galī*, with enough rooms to rent out for additional income. Perhaps most telling of their upward mobility is the fact that, while Auntie-jī never attended school and Uncle-jī finished only the equivalent of eighth grade, all of their children—including their three daughters—would receive college educations. For the Malis, this commitment to educating their children not only marks their belonging in the urban middle classes but distinguishes them from rural counterparts, who they claimed, in both overt and covert ways, did not educate their children (especially daughters) due to a lack of either resources or understanding of the value of education. For the emerging middle classes in Pulan, then, being in-between is a position negotiated within the urban neighborhood *and* between the city and the village.

Implicit in claims to moral superiority among the emerging middle classes in Pulan is also the sense that caste is no barrier to caregiving among middle-class neighbors. While nearly everyone could easily name the *jātī* (lit. birth group, here meaning caste) of each of their neighbors, caste was rarely cited as a factor in determining participants in social or religious gatherings. Deepti once told me directly that, in the city, "caste is no problem." This narrative appears to be part of a broader middle-class rhetoric espousing egalitarian values and rejecting caste as a legitimate grounding for socioeconomic or political discrimination. While my position as a foreigner may have influenced the ways in which some residents expressed this sentiment to me, to claim that "caste is no problem" echoes what Amanda Gilbertson (2018, 100) calls "cosmopolitan castelessness," which she finds to be "a privilege of the middle and upper caste, [which] serves to deny the intimate interconnection between caste and class." While Gilbertson examines how cosmopolitan castelessness among the middle and upper classes reinforces their own power, in Pulan we can see how this narrative trickles down to the emerging middles classes. While caste clearly matters in everyday and ritual life in Pulan, here I suggest that the invocation of a cosmopolitan castelessness is nevertheless a way of asserting a particular understanding of what many residents seem to think *should* be middle-class values, one they claimed was especially evident during Navarātri celebrations because urban neighbors from all castes would celebrate and dance together. Indeed, my occasional suggestions that caste was a factor were often swiftly rebuked, and instead issues of inconvenience or habit were named as the causes.

This movement away from discussing caste is increasingly common in urban areas. As Kathinka Frøystad (2003, 67–68) explains, "When dealing with social inequality in urban India . . . the prohibition of caste discrimination has virtually made it socially unacceptable to admit caste inhibitions, let alone defend them. Thus, urban upper and middle class people who discuss inequality today, often prefer to do so in terms of class, literacy or hygiene—even when reluctantly acknowledging that caste may come into play as well."[3] Although Frøystad's interlocuters were upper caste and wealthier than those in Pulan, this sentiment about caste is similar. However, as the practices of Navarātri make clear, caste identities, communities, and values remain critical for many in the emerging middle classes and are reinforced during Navarātri celebrations even as rural practices become overlaid with emerging middle-class sensibilities.

Gender complicates these negotiations because it is central to the articulation and performance of class and caste values. While families like the Malis are committed to sending their daughters to college as a marker of their middle-class status, they also teach their daughters to regulate their lives and bodies in new ways to avoid violating caste and gender propriety outside of the home (see also Fuller and Narasimhan 2008; Lukose 2009). This balance can be especially difficult for young women, as their bodies have long been the foundation upon which class, caste, religious, and nationalist identities are articulated, performed, and defended (Donner 2008; Hancock 1999; Mankekar 1999; Sarkar 2001). But it is perhaps especially difficult for young women like Arthi and Deepti whose recently urbanized families maintain strong ties to their village communities and the caste and gendered values that predominate there, which may differ from the middle-class values they are expected to perform and embody in the urban neighborhood. It is here that Navarātri, as a festival that is equally defined by class and caste values and aesthetics for families like the Malis, reflects shifts in class and caste practices in modern India and also becomes a public site for navigating them. In particular, Navarātri celebrations show that while caste may be secularizing in terms of politics and economics (Sheth 1999) and may be eschewed in dominant discourse, it remains a critical feature of everyday and religious life, especially for determining middle-class gendered values.

Celebrating Navarātri in Pulan

It is perhaps not surprising that Navarātri is a valuable time for negotiating class, caste, and gender in Rajasthan, as the festival combines both emerging pan-Indian practices and localized, village-specific forms of worship and focuses on the *śakti* (power) of the goddess. Though the nine nights dedicated to celebrating the forms of the goddess are celebrated in some form throughout much of India, the particularities of ritual worship vary across and within regions. In Udaipur, the history of Navarātri is shaped by the traditions of Rajputs, the martial and royal caste that has long been socioeconomically and politically dominant in Rajasthan.

Lindsey Harlan (1992) explains that nearly all the royal Rajput women with whom she worked in Udaipur[4] observed a Navarātri *vrat* (vow, fast) because Navarātri is "*the* Rajput holiday" (45, emphasis in original) due to the fact that it commemorates the military victory of the goddess Durgā. Durgā's conquest of the buffalo demon Mahiṣāsura and his army valorizes the warrior ethics of honor and protection that pervade Rajasthani culture, even among those who are not Rajput. Indeed, among Rajputs, local *kuldevīs*—the family goddesses who are central to domestic worship—are known to have also vanquished demons and therefore join "an omnipresent homology between all *kuldevis* and the Goddess expressed during Navratri." As Harlan explains, "On this day [Navarātri] the *kuldevi* is worshipped as Durga. The *Devimahatmya* or *Durga Path*, a Hindi translation, is recited in great goddess temples and *kuldevi* temples alike. Moreover, *kuldevis* are as often referred to as Durga, Devi, Kali, Camunda, and Shakti, all Sanskrit-tradition epithets, as they are by their individual local names" (61). The significance of these claims for Rajputs is that it aligns their histories with cosmic Hindu histories and imparts cosmic significance to the kings and local sacrifices.[5] The buffalo (or goat substitute) sacrifice that is performed by men for the *kuldevī* during Navarātri is both the sacrifice to Durgā as a goddess and of Durgā as a warrior. Among Rajputs, then, Navarātri is powerful because it reinforces the value and power of the local caste community and its values.

While I did not work with royal Rajput communities[6] like Harlan did, her descriptions of attitudes and practices—both in terms of names and sacrifices—toward *kuldevīs* align with what I encountered in Pulan and Rām Nagar. The *kuldevī* is the first and most important focus of nightly worship, although in urban areas this worship takes place privately in the home with only family members before they attend celebrations of Durgā in her pan-Indian form at public *mūrtis*. This distinction is critical because, as I want to suggest here, it correlates with the kinds of caste and class boundaries that families—and especially young women—in the emerging middle classes must navigate. On the one hand, the *kuldevī* represents one's caste community, history, and values, which in this case are associated with the village. On the other, the Sanskritic forms of the goddess encapsulated in the images of Durgā that are central to public practices in the city are associated with a pan-Indian, middle-class Hindu community and its aesthetics and values, which I describe in detail below. Thus, moving between these devotional communities is the very act of maneuvering between overlapping and sometimes contradictory sets of expectations. These tensions are the basis for the claims of feeling comfortable in the village and the implicit claims of feeling uncomfortable in the city expressed by the Mali siblings and show how Navarātri, unlike other major festivals, such as Ganeśa Caturthī, Holī, or Diwālī, helps us to understand the evolving relationship between class and caste in modern India for upwardly mobile families.[7]

When I asked women in Pulan about the meaning of Navarātri, most responded simply that "it is for the goddess." When I pushed for stories of the goddess, I was often directed to older residents or given newspaper clippings depicting the nine forms of the goddess. One woman asked if I had seen a recent television program about Durgā killing the demons. When I said I had not but had heard that story, she responded bluntly, "Whatever you heard is right." As is evident in these responses, the official textual stories of Navarātri are something about which people are aware but are not central. Rather, domestic practices centering around the *kuldevī* are most important, followed by public practices centering around socializing, entertainment, and dancing. While the *kuldevī* is worshipped daily in domestic *pūjā* practices, these practices become more elaborate during Navarātri, with women decorating their images of the goddess and altars, making special sweets to offer for *prasād* (blessed food), and singing special songs that are not a part of their usual repertoires. These domestic worship practices, which are conducted in the relative privacy of the urban home each evening with only family, are supplemented by public celebrations that center on the goddess in her pan-Indian, Sanskritic form as Durgā. It is in these latter practices that we see the most visible shifts in middle-class practices and aesthetics.

Throughout Udaipur, public Navarātri celebrations center on temporary festival *mūrtis* (images) of the goddess in her form as Durgā Mātā (or occasionally I was told it was Ambā Mātā) displayed in communal spaces.[8] In the early morning of the first day of Navarātri, individuals or groups of neighborhood community members travel to various markets throughout the city to purchase *mūrtis* complete with elaborately painted features and clothing. Some temples sponsor their own *mūrtis* and festivities, such as those in the Suthārvāḍa Mitṛ Maṇḍal, which has one of the largest *mūrtis* in the city and a stage reaching nearly fifty feet high.[9] Most *mūrtis*, however, are collectively purchased by residents of local neighborhoods. The *mūrtis* range in their size and style of decoration, but, unlike the diverse *mūrtis* made for the Gaṇeśa festival, the *mūrtis* for Navarātri are more uniform in their depiction of the goddess.[10] They usually show her seated on a tiger, with different implements representing the range of her *śakti* (power) in each of her arms: a conch shell, a trident, a sword, a bow and arrow, a ring of light, and a lotus bud, and her eighth arm is held up in a *mudrā* symbolizing her protection and blessings.

In Pulan, two *mūrtis* were installed along the main street. One was in a small open lot next to the Śiva temple at the center of the neighborhood, which had been converted into a large *paṇḍal* (tent; figure 6.1). Green felt covered the ground, and a red embroidered cloth provided a makeshift

Figure 6.1. *Mūrti* near the temple. Note the size of the *mūrti*, the sheet in the background, and the relatively simple but extravagant decorations, particularly as they compare to the second *mūrti* in the neighborhood (see Figure 6.2, below). Photo by author.

roof. The cloth sheet that formed the backdrop of the *mūrti* depicted a quintessential American winter scene of two young boys trudging through a snowy, star-filled landscape toward a large, brightly lit home with their toboggan in tow. The *mūrti* of Durgā, reaching about ten feet high, was installed atop a small dais covered with a shiny, white silk cloth. The location of the *mūrti* at the back of the *paṇḍal* created space for devotees to gather within the *paṇḍal*—and therefore off the street—to offer *pūjā* and take *darśan* (sight of the deity). A hired DJ arranged large speakers at the front of the lot, which helped to demarcate the boundaries of the *paṇḍal*. Durgā, sitting astride a tiger, was painted in a sparkling red sari with a matching cloth draped over the golden crown atop her head. A wig of long, curly synthetic hair cascaded over her shoulders and chest, pooling in her lap. The detailed, placid expression on her face, towering over devotees, inspired a mix of calm reassurance and awed respect.

The second *mūrti* was installed ten *galīs* away on a small permanent marble-and-granite stage built into the stone wall that runs along the main street (figure 6.2). Although depicting Durgā in a similar way, this *mūrti* was smaller and had cruder, less-well-proportioned features. An orange cotton sari was draped over the multicolored sari painted onto the statue, and a small, beaded chandelier, which hung directly over the *mūrti*'s unadorned head, was lit with strings of lights. A statue of Gaṇeśa, also smaller than at the first *mūrti*, sat in front of the goddess, surrounded by an array of *pūjā* implements. The small *paṇḍal* housing the *mūrti* was heavily decorated with colored lights and showed a scenic

Figure 6.2. Second *mūrti*. Note the similarities in motif between the two *paṇḍals* but also the differences in size, style, and decorations that display the range of possibilities for public display. Photo by author.

image of a swan in the placid waters of a mountaintop lake. But, as the *paṇḍal* covered only the *mūrti* and the small stage, devotees gathered on the street in front of the image to offer worship and take *darśan*. The DJ hired by the community sponsoring the second *mūrti* had arranged his speakers and equipment on the street in front and to the right of the *mūrti*.

Although I focus in this chapter on the second *mūrti* shown here because it was the one in front of which Arthi and Deepti danced, comparing the two helps us recognize subtle but significant ways in which Navarātri celebrations contribute to class performances. The size, style, and foreignness of the imagery at the larger *mūrti* combined with its presence near the temple, the regular attendance of the Brahmin family who cared for the temple, and the fact that devotees moved off the street into the ritual space of the *paṇḍal* all seemed to add a certain prestige that was lacking at the second, smaller roadside *mūrti*. While it is beyond the scope of this chapter to analyze narratives of how there came to be two *mūrtis*, there were no explicit restrictions on who could celebrate at which *mūrti*, and the makeup of the ritual communities at either was not radically different.[11] But the subtle details of these *mūrtis* show how shared motifs of Navarātri *paṇḍals* link communities to pan-Indian deities and (imagined) middle-class practices—in the forms of tents and DJs—while simultaneously reflecting relative differences in the economic statuses of communities and/or donors. That is, the *mūrtis* and *paṇḍals* themselves are important sites for displaying class status and aesthetic sensibilities and, as we will see, reshaping urban and rural celebrations.

At the smaller *mūrti*, where Arthi and Deepti danced, *pūjā* was performed each evening by a male member of the community, followed by hours of dancing to Bollywood songs played by the DJ before a final *ārtī* (flame ceremony) concluded the evening's festivities.[12] Only small crowds gathered for the first *ārtī* in the early evening because nearly everyone remained home to offer *pūjā* to the *kuldevī* first. But everyone came for the dancing.

Dancing was central to every Navarātri celebration I witnessed throughout Udaipur and was a popular conversation topic among women. In Pulan, an area of the street in front of the *mūrti* was cordoned off with ropes each evening, and a lattice of decorative lights was strung overhead to demarcate a dance space (figure 6.3). Each evening, women would gather in windows or on front steps, roofs, or mats spread on the ground to watch the dancers. Groups of young men, who traversed the city on motorcycles to watch the dancing in different neighborhoods, formed tight clusters along the perimeter of the ropes. Early in the evenings, small children and younger girls would gather to dance, their attempts to wield adult-sized *ḍaṇḍiyā* sticks providing delight to all who watched (figure 6.4). Later in the evenings, and especially on the later days of the festival, the crowd

Figure 6.3. View of the dance area in front of the second *mūrti* from above. The lights add to the festive feeling and help to mark the street as a middle-class ritual space. Photo by author.

Figure 6.4. Young girls dancing *ḍaṇḍiyā* in Rajasthani outfits. Navarātri is an occasion to purchase new clothes and to see and be seen by others. The dancing, a source of entertainment and leisure, plays a larger role in drawing a crowd than the communal worship of Durgā. Photo by author.

of dancers would shift as teenaged girls and boys displaced the smaller children. A few pairs of older women and men would join, but dancers were primarily young people in their late teens or early twenties.

While I witnessed dancing at every Navarātri celebration I attended in and beyond Udaipur, multiple women told me that dancing only became popular in the past fifteen to twenty years. They also noted that dancing was most popular in the neighboring state of Gujarat (see Shukla-Bhatt in this volume), citing the influence of films and television serials, televised images of Gujarati celebrations of Navarātri, and an increased presence of Gujarati immigrants as sources for the increased popularity of dancing. Even purchasing a *mūrti* was described as a relatively new practice and, along with dancing, was cited as a significant difference between rural and urban celebrations. As one neighbor, Neelima, explained,

> Look, for Navarātri, we do *pūjā* to Mātā-jī [lit. Mother, here meaning the goddess]. They celebrate Navarātri in the village, but they didn't used to dance *garbā*.[13] They just started to dance *garbā* in the last eight or nine years when they got lights and music. They saw a tape of it. But they don't purchase a *mūrti*. There, they just worship the village Mātā-jī in the main place, and they all play *garbā* there. Here, they dance on the main road.

Neelima notes that dancing is a recent phenomenon in her village because the electricity necessary for lights and music came to the village only recently. She also highlights the influence of media and images of outside communities: only after they "saw it on a tape" did the residents of her village take up this new practice. Likewise, women told me that while people used to go to temples to celebrate Navarātri, and one woman even suggested that "everyone in Udaipur" would go to one temple in the Old City, in the past fifteen years, localized communities have begun to purchase *mūrtis* and celebrate separately in public areas.

In both Udaipur and in the village, taking up these new practices of purchasing a *mūrti*, hiring a DJ, and dancing in communal spaces helps to demarcate community belonging and publicly display a community's relative wealth and capacity to conform to emerging-middle-class sensibilities. As a public, communal festival that helps to produce ideas of modernity and authenticity, simultaneously bringing the "global" into the "local" and vice-versa (Gabbert 2007; Magliocco 2001), purchasing a *mūrti* and dancing during Navarātri links localized communities to middle-class communities elsewhere in India. Insofar as public festivals become sites of public scrutiny, in which reputations are managed and status is maintained or enhanced (Rao 2001), Navarātri helps individuals, families, and broader communities to perform middle-class status both to themselves and to outsiders.

The significance of Navarātri in Pulan as a time to see and be seen and to perform middle-class identities was evident in women's descriptions of the festival. Multiple women, most of them younger, enjoyed Navarātri because it offered an opportunity to purchase new clothing. For some, dressing up meant donning their most Western clothing, while for others it meant displaying their most traditional, elaborate Indian clothing, such as newly popular gauzy, bejeweled saris. These choices about clothing become nuanced negotiations of one's relationship to modernity and tradition and effectively display how young people, but especially young women, show that they are middle class without appearing to have become "overly Western" or to lack family values (Gilbertson 2014). While some women lamented that the festival had seemed to lose its devotional value due to the increased consumerism, most looked forward to it as a source of entertainment, a break from the routines of their everyday lives, and a sanctioned time to socialize with friends and neighbors.

These relationships between neighbors were also one of the most common distinctions noted between rural and urban celebrations. As Neelima further explained,

> There are a lot of differences in the village. Like, here, everyone dances *garbā* together. In the village, only the people that we can eat with [meaning people in the same *jātī*] dance together. . . . In the village, the upper ones [higher caste] celebrate separately. The lower ones [lower caste] celebrate separately. They worship different gods. . . . In the village, we take the same amount [of money] from each person [to pay for decorations], but we only take from our caste community [*samāj*]. Depending on how much our debt is, we divide it evenly, and everyone gives the same amount. Here in the city, you take money from everyone.

Whereas in Neelima's village caste determines who celebrates together such that upper and lower *jātī* communities dance separately, in part because they worship different forms of the goddess, she suggests that caste is irrelevant for public celebrations in urban areas. In the city, all people go to the same place to worship the goddess in a pan-Indian form, and all are expected to contribute money to the celebrations. Thus, shared class identities—rather than shared caste identities—are central to public urban ritual celebrations because they display the class status of individuals and the neighborhood and foster community ties within the middle-class neighborhood. The *mūrtis*, the DJs, the clothes, and the dancing that mirror celebrations throughout the city help to mark Pulan as a middle-class neighborhood in socioeconomic and aesthetic terms. The caste of the ritual community—even if only recognizable to the community itself—marks them as subscribing to middle-class morality.[14]

This claim about the shifting significance of caste highlights how the festival can function to foster a sense of community that transcends normative social boundaries, such as caste (De Neve 2000), and create new bases of social cohesion, such as class (Ghosh 2000). Here, we hear the echoes of a middle-class egalitarian ethos in which, as Deepti put it, "caste is no problem." Yet the repeated trope that one can feel more "comfortable" in the village due specifically to caste homogeneity suggests that caste very much still matters for emerging-middle-class families in urban neighborhoods. Reconciling these claims—and deciding which categories of identity should be prioritized in determining propriety and suitable behaviors as one moves between the village and the city—is central to Navarātri celebrations, and it is in this way that the festival becomes a microcosmic experience allowing us to analyze the broader process of becoming middle class in contemporary India.

Celebrating Navarātri in the Village

On the seventh day of Navarātri, Deepti, Arthi, Auntie-jī, and I took a bus to Rām Nagar. When we reached the two-room home they maintain there, the girls and Auntie-jī performed a brief *pūjā* in front of the courtyard temple before beginning to clean and prepare for dinner. After the rest of the family members arrived and we had eaten, the girls ushered me to the three-bedroom home of a neighbor to prepare to dance. The house was owned by the father of Manju, a woman in her late twenties who was married to Auntie-jī's brother and was also their neighbor in Pulan. As Manju offered her opinion on the girls' outfits, I realized that Deepti and Arthi were dressing much more formally than they had in Pulan. In the city, they wore nice cotton *salvār* suits, but nothing that they would not wear for everyday use. In Rām Nagar, however, they donned the vibrant, expensive nylon clothing they had purchased for Kavita's wedding the year before. When Deepti put on a bright pink-and-yellow sleeveless *kurtī* dress with matching tights—a popular style in Udaipur—she turned to Manju for approval. But Manju shook her head and told her to put on a long-sleeved shirt underneath. Concerned, I asked about my own sleeveless *kurtā*, but Manju dismissed my concerns. She explained that while Deepti could wear a sleeveless *kurtī* dress in Udaipur, it would be inappropriate for her to do so in the village, but because I am not Indian, it would be fine for me to do so. The girls carefully applied makeup and jewelry, something they had not done in Pulan, and loosened their ponytails to rearrange their long hair in barrettes such that half of it flowed down their backs, also a popular style in Udaipur. Deepti rearranged the bobby pins holding back her bangs multiple times until they lay at the perfect height.

When the girls were finally satisfied with their appearances, we began walking toward the center of the village.[15] Hearing them speaking in low tones behind me, I asked what they were talking about. Arthi, with her characteristic forthrightness, immediately replied, "We are embarrassed (*śarm lagtā*) that you're here because everyone will be looking at us." Her comment surprised, confused, and slightly hurt me; after all of their assurances that both they and I would feel more "comfortable" dancing in the village, I had not expected their embarrassment. If anything, I had worried they would try to show me off as a status symbol, an experience I had had before. But, as I came to realize and will return to below, I had misunderstood their claim to "comfort" and the ways in which it involved caste propriety.

At the center of the village, a significantly larger crowd of people was gathered than had been present at either of the locations in Pulan. As in urban areas, a large *mūrti* of Durgā was set up inside a *paṇḍal* to one side of the small circle designated for dancing. A DJ blasted music from his perch atop a platform overlooking the dancers, and the dance area was cordoned off with ropes, beyond which plastic chairs were set up for men and boys to watch. Groups of women gathered on mats on the ground on the other side of the circle. When we first arrived, only young girls were dancing. Eventually, other young women in their late teens or early twenties, like Arthi and Deepti, joined, and even a few younger men, although I recognized all of them as being from Pulan. A few younger married women joined as well, including Krishna's wife, who had not danced in the city, although she kept her face veiled and danced only with a female cousin. Very few of the older women joined, and at no point did any older men.

When we arrived at the dance area, feeling embarrassed myself and somewhat self-pitying, I told the girls I would sit alone and simply watch so as not to embarrass them. Arthi reluctantly insisted that I dance with her, although she soon passed me off to Manju, who seemed not to be as embarrassed by my presence. The space was crowded and it was difficult to avoid bumping into other people, so I was relieved when, after thirty minutes, Manju announced that she was tired and asked if

I wanted to go to the temple with her. We walked one block away to a small dead-end street where a crowd of women and men sitting on rugs stretched the length of the street. We quickly found Auntie-jī and joined her where she sat chatting with other women. I peered over their heads at the men gathered in front of the doorway of the last building on the left-hand side of the street. Unlike the surrounding buildings, it was single story, with a thatched roof and a heavy wooden door. I could not see inside but recognized a bright-orange drawing of a trident painted on the outside wall as representing the goddess.[16] As I watched, a man dressed in a white *dhotī* (a cloth tied around the legs and waist into loose pants that is traditionally worn by men) and a turban emerged from the building to mark the trident with *kumkum*, a bright-red vermillion powder used in ritual ceremonies. I asked Manju what was happening, and she explained that everyone on this "side" of the village, who were all from the Mali caste, had come because the men inside were performing a ritual for the goddess of their caste. Everyone comes to the temple, she explained, because it brings *lābh* (good fortune). When I asked why there were only men going inside, she said it was because, for the goddess, men are "higher" (*ādmī ūṃce haiṃ*). While I had never heard this claim about the goddess in Pulan, and women were largely responsible for conducting daily *pūjā* to the *kuldevī* at home altars, men's heightened ritual roles at temples in Pulan and Rām Nagar during these Navarātri festivals are reminiscent of those described by Harlan's Rajput interlocuters and mark the heightened power of the goddess during Navarātri.

We sat chatting for about thirty minutes, at which point Deepti and Arthi joined. Arthi said we had to "wait for the goddess to come" before we could leave. About thirty minutes later, the men inside the temple began ringing bells and banging pots with increased fervency, signaling the appearance of the goddess. After a few minutes, the sound receded, and the men emerged from the temple to hand out *prasād* (blessed foods) of small *laḍḍus* (balls of sweetened dough). As Deepti and I waited for the women in the family to finish chatting and move forward for *darśan*, I began nibbling on the *prasād*. Deepti scolded me, saying, "Be careful! You're dropping the *prasād* on the ground!" and held up her own perfectly intact *laḍḍu*. Again, I felt embarrassed and realized that in Pulan, while small amounts of *prasād* had been passed out following the final *ārtī* at the public *mūrtis*, neither Deepti nor Arthi, nor any of the other women with whom I had sat, had taken it. They had already performed *pūjā* at their domestic altars and received *prasād* there. In the village, however, the communal temple ritual took the place of the private, domestic ritual from Pulan, and I had not given proper care to the blessing that had been offered by the goddess.

This different emphasis on the value of the *pūjā* was only one of a number of small details that stood out to me about Navarātri practices in Rām Nagar. To begin with, unlike some women who claimed that rural communities do not invest in *mūrtis* but instead focus on permanent images of local goddesses, the residents of Rām Nagar had purchased a *mūrti* of Durgā and hired a DJ. The features of dancing, a *mūrti*, and a DJ suggest the ways in which popular practices, religious and otherwise, seem to move from urban to rural areas through both media images and migrant families who return regularly. Just as public Navarātri displays enabled residents of Pulan and other emerging-middle-class communities in Udaipur to perform a middle-class identity, so too did they enable rural communities to perform a more urban, cosmopolitan identity, although within limits. For example, none of the boys who lived in the village danced, at least not the night I attended, although many of the young men who live in Pulan did.

The homogeneity of the caste community in Rām Nagar created other differences. Both the *mūrti* itself and the crowd that gathered to dance or observe the dancing were much larger than in Pulan because residents throughout most of the village had donated money to purchase one *mūrti*. Whereas in Pulan *pūjā* to localized goddesses was domesticated and private, in Rām Nagar the Durgā *mūrti* and dancing were located alongside communal worship to a local, caste-specific goddess. There was no explicit relationship stated between this local form of the goddess and that of Durgā, but the fact that older women had relatively little interest in the celebrations taking place in front of the festival *mūrti* suggests that the devotional practices remained centered on the village goddess even while the village was able to display the capacity to participate in pan-Indian forms of religiosity and entertainment. Moreover, as Arthi and Deepti's embarrassment of my presence suggests, beyond hoping to avoid drawing unwanted attention to themselves, they were concerned about how I might behave inappropriately. As became clear in the conversations about clothing and my mishandling of *prasād*, I did not know the boundaries of suitable behaviors in the village, which were determined largely in terms of caste and were stricter in many ways than in the city. Their embarrassment and chiding suggested to me that the stakes of violating rules were higher in the village than in the city even if the rules by which to abide were clearer in Rām Nagar, a contradiction I consider in more depth in my concluding thoughts below. What I want to stress here is that, while elements of Navarātri as a middle-class practice are becoming prominent in rural areas, the devotion to the *kuldevī* and the conservative practices of Arthi and Deepti related to clothing and *prasād* demonstrate that Navarātri remains a fundamentally caste-oriented festival among families in the emerging middle classes in Pulan. As families return to the village, they shift into a different set of suitable behaviors and ideals. Most notably, caste—and the significance of caste—becomes not only an acceptable mark of distinction but a critical one that determines the makeup of the ritual community. This reflects and reinforces continued ties to rural caste values and belies the middle-class rhetoric that "caste is no problem" adopted by young women like Arthi and Deepti, revealing the ways in which this assertion may apply only in urban areas and, even then, may be only rhetoric. As Navarātri shows, caste very much still matters, and it may be due to the fact that the tension between rhetoric and practice does not exist in the village that they feel more comfortable there.

Conclusions about Comfort

Examining differences between Arthi and Deepti's experiences of celebrating Navarātri in Pulan and Rām Nagar shows how the festival, the goddess, and Hindu communities in India are increasingly being shaped by middle-class values and aesthetics but also how those shifts must be reconciled with the continuing significance of caste-specific values and practices. Yet this process of reconciliation is difficult and, as Arthi and Deepti's narrative suggests, uncomfortable. This difficulty became clear to me in the ways I misinterpreted their claim about being "comfortable" in the village. I had not anticipated that Arthi and Deepti would get more dressed up and feel embarrassed about my presence, because I had assumed they invoked "comfort" in the way that I might have, primarily to mean that they would feel less self-conscious about their appearance in the village. But the opposite was clearly true. They were significantly more concerned with their clothes and makeup for reasons that appear related to the performance of their urban, middle-class identities. Their brightly colored nylon *kurtī* dresses and tights were in keeping with the latest fashions for young middle-class girls in Udaipur. They and their other cousins from the city stood out among the girls in Rām Nagar, most of whom wore more traditional *salvār* suits. While this is not to imply that the young women in Rām Nagar did not have access to the same fashion trends and clothing, Arthi and Deepti's heightened concern about their appearance does suggest a desire to display their access to their rural counterparts.

Instead, it seems that their claim to comfort had to do with how they did or did not have to manage their bodies and belonging in the village like they did in the city. In Pulan, their class status and community belonging were known, accepted, and shared by most of the other participants due merely to their residence. Yet they had to carefully monitor with whom they danced. As Arthi had explained, they were allowed to dance in Pulan only because of the restriction that they dance with each other or with other members of the extended family. They were careful not to move into the space of other dancers, especially young men, lest they violate the codes of gender and caste propriety laid out by their parents. Managing their bodies along caste (and gendered) lines runs counter to claims that "caste doesn't matter" in the city, because while young women and men from multiple castes did gather to dance in one space, they did not actually dance together as partners.

In Rām Nagar, conversely, Deepti and Arthi's belonging in the community was established through their embodied caste identities. Thus, though they felt a need to heighten the performance of their middle-class status through aesthetics, they did not have to manage their bodies in the same way. They conformed to different standards of appropriate attire—as evidenced by Deepti putting on a long-sleeved shirt under her stylish, sleeveless *kurtī*—but the threat of violating rules of bodily propriety was reduced due to the caste-homogeneous nature of the community, the gender homogeneity of the dancers, and the fact that the task of monitoring proper interactions fell more equally to everyone present. The particular rules guiding interactions were implicitly understood, agreed upon, and maintained by the entire community. While Arthi and Deepti still chose only to dance with one another, which may suggest different class boundaries, they did not have to operate within a rhetoric that caste does not matter. Caste, in this case, was the primary factor determining the ritual participants.

It is this tension between a middle-class rhetoric that caste does not matter and continuing practices in which caste *does* matter that I think makes Arthi and Deepti—and their siblings—feel more comfortable celebrating Navarātri in the village. The prioritization of caste propriety creates a freedom and ease that is lacking in the emerging-middle-class contexts of their urban lives, where they must continually negotiate emerging boundaries of suitability and must abide by caste rules without necessarily claiming they are doing so. Such a double burden is fundamentally uncomfortable. Navarātri celebrations thus reveal the struggle to reconcile caste commitments with class aspirations. In this way, Navarātri reflects the shifts occurring in India related to class, caste, and gender; moreover, it is one of the very sites at which the expanding boundaries of rhetoric and practice are determined and tested by emerging-middle-class families. The movement between different locales, communities, and forms of the goddess mirrors the everyday ways in which middle-class

Hindus, especially young women, have to balance coexisting and sometimes competing expectations and shows how we can and must look to religious arenas to understand how caste and class will continue to be transformed in the rapidly shifting contexts of modern India.

Notes

1. This is not to suggest that globalization is unequivocally and equally productive for all communities. For discussions of the uneven impacts across communities, see Ganguly-Scrase and Scrase (2009) and Oza (2006).

2. See the afterword in Flueckiger (2015) for a similar discussion of Sanskritized practice transforming local deities. See also Srivastava (2012) for a discussion of status maintenance during festival celebrations within gated communities in Delhi and Wadley (2000) for the influence of narratives of science and modernity on middle-class domestic religious practices in urban areas.

3. See also Flueckiger's (2015, 13–17) "A Note on Caste."

4. Rajputs, like many castes in India, are subdivided into distinct *jātīs*. Although the higher *jātīs* of Rajputs have historically been among the highest and wealthiest castes in Rajasthan, Harlan distinguishes between the royal Rajput *jātīs* with whom she works and the *coṭa bhai* (little brother) *jātīs* of Rajputs who were historically bards to the higher-ranked royal Rajputs and are recognized by the state of Rajasthan as OBC. For more on Rajput history in and around Udaipur, see Harlan (1992).

5. The significance of kingship during Navarātri is common. See, for example, the chapters in the section entitled "Navarātri in the Court" in Simmons, Sen, and Rodrigues (2018).

6. The few Rajput families who lived in Pulan, for example, hailed from the *coṭa bhai jātīs*.

7. In this chapter, I focus on issues of performance and aesthetics, although it is important to note that Durgā herself has a complicated identity as both a fierce warrior and a loving, protective mother (see McDermott 2011). While I do not have the data for this, it would be interesting to consider how the public forms of Durgā worshipped in communal spaces may also be gentrified and domesticated like the *grāmmādevatās* that Waghorne (2004) describes in Madurai temples and how, if at all, they may reflect and shape different middle-class values in urban areas versus rural areas.

8. While in some areas of India, such as West Bengal, Navarātri is synonymous with Durgā Pūjā and most images of the goddess depict her in her form as Mahiṣāsuramardinī (i.e., slaying the buffalo demon Mahiṣāsura), this story is only peripheral to celebrations in Pulan.

9. I was told by multiple women in Pulan that this was the best *paṇḍal* in the city and where I should go to understand Navarātri, although none of the women had been there themselves. Instead, their claims were primarily based on what they had seen and read in the local paper.

10. See "Increase in Demand for Murtis," *Mumbai Mirror*, accessed September 2, 2014, http://www.mumbaimirror.com/mumbai/others/Increase-in-demand-for-murtis/articleshow/16166699.cms.

11. See Ortegren (2019).

12. *Ārtī* at the *mūrtis* was performed each night by a different male member of the community. It was explained to me that these men were chosen based on their power in the community, their recognized religious devotion, and/or their relationship to those who had made large donations for the *mūrti*. Although the Brahmin priest who presided over formal temple functions helped perform *ārtī* each night at the *mūrti* near the temple, the prominence of the lay members at both emphasized the communal nature of the festival.

13. Women regularly used the terms *garbā* and *ḍaṇḍiyā* interchangeably to describe the dancing, although they are different styles of dance. Most women I spoke to considered *garbā*, which is traditional to Gujarat and involves more elaborate movements with one's hands, to be more difficult than *ḍaṇḍiyā*, which is usually danced with sticks and is the only style of dancing I witnessed in Rajasthan.

14. See Wilson (2018) for a discussion of negotiations of class, caste, and gender among upwardly mobile women in South India.

15. Manju and the girls warned me that I should not take my phone or my camera with me lest they get stolen, which is why I have no pictures of celebrations in Rām Nagar but may also suggest particular attitudes about the village among urbanized families.

16. The trident is a common image of local goddesses and can be found at the center of most women's domestic *pūjā* shelves, including those of the Malis. When I asked about the image, women usually said, "that is our *Mātā* [lit. mother, here meaning village- and/or family-specific goddess]." When I queried further, most women could name the goddess but usually did not know her story.

References

Atmavilas, Yamani N. 2008. *Of Love and Labor: Women Workers, Modernity and Changing Gender Relations in Bangalore, India*. PhD diss., Emory University.

Brosius, Christiane. 2010. *India's Middle Class: New Forms of Urban Leisure, Consumption and Prosperity*. New Delhi: Routledge.

De Neve, Geert. 2000. "Patronage and 'Community': The Role of a Tamil 'Village' Festival in the Integration of a Town." *Journal of the Royal Anthropological Institute* 6 (3): 501–19. http://dx.doi.org/10.1111/1467-9655.00029.

Donner, Henrike. 2008. *Domestic Goddesses: Maternity, Globalisation and Middle-Class Identity in Contemporary India*. Aldershot: Ashgate.

———, ed. 2011. *Being Middle-Class in India: A Way of Life*. New York: Routledge.

Dwyer, Rachel. 2014. *Bollywood's India: Hindi Cinema as a Guide to Contemporary India*. London: Reaktion Books.

Fernandes, Leela. 2006. *India's New Middle Class: A Democratic Politics in an Era of Economic Reform*. Minneapolis: University of Minnesota Press.

Flueckiger, Joyce Burkhalter. 2015. *Everyday Hinduism*. West Sussex, UK: Wiley-Blackwell.

Frøystad, Kathinka. 2005. *Blended Boundaries: Caste, Class, and Shifting Faces of 'Hinduness' in a North Indian City*. New York: Oxford University Press.

Fuller, Chris J., and Haripriya Narasimhan. 2008. "Companionate Marriage in India: The Changing Marriage System in a Middle-Class Brahman Subcaste." *Journal of the Royal Anthropological Institute* 14 (4): 736–54.

Gabbert, Lisa. 2007. "Situating the Local by Inventing the Global: Community Festival and Social Change." *Western Folklore* 66 (3/4): 259–80.

Ganguly-Scrase, Ruchira, and Timothy J. Scrase. 2009. *Globalisation and the Middle Classes in India: The Social and Cultural Impact of Neoliberal Reforms*. New York: Routledge.

Ghosh, Anjan. 2000. "Spaces of Recognition: Puja and Power in Contemporary Calcutta." *Journal of Southern African Studies* 26 (2): 289–99.

Gilbertson, Amanda. 2014. "A Fine Balance: Negotiating Fashion and Respectable Femininity in Middle-Class Hyderabad, India." *Modern Asia Studies* 48 (1): 120–58.

———. 2018. *Within the Limits: Moral Boundaries of Class and Gender in Urban India*. New Delhi: Oxford University Press.

Hancock, Mary. 1999. *Womanhood in the Making: Domestic Rituals and Public Culture in Urban South India*. Boulder, CO: Westview Press.

Harlan, Lindsey. 1992. *Religion and Rajput Women*. Berkeley: University of California Press.

Liechty, Mark. 2003. *Suitably Modern: Making Middle-Class Culture in a New Consumer Society*. Princeton, NJ: Princeton University Press.

Lukose, Ritty A. 2009. *Liberalization's Children: Gender, Youth, and Consumer Citizenship in Globalizing India*. Durham, NC: Duke University Press.

Magliocco, Sabina. 2001. "Coordinates of Power and Performance: Festivals as Sites of (Re)Presentation and Reclamation in Sardinia." *Folkore Studies Association of Canada* 23 (1): 167–88.

Mankekar, Purnima.1999. *Screening Culture, Viewing Politics: An Ethnography of Television, Womanhood, and Nation in Postcolonial India*. Durham, NC: Duke University Press.

Nisbett, Nicholas. 2006. "The Internet, Cybercafés and the New Social Spaces of Bangalorean Youth." In *Locating the Field: Space, Place and Context in Anthropology*, edited by Simon Coleman and Peter Collins, 129–47. New York: Berg.

———. 2009. *Growing Up in the Knowledge Society: Living the IT Dream in Bangalore*. New York: Routledge.

Ortegren, Jennifer D. 2019. "Gaṇeśa Caturthī and the Making of the Aspirational Middle Classes in Rajasthan." *International Journal of Hindu Studies* 23, no. 1 (April): 61–77.

Oza, Rupal. 2006. *The Making of Neoliberal India: Nationalism, Gender and the Paradoxes of Globalization*. New York: Routledge.

Radhakrishnan, Smitha. 2011. *Appropriately Indian: Gender and Culture in a New Transnational Class*. Durham, NC: Duke University Press.

Rajagopal, Arvind. 1999. "Thinking about the New Indian Middle Class: Gender, Advertising and Politics in an Age of Globalisation." In *Signposts: Gender Issues in Post-independence India*, edited by Rajeswari Sunder Rajan, 57–100. New Delhi: Kali for Women.

Rao, Vijayendra. 2001. "Poverty and Public Celebrations." *Annals of the American Academy of Political and Social Science* 573 (1): 85–104.

Säävälä, Minna. 2001. "Low Caste but Middle-Class: Some Religious Strategies for Middle-Class Identification in Hyderabad." *Contributions to Indian Sociology* 35 (3): 293–318.

Sarkar, Tanika. 2001. *Hindu Wife, Hindu Nation: Community, Religion, and Cultural Nationalism*. Bloomington: Indiana University Press.

Sheth, D. L. 1999. "Secularisation of Caste and Making of New Middle Class." *Economic and Political Weekly* 34 (34/35): 2502–10.

Simmons, Caleb, Moumita Sen, and Hillary Rodrigues, eds. 2018. *Nine Nights of the Goddess: The Navarātri Festival in South Asia*. Albany: State University of New York Press.

Srivastava, Sanjay. 2012. "National Identities, Bedrooms, and Kitchens: Gated Communities and New Narratives of Space in India." In *The Global Middle Class: Theorizing through Ethnography*, edited by Rachel Heiman, Carla Freeman, and Mark Liechty, 57–84. Santa Fe, NM: School for Advanced Research Press.

Wadley, Susan S. 2000. "From Sacred Cow Dung to Cow 'Shit.'" *Journal of the Japanese Association for South Asian Studies* 12:1–28.

Waghorne, Joanne. 2004. *Diaspora of the Gods: Modern Hindu Temples in an Urban Middle-Class World*. New York: Oxford University Press.

Wilson, Nicole A. 2018. "*Kolus*, Caste, and Class: Navarātri as a Site for Ritual and Social Change in Urban South India." In Simmons, Sen, and Rodrigues 2018, 237–56.

7

Female Agency during Tamil Navarātri

INA MARIE LUNDE ILKAMA

This chapter investigates the Navarātri festival in Kāñcipuram and its alleged nature as a women's festival through the exploration of two cases: one domestic and one temple celebration.[1] The domestic *kolu* display of dolls is a particularly female setting in which women have clear-cut ritual roles. *Kolu* is also a rapidly growing ritual practice in contemporary Tamil Nadu. But the role of women is also more pronounced in temples during the festival, seen, for example, in *pūjās* performed for or by women. However, women's roles are expressed very differently in the temples compared to domestically,[2] and they also vary significantly between individual temples. In this chapter, I show how individual agents creatively deploy *kolu* for their own purposes, as is the case with Ms. Madhumita, introduced below, whose *kolu* has a special twist, and how temples accommodate rituals for women during Navarātri, as in the case of the small but popular temple of the village goddess Paṭavēṭṭammaṉ.

Domestic Navarātri

Tiered altars of dolls, known in Tamil as *kolu* or *pommai kolu,* are set up in many households during Navarātri. These *kolus* are worshipped during the festival as manifestations of the goddess in the home. They consist of dolls, usually fashioned of clay or papier-mâché, displayed hierarchically on steps. The dolls depict various deities, saints, and mythological and cultural/religious events and are arranged along with children's toys, souvenirs, and various trinkets. Here I discuss a *kolu* that is a bit out of the ordinary, namely that of Ms. Madhumita, a thirty-two-year-old teacher whose home I visited repeatedly during Navarātri in 2015. This particular *kolu* displays and represents Madhumita's agency and innovative power; it shows what she *does* with ritual while simultaneously performing the traditional *kolu* rituals, as so many women throughout Tamil Nadu do during these nine nights. Madhumita's *kolu* therefore illustrates what *kolu* commonly conveys in terms of female ritual agency and allows for a discussion of *kolu* in general, as well as demonstrating this ritual's processes of adaptation and appropriation.

Ms. Madhumita's *Kolu*

The small living room in the house of Madhumita's mother[3] abounds with dolls during Navarātri. A *kolu* of seven steps rises in the middle of the room (figure 7.1), and on the floor on each side, as well as on a table in the corner, there are several more dolls, including wedding and procession sets, Gaṇeśas, and three dominating self-manufactured dolls depicting Aiyappaṉ, Ardhanareśvara (half Śiva, half Śakti), and Rājarajeśvarī. The floor in front of the three dolls is spread with baby dolls, plastic fruits, and stuffed animals, and the hallway is decorated with children's toys such as trains, Disney figurines, and a toy tea set. On top of the *kolu* stands the pot (*kalaśa*) into which the goddess is invoked, flanked by representations of Mīnākṣī and Kāmākṣī.

The pot is not the only manifestation of the goddess in this home during this festival; the goddess often manifests herself in Madhumita during Navarātri evenings, when visitors come to see her *kolu*. Then she speaks prophecy (Tamil: *aruḷ vākku*) for the visitors, who may confront the goddess with their problems or desires. One evening while I visited, as Madhumita's mother chanted the *Mahiṣāsura Mardinī Stotram*, Madhumita's body suddenly started to gently rock back and forth while her eyes were closed, a blissful expression was on her face, and her tongue occasionally slipped out of her mouth like a lizard searching for an insect. The goddess was quickly welcomed into Madhumita's body as her mother smeared her face, arms, and feet with turmeric and vermillion powder and presented her with a plate filled with fruits and a sari. After Madhumita's mother had sung some Tamil devotional songs and waved the *āratī* lamp before the goddess, a woman among the guests approached Madhumita

Figure 7.1. Ms. Madhumita's *kolu* (Kāñcipuram, 2015). Photo by author.

with another plate filled with bananas, apples, a coconut, betel leaves, incense, and a sari. Madhumita as the goddess draped the cloth around herself as she continued rocking peacefully back and forth. The woman then engaged in a conversation with the goddess, all the while looking deeply moved, joining her palms, and almost inaudibly whispering her questions and replies to the goddess (figure 7.2).

As the conversation went on, it was revealed that she had trouble with her husband and wanted her family to stick together, and that this was her second approach to the goddess to find a solution to this problem. The woman and the goddess talked back and forth about how the husband had little time to go to the temple, which had been the remedy previously prescribed by the goddess. The goddess stood her ground: "If you follow whatever I say without failure, you will get whatever you want. . . . When I say a remedy for someone, they have to follow it. If you don't, what can I do? Once you do, come and tell me!" The woman then continued asking for the well-being of her brother and his wife, who do not live together anymore, and of a baby on behalf of an acquaintance. The goddess took the opportunity to campaign for more visitors, replying that they had to come and see her themselves to get their desires fulfilled: "If she is hungry, can you eat for her?!"

Every year on Vijayadaśamī, the festival's tenth day, Madhumita's mother performs an ablution (*abhiṣeka*) for Madhumita as the goddess with

Figure 7.2. Ms. Madhumita as the goddess speaks prophecy for a female visitor (Kāñcipuram, 2015). Photo by author.

the water from the pot on the *kolu* in which the goddess had been ritually installed. Madhumita explained in an interview how this ablution is related to the killing of Mahiṣa (the myth in the *Devīmāhātmya*) and thus connected her own possessions with the Navarātri festival's master narrative: "That will be the very grand day, the last day [i.e., Vijayadaśamī]. The last day was Mahiṣāsuramardini [the killing of the buffalo demon], so Ampāḷ [Tamil for "the goddess"] will be very angry. To destroy [Mahiṣa], she will be getting very angry, and she will be in an *ugram* [fierce] state. To reduce that, we will have the *kalaśa abhiṣekam* [ablution from the pot]." Madhumita explained to me that people mainly approach her for issues regarding fertility, marriage, disease, and getting rid of evil spirits. "That is very special here when comparing to other homes and other *kolus*," Madhumita explained. "Here, Ampāḷ is lively, coming and speaking prophecy to all those fellows." Deity or spirit possession is a practice commonly associated with lower castes (see, for example, Ram 2013; Trawick 1992).[4] Keeping *kolu*, on the other hand, has traditionally been a practice in households of Brahmins and other higher castes, running in the family hereditarily (Chettiar 1973, 100; Reiniche 1979, 51n16; Logan 1980; Tanaka 1999; Hancock 1999; Wilson 2015, 2018; Narayanan 2018; Sivakumar 2018). A family's collection of dolls traditionally starts when a couple marries. The bride is then presented with a pair of wooden *marappāccipommaikaḷ* (Tamil for "dolls prepared from wood") by her mother, and other dolls are also passed from mother to daughter. However, my own fieldwork, as well as recent studies by Wilson (2015, 2018), shows that *kolu* is currently being taken up by other families of various social standings, on the initiatives of women (and their children). This has been happening for the past two decades or so, and *kolu* continues to become more and more popular. In Tamil Nadu, as in India in general, there is currently a growing middle class and a powerful desire to acquire middle-class status. With its public display of economic power manifested in the abundance of dolls and gifts given to guests, keeping *kolu* is one key ritual that may communicate middle-class-ness. Wilson (2015, 2018) further links *kolu* to a Brahminization process,[5] in which people from lower strata of society move upward in the social hierarchy through emulating practices prevalent in higher castes. However, I propose that Madhumita's case points toward what could be called a de-Brahminization of the *kolu*, as some people appropriate the ritual and make it their own without necessarily becoming more Brahmin-like in their habits. Through taking the creative turn of including possession and prophecy in her performance of *kolu*, Madhumita appropriates and adapts this ritual practice to her own caste background (figure 7.3).[6]

Figure 7.3. Ms. Madhumita, sitting in front of the *kolu*, being possessed by the goddess (Kāñcipuram, 2015). Photo by author.

Making the Domestic Public

While Madhumita's *kolu* stands out, since people visit during Navarātri in order to approach the goddess with their problems, the visits themselves are not out of the ordinary: it is an important part of the nine festival evenings that friends, relatives, and neighbors visit in order to view the *kolus*. This is considered a female activity, since it is women, often along with their children, who go for such visits during Navarātri evenings. This is a joyous occasion to dress up in their finest silk saris, and the children might even be dressed up as various deities. During the visits, the displays are admired, the dolls chatted about—both the particular dolls and their mythological backgrounds—and the women sing Tamil devotional songs (if they are Brahmins, they also recite Sanskrit *ślokas*) and receive the specially prepared snacks, which had been first offered to the goddess on the *kolu*. These are usually various types of pulses or chickpeas (Tamil: *cuṇṭal*), regarded as "heating" dishes within Tamil typography (see Eichinger Ferro-Luzzi 1977, 547), which increase the feminine power (*śakti*) of the consumers, thus strengthening their connection with the goddess.[7] Some women play musical instruments, and children may perform anything from recitations to yoga in front of the gods and the other figures on display. As the women leave, they are presented with a plate of gifts known as the *tāmpulam* (Tamil; figure 7.4), which usually includes a string of jasmine flowers to put on their hair, glass bangles, a sari blouse piece, vermillion powder, betel leaves, and sometimes a plastic bowl. The gifts are given to auspicious married women (*sumaṅgalī*) and girls of marriageable age and bear connotations of female auspiciousness, beauty, fertility, and domesticity (Hancock 1999, 3–4). While many of the *tāmpulam* gifts during Navarātri (pocket mirrors, *mehendi* cones, and flowers to put in the hair) point to feminine beauty, bangles are widely associated with fertility (Allocco 2009, 313), and the blouse piece, which is to be sewn for a sari, represents the dress commonly worn after marriage. The gifts are only presented to women and never to men. Children might receive a pen and a notebook, particularly on the ninth day, which is the day of the Sarasvatī Pūjā.

The fact that women visit one another and go from home to home in the evening sets Navarātri apart from other festivals celebrated in Tamil Nadu. Women, whose movements are usually restricted after darkness, claim the neighborhood streets while *kolu* hopping in the evenings without their husbands (cf. Wilson 2015, 20; 2018, 315). The *kolus* they visit also

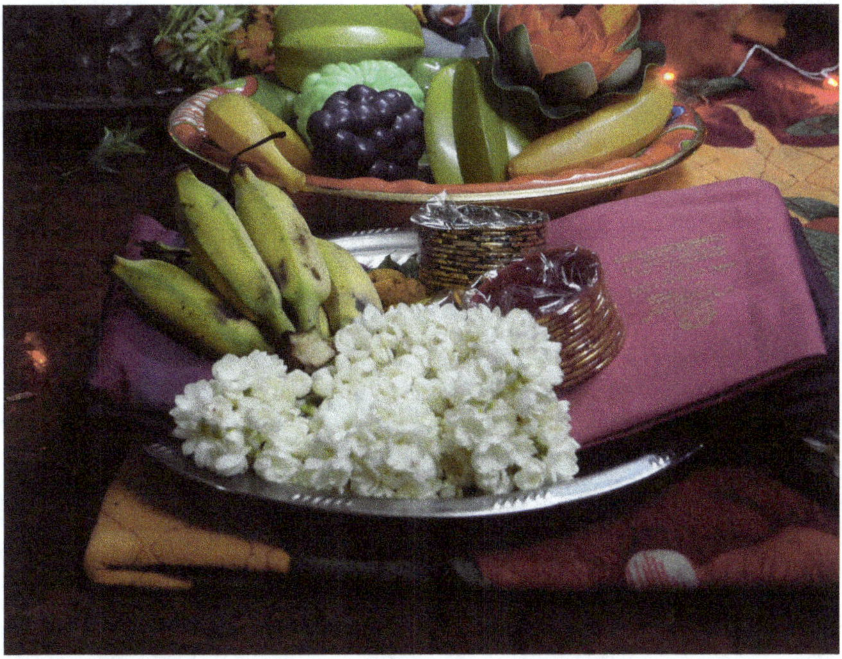

Figure 7.4. The *tāmpulam* (Kāñcipuram, 2015). Photo by author.

blur the distinction between the private and the domestic (Hancock 1999, 6),[8] in that homes are opened up and on display through the creativity of women, who are the religious specialists and the intermediaries between visitors and the goddess. Indeed, an overwhelming majority of respondents emphasized in interviews that having visitors over was their main enjoyment in Navarātri or their reason for starting with *kolu* in the first place; it is an arena for socializing and for maintaining and even developing friendships with other women. One woman said, "We celebrate all kinds of festivals, like Diwali. But we celebrate this with our family. Similarly, for Poṅkal[9] we invite only our relatives. Only during Navarātri we invite everyone. We unite people. Among the crowd present here, some are my relatives, some are friends. As far as Navarātri goes, irrespective of whether you are invited or not, people can come. It is a festival that women celebrate together." Many also compared their homes to temples, as did Madhumita, stating that "this is not a home; it is a temple. So it will look like a temple." Importantly, people may also come to a *kolu* unannounced or uninvited, and even strangers are welcomed. Taking this into account—the practice of opening homes for fellow women as domestic temples and possibly receiving also strangers—Navarātri may be characterized as even more public than weddings and other functions.

Newly Started Kolus

The practice of *kolu* is no small commitment, as the general notion of how to keep it is that (1) it is a lifelong commitment (only when someone has recently died in the family would one discontinue the *kolu* for that year),[10] (2) there is a need to buy at least one doll each year, (3) the *kolu* should be set up in a clean space at a particular auspicious time, and (4) it should be worshipped daily with particular foods and particular *stotras*. The practice is not only demanding and time-consuming but also requires a solid income allowing a family to commit to repeatedly buying new dolls and repainting old ones. Madhumita's family had been keeping *kolu* for the past seven or eight years when I visited in 2015. Indeed, it was the goddess herself who initially told Madhumita to keep *kolu*: "After getting Ampāḷ on my body, she told [us] to keep *kolu*. We have to keep the *kolu*," Madhumita told me. Being impelled like this by the goddess herself is an exceptional case. In general, I detected three reasons among my respondents who had started keeping *kolu* over the past two decades for why they started the practice: (1) observing Brahmins and wanting to do the same, (2) seeing others in the same community who had recently started with *kolu* and prospered, and (3) as a vow to the goddess.

A relatively young but popular practice in Kāñcipuram is to keep particular types or sets of dolls in the *kolu* as a vow (Tamil: *vēṇṭutal*) to the goddess, as the third reason alludes to. These are usually wedding (*kalyāna*) sets for getting married and *sīmantam*[11] sets (marketed as baby-shower sets in English) or baby Kṛṣṇas for conceiving a child. Such votive dolls or sets are also bought by people who do not keep *kolu*: they buy them as a vow and donate them to other people's *kolus* or to temple *kolus* and may in turn vow to keep their own *kolu* once their vow is fulfilled. A doll maker in Kāñcipuram explained to me that most of the dolls he sells these days are such votive dolls and that this is a quite recent development: "Now *kalyāna* sets and *sīmanta* sets are most popular. Previously, *sīmanta* sets were not known, but now they are very popular. Those who don't have kids keep the dolls in their own *kolu* or give it to temples. Then, the following year, they come to us and say that they now have a child." Votive dolls were also present among the dolls on Madhumita's *kolu*, including a wedding set, a Kṛṣṇa *uñcal* (Tamil for "swing") and a few baby Kṛṣṇas that had been given by people who had approached the goddess desiring to marry or to conceive. Madhumita herself had also fashioned an image of Balā (child) Kāmākṣī, since she, too, recently married, desires offspring.

Kolu Rituals

In its initial stage, the *kolu* may be arranged by a family together or by the women and children, but the eldest married woman is generally the one in charge of how the dolls are displayed on the steps and what goes where. Certain unwritten rules are followed when placing the dolls on the steps (usually the gods are put on top and the inanimate objects on the bottom), but one is quite free to arrange the *kolu* according to one's convenience or creativity. Madhumita's *kolu*, for instance, was arranged according to the height of the dolls. Others create themes or original setups in their *kolu*, although the themes are not as innovative in Kāñcipuram as they are in *kolu* competitions in Chennai or online.[12] The aesthetic agency of women is expressed not only in the arrangements of the dolls but also in the pots and oil lamps (Tamil: *viḷakku*) that become goddesses in their hands, decorated (often elaborately) and consecrated as the goddess and placed on or near the *kolu*.

Although Madhumita performs most of the *kolu* ritual procedures in her mother's home, it is commonly the eldest married woman of the household who performs these rituals, accompanied by her unmarried daughters or daughters-in-law or both. She is also the one who invokes the goddess in the pot at an auspicious time. Following this invocation, once the pot is placed on the *kolu*, she will draw a *kolam* (auspicious geometrical patterns made of rice flour) on the floor in front; henceforward, the *kolu* is treated as a sacred space. Madhumita and her mother change the flowers of the pot, draw fresh *kolams*, perform *pūjās*, cook and offer pulses and other food items, recite various *ślokas* (verses), and sing *stotras* (hymns) daily. Madhumita also performs a *kanyā pūjā* to her seven-year-old niece in front of the *kolu* every Navarātri evening and will continue to do so until the niece comes of age. She worships the girl as a goddess by applying turmeric and vermillion powder to her hands (figure 7.5),

Figure 7.5. Ms. Madhumita performing a *kanyā pūjā* (Kāñcipuram, 2015). Photo by author.

gives her a new dress and a plate filled with fruits and flowers, feeds her, and sings devotional songs, and finally the whole family prostrates themselves before her. She explained that this was "because the child is equal to God." Mainly Brahmin families perform such worship of young girls (*kanyā*, Tamil: *kaṉṉi*) and often also for married women (*sumaṅgalī* or *suvasinī pūjā*), although it is performed in some non-Brahmin homes as well, such as that of Madhumita. In *pūjās* like these, women are explicitly seen as the goddess's manifestations. Navarātri is a time during which the divine in female form, and also in human form, is celebrated and worshipped.[13] It is widely believed that the goddess is among the guests visiting the *kolu* and that the gifts presented to the women ultimately reach the goddess. One respondent said, "We believe that among all the guests who come here one will surely be the goddess herself. That is why we offer turmeric and bangles." Thus, women's reciprocal role functions on two levels: women go *kolu* hopping for *darśana* of the goddess on the *kolu*, and the guests who come are received *as* the goddess.

Transmission of Female Knowledge

Knowing what food to make, which *kolam* to draw, and which songs to sing is crucial for the performance of any ritual. Songs, stories, and food recipes, as well as the unwritten role of female ritual behavior, are all considered specific female knowledge, all of which is expressed in *kolu*. Non-Brahmin women with newly started *kolus* would ask Brahmin women when in doubt or consult religious magazines or pamphlets, which explain how to perform certain rituals and which deity to worship when. One woman who kept *kolu* explained to me, "I have a book . . . which mentions how each Devī is to be worshipped with *prasāda* [food offerings], mixed rice, *kolam*, etc. We will follow whatever we can from this. Some things only the Iyers [a Brahmin caste] will know." Such books indicate a shift in the transmission of tradition. While women's rituals traditionally have been transmitted orally and through performance, in contrast with the sanctioning of male rituals through the scriptures, women's rituals are now also appearing in writing (see also Hüsken 2013).[14]

Prosperity and Auspiciousness

It is a prevalent belief that keeping *kolu* brings prosperity and abundance to the household and ensures women long lives as *sumaṅgalīs*. Concerns attributed mostly to women, such as the well-being of the family, fertility, marriage, and domestic prosperity, are emphasized and expressed in the *kolu* and its rituals, such as in the gifts presented to auspiciously married women or women of marriageable age and in the *pūjās* to *sumaṅgalīs* and prepubescent girls. However, even though the *kolu* serves to celebrate femininity and expresses a set of feminine values, the festival clearly prioritizes certain states of womanhood over others (see also Rodrigues 2005). The *pūjās* to the goddess as a woman, the gifts, and the attendance of women and children all point to an emphasis on women's fertility: the auspiciousness of the *sumaṅgalī* depends on her possessing a (living) husband and her ability to bear children, and the *kanyā* is a potential *sumaṅgalī*. Although none of my respondents mentioned it, according to Logan (1980, 256), Navarātri is considered a good time to "come of age." Rodrigues (2009) further connects the worship of young girls in the Tantric *pūjā* to the onset of their menstruation and thus their transformation into fertile women. Evidently, only specific types of women, rather than womanhood in general, are celebrated (and the link between *kolus*, fertility, and marriage is even more pronounced in non-Brahmin environments, where particular *kolu* dolls are connected to the desire for conception and marriage). In consequence, views on the participation of widows (*amaṅkali*) during *kolu* varied greatly among my respondents. Some regarded all women as equal and encouraged the participation of widows (that is, offering them the *tāmpulam*); others discouraged it, thinking it meant bad luck. Also, if a girl or woman is in what is considered an impure state such as menstruating, or if a death has occurred in the family recently, she should not go near the auspicious *kolu*.

Accordingly, the dolls themselves should be auspicious, and fierce (*ugra*) deities like Kālī are rarely represented on a *kolu*. Demons are, however, not uncommon, as they form part of mythological sets. Some dolls are themselves manifestations of their keepers' desire for prosperity: Madhumita kept the Aṣṭalakṣmī (the eight forms of Lakṣmī, goddess of wealth and abundance) with two trays of money in front of her, and she performed a Lakṣmī *pūjā* during Navarātri, explaining to me that she wanted more money. At the same time, the family spends some 50,000–60,000 rupees on their *kolu* every year, for dolls, decorations, and gifts. Keeping a *kolu* thus also represents economic agency in the hands of women.

Where Are the Men?

While husbands and male family members may be present in the home when guests are being received during *kolu* viewings, they rarely go for *kolu* visits themselves, as it is considered a female activity. When I asked about the different roles of men and women in their families during Navarātri, a female respondent said, "So as far as Navarātri period is concerned, it is the ladies who do much work. The role of men is mainly in the initial stage of arrangements, dismantling the [*kolu*] in the end and some house-related stuff like buying things required for *pūjā*, etc. If the *sumaṅgalīs* start coming by five or five thirty in the evening, one or the other will be coming till eight or eight thirty. Women will have continuous work." Indeed, I visited nearly fifty *kolus* during the Navarātri season of 2014–15 and have no memory of men showing up during any of my evening visits—that is, of course, apart from those who lived in the households in question. On the contrary, rooms could be filled to the brim with women and children. This being said, and while women generally are the ones in the family who take most interest in the *kolu*, I also met men with a huge interest and pride in their families' doll collections. These included male Brahmin priests, who often had strong opinions on how to arrange the *kolu*. Hüsken (2012, 189; this volume) suggests that this reflects their expertise as *alaṃkāra* (ornamentations of the goddess) makers in the temple. I also visited the *kolu* of a married couple where the husband, like Madhumita, regularly became possessed by the goddess. However, also in these households, it is the women who perform the rituals for the *kolu* and offer *tāmpulam* to the visitors. Thus, despite occasional male interest, *kolu* remains predominantly a scene for female agency—ritual, aesthetic, and economic—and it revolves around women and feminine values.

Navarātri in Kāñcipuram Temples

Navarātri is celebrated in the majority of temples in Kāñcipuram and is particularly important in temples dedicated to independent goddesses, known as *amman̲* (Tamil for "mother"). It is also marked in temples where the goddess is represented as a consort of a male deity, such as the well-known temple of Varadarāja (Viṣṇu) (see Hüsken 2018).[15] While the Sanskritic Brahmin tradition is particularly male dominated, emphasis on women may also be found here. This is, for instance, the case in the Kāmākṣī temple, which houses the principal goddess of Kāñcipuram, where *kanyā*- and *sumaṅgalīpūjās* are performed daily.[16] However, when turning to certain *amman̲* temples where the goddess is served by priests from lower castes (Tamil: *pūcāri*), female agency becomes more visible. This is the case of the small temple of the village goddess Paṭavēṭṭamman̲, whose Navarātri celebrations I will turn to shortly.

First, we note that, while temples celebrate Navarātri differently, there are some commonly shared rituals. For instance, there will be special ornamentations (*alaṃkāra*) of the goddess, a major attraction in most *amman̲* temples and something for which the Paṭavēṭṭamman̲ temple is particularly famous. Temple priests will perform more elaborate worship of the goddess during the festival, including fire rituals (*homa*), *pūjās*, ablutions, and invocations of the goddess in pots. *Kolus* are also set up in some temples, where devotees donate dolls, but not in all of them, and this is a recent development in Kāñcipuram, probably in connection with the increase of votive dolls and in non-Brahmin families partaking in *kolu*. Finally, fights between the goddess and the demon (Tamil: *curasaṃhāra*) might be enacted during Navarātri, but this is not the case in all temples.[17] None of these Navarātri rituals, except the worship of prepubescent girls and auspiciously married women, show any focus on women, and they are performed by men or male priests. Women do, of course, form part of the audience, often along with their families, but not necessarily as an overwhelming majority.

Navarātri in the Paṭavēṭṭammaṉ Temple

The modest Paṭavēṭṭammaṉ temple is situated slightly outside the city center toward the south of Kāñcipuram and celebrates Navarātri lavishly. While there is no doubt that its famed and themed *alaṃkāras* are one of the reasons for the temple's popularity during this festival, I suspect another is the active involvement of the devotees. The crowd attending Navarātri celebrations in the Paṭavēṭṭammaṉ temple grows visibly from year to year. Many come every evening, and many tie protective cords (*rakṣabandhana*, Tamil: *kāppu*), signifying their vows to Paṭavēṭṭammaṉ. A smaller group of men, women, and girls among the devotees who tie the *kāppu* belongs to the temple trust.[18] During Navarātri they are dressed uniformly in saffron-colored clothes and are allotted special tasks in the temple. The tasks include distributing flowers or *prasāda*, serving food, helping with ritual preparations, and handling the huge crowd of devotees within this small space so that no one is hurt. Because of the tying of protective cords, it is mainly the same people who attend the Navarātri celebrations here daily, and, importantly for those who tie them, Navarātri is a pure temple celebration.[19]

This particular temple has taken its own twist and incorporated some rituals that are associated more with the Āṭi festival[20] into their Navarātri celebrations. Each evening, the festival is a big public spectacle, with the unveiling of the themed *alaṃkāra*, music from loudspeakers, entertainment on a stage, and huge crowds. As devotees partake in vows, *pūjas*, and processions during Navarātri, women interact directly with the goddess, not only as her representatives or as recipients of worship, as in the Kāmākṣī temple. The devotees on vows include men, women, and some children, but the majority are women and girls, who have certain rituals reserved to them. The involvement of women in this temple is not specific to Navarātri, says the priest Mr. Venkatesh, who points to the ritual expectations of women on behalf of their family:

> Anything related to temple, only ladies mostly participate. . . . If you see, the women will have more expectation and worries. Only a mother can understand the problem of the children. Men go out for work; at that time, only the ladies pray for their safety. There are plusses and minuses for everybody, even ladies have, but when they tie the protective cord and carry the milk pots [in the procession that is held the day after Vijayadaśamī], they will do it with full devotion. That is why there are more ladies [during Navarātri].

In the following, I will describe the Navarātri rituals in this temple where women play a part. The *tāy cir koṇḍu varutal* (Tamil for "bringing gifts to the Mother") initiates the festival. This is a procession where women bring auspicious gifts for the goddess.[21] In 2015, one woman carried a plate entirely filled with sugar, another brought a sewing kit, but most brought bangles, saris, flowers, and fruits. Leading the procession was the goddess installed in a pot, carried by a woman on the top of her head (figure 7.6). Afterward, the pot was kept in the temple's sanctum for the duration of the festival. This ritual is not connected to the fulfillment of

Figure 7.6. Woman carrying the goddess as a pot in the *tāy cīr* procession (Kāñcipuram, 2015). Photo by author.

vows but is an act of devotion toward the goddess. After the procession reached the Paṭavēṭṭammaṉ temple and the women presented their plates to the goddess, the priest tied protective cords to the wrists of all the devotees who took a vow (*vrata*) during the festival. These vows are usually to do with petitions for marriage, conceiving a child, or being relieved from illness.

There is no worship of prepubescent girls or auspiciously married women in this temple, but on the evening of Navarātri Friday women perform an oil-lamp *pūjā* (Tamil: *tiruviḷakku pūjai*) in the temple dedicated to Lakṣmī, praying for the prosperity of the household (figure 7.7). The priest told me they used to perform various *pūjās* daily during Navarātri (also for *kanyās* and *sumaṅgalīs*) up to the 1990s, but due to time constraints the lamp *pūjā* is the only one that has been continued up to the present.

Another procession ends the Navarātri festival, when a crowd of women carry milk pots (Tamil: *pālkuṭam*) and, finally, pour the milk over the goddess's image in the sanctum. This procession includes a piercing ritual, during which some of the devotees manifest their vows through ritual piercing (Tamil: *alaku*). The vows signified by the piercing can be taken for one's own sake or on behalf of others, and some people are also pierced as thanks for a vow that has already been fulfilled. In 2015, both men and women were pierced, usually with a spear (Tamil: *vēl*) or trident (Tamil: *cūlam*) through the cheek or tongue (figure 7.8), but a few men were, in addition, pierced by a porcupine-like structure of 108 spears in their upper bodies (cf. Kapadia 2001, 189). Another one had hooks pierced in his back to drag a cart, and another had limes sewn onto his forehead, back, and chest with needle and thread (these piercings all require a naked upper body, which may be why they are not suitable for women). Some were also possessed. The women were uniformly clad in the colors of the goddess—yellow and red—for the occasion and carefully prepared their pots with turmeric and vermillion powders as well as *nīm* and banana leaves and flowers; after, these were filled with milk, and all joined in the procession (figure 7.9). The ablutions of milk that the women then performed to the temple image, one by one, were done to cool down the goddess after her ferocious fight with the demon, which had been enacted in the temple during the previous evening of Vijayadaśamī. Men did not carry milk pots, as this ritual is reserved for women, but men who undertook vows performed an ablution with 108 conches, following the women's ablutions of milk.

However, while what could be classified as women's rituals form important parts of the Navarātri festival in the Paṭavēṭṭammaṉ temple,[22] in most other temples the involvement of women tends to be limited to their passive participation in *kanyā* or *sumaṅgalī pūjās*.

Figure 7.7. Women performing a lamp *pūjā* (Kāñcipuram, 2014). Photo by author.

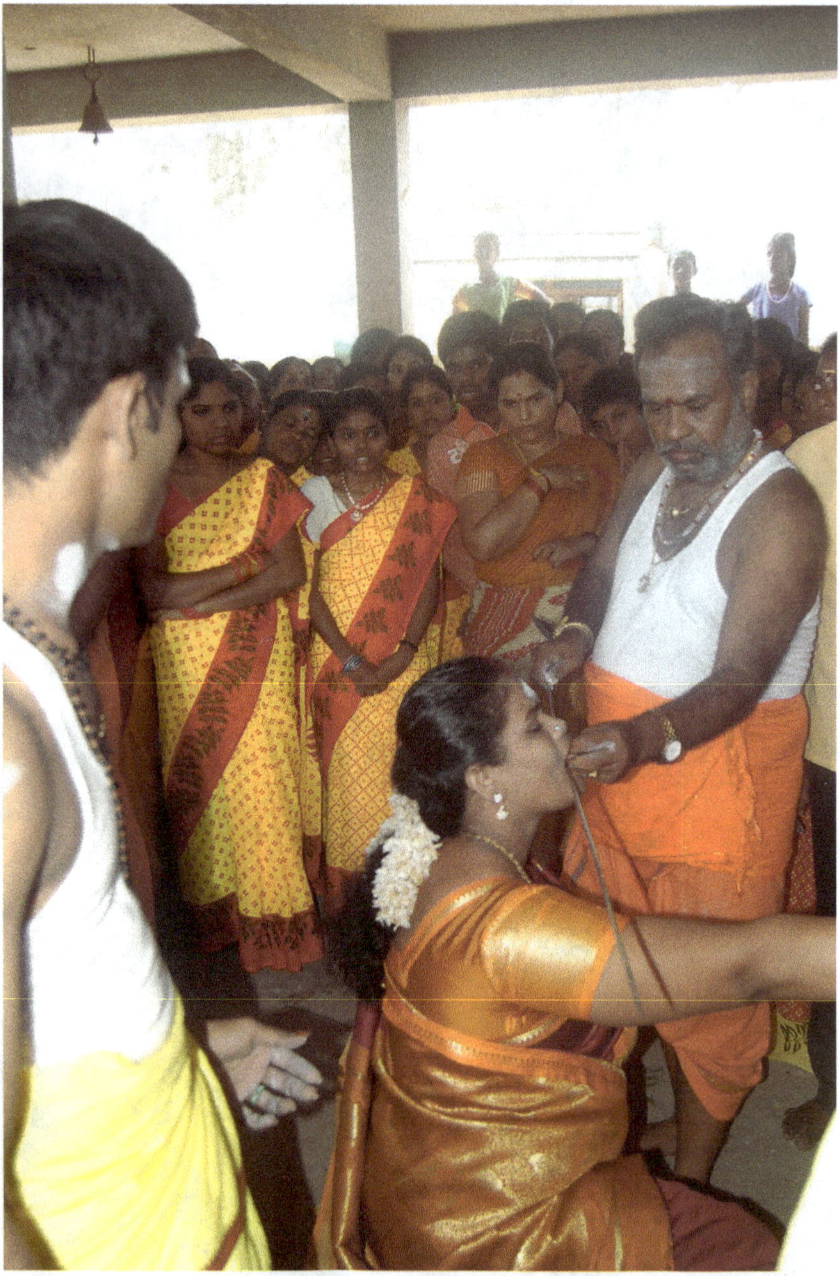

Figure 7.8. The priest (*pūcāri*) pierces a female devotee (Kāñcipuram, 2011). Photo by author.

Figure 7.9. A group of women in the milk-pot procession (Kāñcipuram, 2014). Photo by author.

Navarātri as Women's Festival

Contemporary Navarātri in Kāñcipuram is a women's festival in that women, femininity, and values commonly attributed to women are emphasized and expressed throughout the festival. Culturally determined female concerns, such as the well-being of the family and the prosperity of the household, that are connected to women's roles as wives and mothers and the wish to gain and maintain the status of the auspicious married *sumaṅgalī* are expressed during the festival time.[23] Moreover, women act as guests, as hosts, and as ritual specialists near the *kolu* and are identified with the goddess in the course of Navarātri. This all confirms a stereotype of female religiosity, which, as Pintchman (2007, 6) points out, tends to emphasize women's important relationships and the domestic realm around which their everyday lives mostly revolve. These values are expressed not only with regard to the *kolu* tradition but also in the context of vows manifested in the milk-pot and piercing rituals of the non-Brahmin Paḍavēṭṭammaṉ temple.

As we have seen, it is particularly the *kolu* and its auspicious rituals performed on the household level by women that emphasize female values such as generosity, hospitality, fecundity, domesticity, and feminine beauty. In temples, on the other hand, the emphasis lies on *alaṃkāras* and enactments of the cosmic battle of the goddess and the demon during Navarātri. As Fuller and Logan (1985) have argued in their influential article on Navarạtri in Madurai, the Mīnākṣī temple and the homes surrounding the temple form complimentary spheres in the course of the festival: while goddess Mīnākṣī fights the demon within the temple premises, the world order is maintained in the homes, represented by the entirely auspicious *kolu*. While at first sight their theory also seems to fit the instances of Navarātri in Kāñcipuram, a closer look at contemporary practices does not allow us to draw such clear-cut boundaries—first, because fertility is hinted at also in temple rituals: temple priests of the Kāmākṣī temple, for example, worship potentially fertile prepubescent girls, along with childbearing, auspiciously married women. Fertility is also an issue in the Paṭavēṭṭamman̲ temple, since the women, in order to cool down the goddess after her ferocious fight with the demon, offer milk to her, the signifier of motherhood.[24] It should also be mentioned that the installation of the goddess in pots, or wombs, which is so important during this festival (although this is by no means exclusive to Navarātri) bears strong associations with fertility and fecundity in earth, soil, and women (cf. Rodrigues 2005, 98). Second, many temples do not enact the goddess's fight with the demon and hence have no particular emphasis on the battle. Instead, the immensely popular *alaṃkāras* are the main attraction in nearly all temples that celebrate Navarātri. Furthermore, many households that are connected to the temples where the fight is enacted do not keep *kolu* (for instance, this is the case in the Paṭavēṭṭamman̲ temple). The sharp contrast between harmony and order in homes and battle and subjugation of demons in temples is therefore superficial.

During Navarātri, women exercise ritual agency in many ways: they are recipients of *pūjās*, they are performers, they are consumers and audience, and they are authors of tradition, as illustrated by Madhumita's appropriation of *kolu* when she includes prophesying and possession in her performance of this ritual. While it is not surprising that women are ritual specialists in homes, Navarātri also exemplifies the agency of women in the male-dominated context of Hindu temples. Through the ethnographic data, we catch a glimpse of a sliding scale of female agency from Brahmin temples to non-Brahmin temples and to the domestic. In the Kāmākṣī temple, daily *pūjās* are performed *to* women, whereas in the Patavēṭṭamman̲ temple, several rituals, including an elaborate milk *abhiṣeka*, are performed entirely *by* women. In the female sphere of the home, we have the rituals of the *kolu*, performed entirely by and for women. Women's agency, as I have explored it in this chapter, is more than free will and resistance (which is a secular conception of the term).[25] My view here thus contrasts with Tanaka's that the Navarātri festival "demonstrates the limitations of women" because it does not openly challenge patriarchy (1999, 134). *Kolu* may be said to reaffirm stereotypical patterns, but women gain and enact powers as *sumaṅgalīs* as they appropriate the goddess's powers. Women maneuver for power within existing social structures and life circumstances. Their agency may even be present in conformity and the ability to maintain things, and it has active, transformative, and creative aspects.

Notes

1. The findings presented in this chapter come from interviews and participant observations in Kāñcipuram during Navarātri seasons 2014–15 and participant observations during Navarātri in 2009 and 2011. Names are anonymized. I have favored Sanskrit terminology throughout, and when Tamil is used this is indicated.

2. To make a broad generalization, women's rituals in India are conceptualized as taking place in the private (domestic) sphere rather than the public (such as in temples or politics). They are based on *pūjā* (devotional rites) rather than the Vedic fire sacrifice, and they are informal rather than formal (seen, for example, in the lack of written invitations). Furthermore, they are transmitted orally in vernaculars and through performance, in contrast to Brahmin men's rituals, which are transmitted through texts pertaining to the Sanskrit textual tradition and therefore held in higher esteem (see, for example, Hüsken 2013; Wadley 1995). Non-Brahmanical rituals also lack this textual authority provided by the elitist Sanskrit tradition and have suffered the same fate along with women's rituals of being overlooked as lower and less important, often being labeled as folklore.

3. While Madhumita married about a year previous to my visit and kept a modest *kolu* in the home she shares with her husband for the first time in 2015, she also assists her mother in arranging the *kolu* and performing rituals in her natal home, which is reachable by a short motorbike ride. Madhumitha's prominent role in her mother's *kolu* after marriage probably stems from her authority as embodying the goddess, to be described shortly, and instead of bringing her clientele with her to her married home, she continues to perform these practices in her natal home. While Madhumita is a middle-class woman, I unfortunately do not know which community she belongs to. It is, however, plausible to assume she is non-Brahmin, due to the practices of her household (e.g., possession), their family deity being Aṅkāḷa Paramēcuvari Amman̲ of Mel Malayanoor (a deity associated with lower castes), and the fact that her father and her husband wore no sacred threads (the sacred thread indicates initiation in Vedic studies).

4. However, see Osella and Osella (2000) and Hancock (1999, 144ff.) for Brahmin possession.

5. See Srinivas (1952, 1956) and Kapadia (1995).

6. Another example of this kind of appropriation is how the Pattunoolis, a community of silk workers in Kāñcipuram, offer meat and alcohol to the goddess on their *kolu*.

7. Pulses are a common offering to goddesses in temples as well as homes during Navarātri. See Fuller and Logan (1985, 84–85, 98) and Tanaka (1999, 128–34).

8. However, as Harlan (2007) shows in her essay on women's rituals in Rajasthan, the domestic is never entirely shut off from the public. Women get inspiration and impressions from traveling (also between homes), and public rituals (such as rites of passage) are also performed in the home.

9. Poṅkal is a harvest festival celebrated in January.

10. A prerequisite for keeping *kolu* is to be a *sumaṅgalī* (auspicious married woman), and at the death of the husband the family's *kolu* continues only if you reside with a daugther-in-law in a joint household.

11. The *sīmantam* is the prenatal rite of passage of parting the hair, performed during a woman's pregnancy. Interestingly, the set depicts the rituals of women surrounding the Brahmanical ritual and not the actual parting of the hair, which is done by the husband and male Brahmins. This reflects the *kolu* as a predominantly female scene.

12. Some themes in these competitions and campaigns, such as women's or equality rights (see, for instance, Sadasivan 2016), lead one's thoughts to the theme-based *paṇḍals* of the Bengali and Benarsi Durgā Pūjās, which can be quite controversial (see, for example, McDermott 2011; Sen 2018; Einarsen 2018). During fieldwork in Kāñcipuram, I encountered instead *kolus* based entirely on social events (such as marriages), for example, or the *itihāsas* (mythological stories from *Ramāyaṇa* and *Mahābhārata*), or elaborate scenes from temple festivals of the major temples in Kāñcipuram.

13. *Kanyā pūjās* are a well-known and widespread devotional practice in honor of the goddess in many parts of India as well as Nepal, and they are not confined to Navarātri, although they form an important part of this festival (see Luchesi 2018). Rodrigues (2005, 90) rightly notes that *only* women are identified with the goddess and there are no equivalents where males are worshipped as embodiments of male gods during any festival. Possession would be the exception here, since both men and women may be possessed by male and female deities.

14. Women's rituals (inclusive of recipes) are also appearing on several web pages or blogs, including ones that tell how to keep *kolu* (e.g., Sendhil 2014). The blogs are written by women and for women.

15. In the Ekāmranatha (Śiva) temple of Kāñcipuram, the festival is currently only celebrated by decorating the goddess and performing ablutions to her.

16. The ritual handbook *Saubhāgyacintāmaṇi*, which is referred to as an authority in the Kāmākṣī *ammaṉ* temple, acknowledges the prominence of women during Navarātri (*Śrīsaubhāgyacintāmaṇi mahānavamīmāhātmyam* 31b–35a, translation mine):

> At this day in particular [i.e., the ninth lunar day of the month Āśvina] [the Great Goddess] abides in all the *śaktis* [female forms] that are on earth, [and] she receives the *pūjā* instantly. Therefore, one should honor

them greatly, those beautiful women, who on this day in particular should not be treated with disrespect by those desirous of welfare. On this day, beautiful clothes, ornaments, and so on should be given to them, yielding infinite fruits [and] causing pleasure to the supreme Śakti. But those who do not worship the supreme mother on the great ninth day will become poor and stupefied birth after birth.

tasmin dine viśeṣeṇa yāḥ kāścicchāktayo bhūvi ||31||
tās sarvāsamadhiṣṭāpya pūjāṃ gṛhṇāti sāñjasā |
tasmāt saṃpūjayed etā yāḥ kāścid vā varāṅganāḥ ||32||
nāvamānyā viśeṣeṇa dine tasmin śubhārthibhiḥ |
tābhyas tasmin dine dattaṃ sadvāsobhūṣaṇādikam ||33||
bhaved anantaphaladaṃ parāśaktipriyaṅkaram |
mahābhūtatithau ye tu nārcayanti parāmbikām ||34||
te tu mūḍhā daridrāś ca bhaveyur janmajanmani |

17. See Ilkama (2018a, 2018b) for more detailed descriptions of these rituals.

18. The trustees who do temple service during Navarātri belong to the dance class of the *pūjāri*'s (non-Brahmin priest) son, who also fashions Paṭavēṭṭamma<u>ṉ</u>'s *alaṃkāras*, a main attraction in this temple during Navarātri (see Ilkama 2018b). According to the *pūjāri*'s calculations, the trust consists of approximately thirty to forty people out of the couple hundred people who tie the *kāppu* altogether.

19. I was only able to locate one devotee in the Paṭavēṭṭammaṉ temple who kept *kolu*: a Brahmin teacher and her family who lived very close by. She did not, however, attend many of the festival's Navarātri rituals, apart from *darśana* of the goddess in her Navarātri *alaṃkāra* every festival evening, because of her *kolu* duties at home.

20. Āṭi is a festival for the goddess that is celebrated in many *ammaṉ* temples in Tamil Nadu from mid-July to mid-August. According to Allocco (2009, 271), Āṭi is considered the most appropriate month in which to undertake vows and petitionary prayers to the goddess.

21. The ritual is modeled on bringing *cīr* (Tamil for "prosperity" or "wealth") to the husband's family for a wedding.

22. Although I have singled out these rituals in this chapter, there is also very much an emphasis on the decorations of the goddess in the Paṭavēṭṭammaṉ temple, and another festival highlight is the Vijayadaśamī fight where the priest is possessed by the goddess and kills the demon in the form of a banana tree.

23. These oppose so-called male values of maintaining purity (for Brahmins), securing a good wheat crop, ridding the village of disease, and so on (Wadley 1995, 126).

24. This argument is following Hüsken (2018), who argues similarly with regard to the *viśvarūpadarśaṇa* in the Varadarāja temple, the principal Viṣṇu temple of Kāñcipuram. There, a cow, a calf, and the goddess are venerated together during the Navarātri celebrations.

25. Here I follow Sax (2006, 474), who emphasizes the transformative aspects of ritual and distinguishes agency from action in defining *agency* as "the ability to transform the world."

References

Allocco, Amy. 2009. "Snakes, Goddesses, and Anthills: Modern Challenges and Women's Ritual Responses in Contemporary South India." PhD diss., Emory University.

Chettiar, S. M. L. Lakshmanan. 1973. *Folklore of Tamil Nadu*. Delhi: National Book Trust.

Eichinger Ferro-Luzzi, Gabriella. 1977. "The Logic of South Indian Food Offerings." *Anthropos* 72 (3/4): 529–56.

Einarsen, Silje Lyngar. 2018. "Navarātri in Benares: Narrative Structures and Social Realities." In Simmons, Sen, and Rodrigues 2018, 139–56.

Fuller, Chris J., and Penelope Logan. 1985. "The Navarātri Festival in Madurai." *Bulletin of the School of Oriental and African Studies* 48 (1): 79–105.

Hancock, Mary. 1999. *Womanhood in the Making: Domestic Ritual and Public Culture in Urban South India*. Boulder, CO: Westview Press.

Harlan, Lindsey. 2007. "Words That Breach Walls: Women's Rituals in Rajasthan." In *Women's Lives, Women's Rituals in the Hindu Tradition*, edited by Tracy Pintchman, 65–84. Oxford: Oxford University Press.

Hüsken, Ute. 2012. "Training, Play, and Blurred Distinctions: On Imitation and 'Real' Ritual." In *Religions in Play: Games, Rituals, and Virtual Worlds*, edited by Philippe Bornet and Maya Burger, 177–96. Zürich: Pano Verlag.

———. 2013. "Denial as Silencing: On Women's Ritual Agency in a South Indian Brahmin Tradition." In "The Denial of Ritual and Its Return," edited by Pamela J. Stewart and Andrew J. Strathern, special issue, *Journal of Ritual Studies* 27 (1): 21–34.

———. 2018. "Ritual Complimentarity and Difference: Navarātri in Kanchipuram." In Simmons, Sen, and Rodrigues 2018, 179–96.

Ilkama, Ina Marie Lunde. 2018a. "Dolls and Demons: The Materiality of Navarātri." In Simmons, Sen, and Rodrigues 2018, 157–78.

———. 2018b. "The Play of the Feminine: Navarātri in Contemporary Kanchipuram." PhD diss., University of Oslo.

Kapadia, Karin. 1995. *Siva and Her Sisters: Gender, Caste, and Class in Rural South India*. Boulder, CO: Westview Press.

———. 2001. "Pierced by Love." In *Invented Identities: The Interplay of Gender, Religion and Politics in India*, edited by Julia Leslie and Mary McGee, 181–202. London: Oxford University Press.

Logan, Penelope. 1980. "Domestic Worship and the Festival Cycle in the South Indian City of Madurai." PhD diss., University of Manchester.

Luchesi, Brigitte. 2018. "Navarātra and Kanyā Pūjā: the Worship of Girls as Representatives of the Goddess in Northwest India." In Simmons, Sen, and Rodrigues 2018, 299–315.

McDermott, Rachel Fell. 2011. *Revelry, Rivalry, and Longing for the Goddess of Bengal: The Fortunes of Hindu Festivals*. New York: Columbia University Press.

Narayanan, Vasudha. 2018. "Royal *Darbār* and Domestic *Kolus*: Social Order, Creation, Procreation, and Re-Creation." In Simmons, Sen, and Rodrigues 2018, 275–98.

Osella, Caroline, and Filippo Osella. 2000. "Movements of Power through Social, Spiritual and Bodily Boundaries: Aspects of Controlled and Uncontrolled Spirit Possession in Rural Kerala." In *La possession en Asie du sud: Parole, corps, territoire*, edited by Jackie Assayag and Gilles Tarabout, 183–210. Puruṣārtha, vol. 21. Paris: Éditions EHESS.

Pintchman, Tracy. 2007. Introduction to *Women's Lives, Women's Rituals in the Hindu Tradition*. Edited by Tracy Pintchman, 3–15. New York: Oxford University Press.

Ram, Kalpana. 2013. *Fertile Disorder: Spirit Possession and Its Provocation of the Modern*. Honolulu: University of Hawai'i Press.

Reiniche, Marie-Louise. 1979. *Les dieux et les hommes: Étude des cultes d'un village Tirunelveli, Inde du Sud*. Paris: Mouton.

Rodrigues, Hillary. 2005. "Women in the Worship of the Great Goddess." In *Goddesses and Women in the Indic Religious Tradition*, edited by Arvind Sharma, 72–104. Leiden, Netherlands: Brill.

———. 2009. "Fluid Control: Orchestrating Blood Flow in the Durgā Pūjā." *Studies in Religion/Sciences Religieuses* 38 (2): 263–92.

Sadasivan, Shridhar. 2016. "Occupy Navratri: A New and Meaningful Way to Celebrate Navratri in Your Home!" *Women's Web*, October 1, 2016. http://www.womensweb.in/2016/10/occupy-navratri-challenging-stereotypes-creating-awareness/. Accessed August 15, 2017.

Sax, William. 2006. "Agency." In *Theorizing Rituals*. Vol. 1, *Issues, Topics, Approaches, Concepts*, edited by Jens Kreinath, Jan A. M. Snoek, and Michael Stausberg, 473–81. Leiden, Netherlands: Brill.

Sen, Moumita. 2018. "Politics, Religion, and Art in the Durgā Pūjā of West Bengal." In Simmons, Sen, and Rodrigues 2018, 105–20.

Sendhil, Chitra. 2014. "Navratri Golu Ideas—How to Keep Golu/Kolu at Home." *Chitra's Food Book*, September 23, 2014. http://www.chitrasfoodbook.com/2014/09/navratri-golu-ideas-how-to-keep.html.

Simmons, Caleb, Moumita Sen, and Hillary Rodrigues, eds. 2018. *Nine Nights of the Goddess: The Navarātri Festival in South Asia*. Albany: State University of New York Press.

Sivakumar, Deeksha. 2018. "Display Shows, Display Tells: The Aesthetics of Memory during Pommai Kolu." In Simmons, Sen, and Rodrigues 2018, 257–74.

Srinivas, Mysore Narasimhachar. 1952. *Religion and Society among the Coorgs of South India*. Oxford: Clarendon Press.

———. 1956. "A Note on Sanskritization and Westernization." *Journal of Asian Studies* 15 (4): 481–96.

Śrīsaubhāgyacintāmaṇiḥ. n.d. Pudukkottai, India: Sarma's Sanatorium Press.

Tanaka, Masakazu. 1999. "The Navarātri Festival in Chidambaram, South India." In *Living With Śakti: Gender, Sexuality and Religion in South Asia*, edited by

Masakazu Tanaka and Musashi Tachikawa, 117–36. Osaka: Museum of Ethnology.

Trawick, Margaret. 1992. *Notes on Love in a Tamil Family*. Berkeley: University of California Press.

Wadley, Susan S. 1995. "Women in the Hindu Tradition." In *Women in India: Two Perspectives*, edited by Doranne Johnson and Susan S. Wadley, 111–36. Columbia, MO: South Asia Publications.

Wilson, Nicole Alyse. 2015. "Middle-Class Identity and Hindu Women's Ritual Practice in South India." PhD diss., Syracuse University.

———. 2018. "*Kolus*, Caste, and Class: Navarātri as a Site for Ritual and Social Change in Urban South India." In Simmons, Sen, and Rodrigues 2018, 247–56.

Navarātri as Instrument of Power

8

Who Kills the Buffalo?

Authority and Agency in the Ritual Logistics of the Nepalese Dasaĩ Festival

ASTRID ZOTTER

Introduction

In establishing and maintaining religious identities and in demarcating their boundaries, negotiation processes often revolve around particular issues and things where it becomes manifest who is in and who is out—or, more fitting in the Hindu context, who is above and who is below. Such bones of contention invite a methodological approach developed in the quickly rising field of material religion, which, on the level of practiced religion, looks at what happens materially, in agents' engaging with physical forms.[1] Adopting such a bottom-up perspective that takes " 'the singular' or 'the particular' as a methodological entry point" (Meyer and Houtman 2011, 3), in the present chapter, I will look at the materiality of the Asian water buffalo (*Bubalis bubalis* L.) and its sacrifice in the course of the Nepalese Dasaĩ festival as a node where visions of religion and society crystallize and are negotiated. As in other Navarātra traditions in the Nepalese Dasaĩ, buffalo sacrifice forms a—or even *the*—climax of the whole festival complex (cf., e.g., Biardeau 1984; Sarkar 2017, 66, 215) and is an enactment of Durgā's central mythological feat, the killing of the buffalo demon (Mahiṣāsura).

Analyses of buffalo sacrifice in South Asia have typically revolved around what the buffalo stands for or what taking its life symbolizes (e.g., Biardeau 1984; Hiltebeitel 2011; Michaels 2016). Here, a different path will be taken in not exclusively focusing on the buffalo's killing but viewing the ritual performance of its death as a phase in its "social life" (Appadurai 1986), or maybe more appropriately its sacrificial life, assuming, with Arjun Appadurai, that in order to "illuminate the concrete, historical circulation of things . . . we have to follow the things themselves, for their meanings are inscribed in their forms, their uses, their trajectories" (5). Rather than following buffaloes and their lives in situ, being a textual researcher, I will look at written material on the logistics of buffalo sacrifice. It will be shown that the trade of sacrificial animals became a major budgetary and logistical concern and indeed a state affair after Nepal developed into a larger territorial state with the conquests of the Shah kings of Gorkha, from roughly the second half of the eighteenth century onward. Administrative papers issued on the subject in the early Shah (1768–1846) and Rana (1846–1951) periods will form my main sources.

The material being researched in itself thus exhibits a double-layered materiality. First, there are the animals themselves that are channeled through a state-run system of exchange directed at sacrifice. Second, the texts as material forms not only bring into focus the ritual-economic complex around buffaloes in a specific historical context but also raise questions about why so much ink, paper, and effort were spent on and around buffalo sacrifice and about which details in particular were captured or left out in the state's documentary practices. Looking at this material with a view to the overall topic of this volume, I will ask further what this excessive materiality, which one may call a hypermateriality, does or achieves.

Even apart from the second-layer materiality just introduced, one very obvious achievement to be noted at the outset is the almost-stereotypical kind of reaction by Western observers to the hypermateriality of buffalo sacrifices. Travelogues stress their material abundance—Percy Brown (1912, 117) speaks of buffaloes "slaughtered by the thousand"; Henry Ambrose Oldfield (1880, 351) was told that nine thousand buffaloes were sacrificed in Nepal but took this to be an exaggeration—and devote long passages to them. Brown, who visited Nepal at the beginning of the twentieth century, delivers a typical description:

> Passing through a doorway, a wild scene greets the eye. . . . a curious combination of a battlefield and a shambles. The participants . . . are grouped around the four sides of the courtyard . . . leaving the centre free for the sacrifice. Here

> are grouped the stands of colours. . . . In front of each stand is the sacrificial post, and beyond that a great mound of decapitated animals, mute and gory witnesses of an inexplicable custom. . . . A living victim is dragged forward and tied by the neck to the post. . . . The executioner approaches, . . . and . . . dexterously severs the head of the animal with one powerful blow. This action is the signal for a blare of trumpets, the energetic firing of guns, and every one making some sign of his gratification at the sacrifice. (117–18)[2]

The blood-sacrifice scene with its knee-jerk rejection runs like a red thread down to the present. It may be seen as one of the building blocks in exotic imaginings of Nepal and usually goes along with moral condemnation and expressions of incomprehension, to put it mildly, and often of sheer disgust, especially about the enthusiasm with which sacrifice is performed and also received by the public. Nepalese wielding the sacrificial sword or watching that scene are stereotypically depicted as backward and uncivilized. As others did, Wilhelm Filchner, after his visit to Nepal in the 1940s, expressed the hope that "the new government of Nepal [formed after the end of the Rana regime in 1951], which makes such efforts to be listed among the progressive nations, will surely abolish this barbarian custom" (Filchner and Maráṭhe 1953, 136, translation mine).

Despite repeated appeals to stop the Dasaĩ buffalo sacrifices, they have persisted. While the act of explicitly killing the large bovine has been curtailed in many festival traditions of the South Asian subcontinent, either by substituting buffaloes with smaller animals or vegetarian offerings or by keeping the rite away from the public gaze, in Nepal it has formed one of the major public features and popular attractions of the festival. No doubt in many Nepalese households sacrificial animals are substituted with vegetarian offerings (figure 8.1). Blood sacrifices are debated, especially during the Dasaĩ festival period and other large-scale sacrificial events, such as the Gadhimai festival, which takes place every five years (see, for example, Adhikari and Gellner 2016; Letizia and Ripert, forthcoming; Michaels 2016). In republican Nepal, antisacrifice voices closely aligning with the just-quoted early outsiders' views gain prevalence. In a judgment in 2016, the Supreme Court of Nepal, responding to petitions against the Gadhimai sacrifices, condemned animal sacrifice as a "bad thing" (*galat kurā*) and "blind belief" (*andhaviśvāsa*) that is "contrary to the progressive development of society" and "not part of (proper) Hinduism," obligating the government to work toward its abandonment (Letizia and Ripert, forthcoming). But in debates on blood sacrifice there are also voices raised in its favor. These sacrifices are often seen as the "most effective way to obtain a boon, to satisfy the gods, or to contain

Figure 8.1. An animal made of cucumber is sacrificed on the occasion of Mahānavamī in a private worship room set up for Dasaĩ (*dasaĩghara*) in a modern Kathmandu suburb (October 2007, photo by author). The sacrifice of such vegetarian animals, typically made of cucumbers or other gourds, has also been reported since the 1940s as being a legitimate substitute for people who cannot afford to buy a real animal (Filchner and Maráṭhe 1953, 133).

or divert these divinities' anger" (Lecomte-Tilouine 2013, 39). Not only are they upheld by their own logic, including referring to the simple fact that in order to eat animals they must first be killed, but the buffalo sacrifices performed under state patronage also constituted, as I hope to show, a rule-governed ritual activity that was to stage and communicate specific messages—that had a performative rhetoric, if you will—rather than being the mindless and barbarian carnage Western observers and modern-day opponents have usually conceived them as.

After introductory remarks on the water buffalo's "social life" in South Asia, with its ambiguities, I will turn to the sacrifice of buffaloes in a specific historical context: the rising Gorkhali state. On the basis of state paperwork, the ritual logistics around sacrificial buffaloes—pragmatically distinguishing the phases of procurement, sacrifice, and re- or after-use—will be discussed, especially with regard to the questions of what the attendant practices of exchange, killing, and consumption reveal about the buffalo as a complex cultural entity and how, in turn, these practices aid in constructing the agents involved. The documentary practices of the state prove especially instructive about official claims to authority and agency. When finally contrasting the official perspective gleaned from the documents with examples of other sacrificial practices that exist parallel or as reactions to the state-managed sacrifices, the potential of the buffalo for complex and shifting attributions of meaning becomes especially evident.

The Social Life of the Water Buffalo

Generally speaking, the water buffalo is an incredibly useful creature. It is the major milk animal all over South Asia. Along with Brazil, India has been leading the list of exporters of beef in recent years, but in the latter case the entire lot consists of buffalo meat (also known as *buff* or *carabeef*),[3] as cattle slaughter is banned by law there. In Nepal, too, cow slaughter is a crime (Michaels 1997), whereas the buffalo is the number-one species in terms of milk and meat production (Osti 2007). Apart from professional buffalo farming, many households, especially in rural areas, keep at least one buffalo cow for their dairy supply. The selling of male calves creates a good source of extra income.

Strangely, when looking at the two related bovines of the subcontinent, the Indian zebu (*Bos taurus indicus* L.) and the Asian water buffalo (*Bubalis bubalis* L.), economic usefulness and cultural appreciation seem to be inverted (see Simoons 1994, 118; Hoffpauir 1982). While a buffalo cow yields two to three times more milk than a zebu cow—the butter-fat content of which is much higher—and while it can live on low-quality fodder, it is met with antipathy in Brahmanical texts. The buffalo is associated with stupidity, bad luck, sickness, death, and demons. The buffalo is reckoned to be a tendentially impure animal in the world of Vedic sacrifice.[4] Buffalo milk, though it may be consumed by humans, is excluded from ritual use. Puranic mythology depicts the buffalo as the creation of the anti-gods, the *asuras*, reacted upon by the countercreation of the gods, the *devas* (Stietencron 1983, 121).

In accord with the reservations toward the buffalo, high-caste people, especially Brahmins, do not eat buff (Lecomte-Tilouine 2013, 50; Simoons 1994, 119), not because the animal is considered too pure, as the cow is, but because buffalo meat is regarded as impure food. So, at least from the mainstream Brahmanical viewpoint, the social life of the buffalo is characterized by high economic value on the one hand and religious antipathy, or at least ambiguity, on the other.

In contrast, buffalo sacrifice has been a highly popular and time-honored hallmark of worshipping goddesses, especially (but not only) on the occasion of Navarātra (Biardeau 1984; Hiltebeitel 2011). Asko Parpola (2018) even connects this with depictions of buffaloes on the seals of the Indus civilization. As Bihani Sarkar (2017, 215) has recently shown, it has been a core feature of what she has dubbed *heroic Śāktism*: "Buffalo sacrifice formed the earliest ritual worship of the goddess, and when her rituals changed over time it continued to serve as one of the most crucial propitiatory acts." The choice of the buffalo as the number-one sacrificial victim for worshipping goddesses, especially those of a martial character, may not necessarily constitute a "Tantric transgression," as Hugh Urban (2001, esp. 780–81) suggests. Rather, it seems that the water buffalo has been thriving as a prominent sacrificial victim in traditions that surely developed outside, but not inevitably in rejection of, Vedic Brahmanism. Buffalo sacrifice has been part of diverse worship traditions, not only of doctrinally Tantric ones. The intimate connection between the goddess and the buffalo is epitomized in the scene depicted, worshipped, and enacted in Navarātra, that of Durgā as Mahiṣāsuramardinī, "Crusher of Buffalo Demon." As part of that scene, Mahiṣāsura, the demon enemy of the goddess, often becomes a receiver of worship himself in popular religion. The development of a benevolent image of the archetypical buffalo is also attested in versions of the attendant narrative. As Heinrich von Stietencron (1983) has shown, in some Śākta Puranic texts, Durgā and Mahiṣāsura are connected by a dramatic story of fate, love, and devotion, culminating in his killing by her hand as an act of liberation: "Hate turns into love, and the gods' adversary of low descent and brazen usurper of rule over the three worlds becomes an ascetic of Brahmanical descent and finally a partial incarnation of the god Śiva. What was loathsome has become worthy of worship: Mahiṣa appears as a symbol or prototype for the successful devotee (*bhakta*) who has attained highest devotion (*prapatti*) and is rewarded with liberation from the cycle of rebirth" (127, translation mine). Ambiguities about the buffalo—the most important sacrificial animal for Durgā, and yet, from certain perspectives, an impure creature—as well as subversions of the dominant Navarātra narration are also at work in the Nepalese Dasaĩ sacrifices.

Dasaĩ and Buffalo Sacrifice in Nepal

Nepal as we know it today was created under the Shah kings, who, from the middle of the eighteenth century onward, expanded their territory from the little kingdom of Gorkha to surrounding realms through military conquests and political alliances. As diversified as the groups living in the conquered territories were their religious practices that entertained looser or tighter ties with textual Hinduism or Buddhism. The Gorkhalis promoted their own form of practiced religion—namely, an explicitly Hindu one with close ideological links to Indian models. The ruling elite styled themselves Rajput Kshatriyas and placed their Brahmins at the top of the caste hierarchy. Key to the religious integration of the newly formed state was the propagation of a minimal Hinduism, which included cow protection and festival participation. The one festival raised to national importance and, in course of time, imposed on people of all castes and creeds was Dasaĩ.

Practically and materially speaking, animal sacrifices loomed large in the Dasaĩ rituals performed by and for the Nepalese king and state. From early on, the Gorkhali rulers patronized blood sacrifice on Dasaĩ, mostly of male[5] buffaloes, goats, and rams but also of cocks and boars in major temples and, notably, all military companies in their realm. In arrangements for temples, they struck a delicate balance between the continuation of rituals on the one hand—by taking over previous patronage relations and confirming specialists, thereby absorbing local traditions—and recalibrations and additions on the other (Zotter 2018a, 2018b). As can be grasped from eyewitness accounts by European observers (such as those discussed above), in the consolidated Nepalese state the publicly staged buffalo sacrifices were of an overwhelming magnitude. In the state's attempt to impose the observance of Dasaĩ on its subjects, too, animal sacrifices played a key role (as discussed in the section that follows).

The state files of that period bear testimony to official measures to establish structures for the supply of sacrificial buffaloes to the state-sponsored sacrificial arenas and provide insights into the actual killing and afterlife of the animals.

Procuring Buffaloes: Forced Participation

In order to feed state-managed arenas for Dasaĩ sacrifices with sufficient material, huge resources needed to be mobilized. While travelogues occasionally highlight the large number of buffaloes sacrificed, they do not deal with where all these animals came from. Official paperwork reveals the attendant large-scale administrative endeavors. Judging from a cursory inspection, the state entertained an expanding infrastructure for the supply of uncastrated male animals—mostly goats and buffaloes[6]—which involved multiple channels to make sure that enough animals arrived in time where they were needed.

For individual temples, endowments were set up according to the traditional *guṭhī* system, in which the king typically donated land, earmarking it for satisfying the material needs of religious institutions. Custodians specified in the founding charters were to ensure that from the produce of the land the stipulated items were provided. Examples include a royal land endowment in 1763 with which to provide, inter alia, animals for each Dasaĩ to the Manakāmanā temple (Vajrācārya and Śreṣṭha 1980, 68–69) and one to two banners (*nisānā*) donated to Kathmandu's Digutaleju in 1807.[7] In other cases, certain localities had to provide the sacrificial animals according to a fixed scheme. Around the old palace of Gorkha, the supply of buffaloes and goats formed an annual tribute to the king and his royal goddess (Unbescheid 1996, 121).

Apart from such more-stable arrangements, state functionaries were sent out to buy animals in the vicinity of the capitals. The oldest document known so far that has been connected to such acquisition is a record of the income and expenditures of the Gorkha palace, which lists the purchase of seven buffaloes (Panta 1988, 763–64; Bhaṭṭarāī 1997, 25–26). It hails from the time of Narabhupal Shah (1697–1743), father of the conquering Prithvinarayan. Later on, too, officials were charged with the task of buying buffaloes and goats around Gorkha (e.g., Bhaṭṭarāī 1997, app. 35, 47; Regmi 1980, 62). Similarly, after Kathmandu became the new capital in 1768, administrators of surrounding localities were ordered to purchase buffaloes from villagers—usually one or two animals per locality—and deliver them before Dasaĩ to the capital.[8] Over time, this system seems to have expanded further and become more thoroughly organized. Documents that specify growing numbers of animals to be bought and procedures to be followed testify to veritable animal treks conducted from individual districts in the Tarai to Kathmandu in the Rana period.[9]

All costs were covered by the state budget, invariably forming the largest item of expense by far for ritual material. And this was even despite the government's policy, attested in the documents, of paying only low and prefixed prices. Moreover, sale was mandatory. A typical *sanctio* in such documents reads, "He who has raised [such animals] and does not give [them] up [for sale], even if he were to receive the appropriate price fixed by the local council (*paṃca*), and who [thereby] becomes entangled in hindering the worship will be [considered] a rebel" (King Gīrvāṇayuddha 1806). That this method of forced exchange could even assume the character of confiscation, perceived as oppressive and stirring up resistance, is evidenced by a complaint by villagers recorded in an official order from 1859:

> The subjects of Bandipur came to complain: "We also have to bring seventeen or eighteen buffaloes and twenty-five or twenty-six goats for Dasaĩ to the sacrificial posts (*maulā*) in our [own town] Bandipur. Those coming from Gorkha confiscate as many buffaloes and goats as they can find, and we cannot raise [our] cattle." Therefore, it appears that there at Bandipur, too, many buffaloes and goats are needed at the sacrificial posts during Dasaĩ. We signed an order (*bandeja*) stating, "You, too, should

> pay the customary prices for the buffaloes and goats fixed in consultation with administrators (*amāli*) and elders (*tharī*). You should not confiscate [animals] from subjects in rural areas (*gā̃ughara*). If subjects willingly sell [the animals], pay the appropriate price." (Raṇa Uddīpasiṃha Kũvara Rāṇā 1859)

The complainants' issue also shows that the official demand for sacrificial animals could reach down to localities by different channels, which in the case of Bandipur involved a double bind for the villagers, who had to materially furnish the local Dasaĩ sacrifices and, moreover, were forcefully deprived of animals by functionaries from Gorkha. The abolition of this system of forced exchange is credited to Prime Minister Chandra Shumshere Rana in the early twentieth century and lauded as one of his social and economic reform measures (Regmi 1984, 10): "The peasant of Nepal is no longer compelled to furnish the beasts required for the annual sacrifices of the Durga Juja [*sic*] festival at low or even nominal rates. Nothing perhaps has brought so directly to the knowledge of the people the new spirit which actuates the Nepal Government than this relief" (Landon 1928, 160). But prices paid by the government for animals before and after these reforms often remained the same, especially those bound by endowment. There is, however, also evidence that at least some were bought at considerably higher prices in the market.[10]

Though the details of the state's animal supply, especially in its historical development, need to be studied in more detail, and though it is too early to draw further conclusions—for example, as to how far state demand for buffaloes promoted or hindered the development of buffalo farming—one thing becomes clear. The capitals' surroundings and eventually the whole realm was made part of His Majesty's sacrificial logistics. Staging Dasaĩ throughout the realm in a synchronized way might be interpreted as leading to a shared temporality (Zotter 2018a). Looking at the procurement of sacrificial animals suggests a shared materiality, although one imposed through imbalanced and mandatory exchange practices. To be sure, price fixing for goods and tributes in cash and kind to equip royal ritual materially was not limited to Dasaĩ but was a general economic policy under the Shahs. Yet still, along with the annual collections of taxes, Dasaĩ certainly was one of the regular occasions when state power was experienced materially down to the level of the individual localities.

Sacrificing Buffaloes: Staging the Warrior

The Gorkhali state sponsored buffalo sacrifices all over the country, probably from an early stage onward. It might not be too far-fetched to speculate that the court rituals of Gorkha may have formed the model for these sacrifices, which were expanded and ramified according to locality and over the course of time. Though we do not have evidence of what court ritual looked like under the preconquest Shahs and later, today buffalo sacrifices are carried out at the old palace at Gorkha on the eighth, the ninth, and the fourteenth of the bright lunar fortnight of Āśvina.[11] The exact number of buffaloes seems to have fluctuated, but, as a fixed point, the first and last buffalo of each series, known as the senior (*jeṭho*) and the junior (*kāncho*), are singled out and sacrificed by a member of the Rana family—one of the "six clans" (*cha thara*) whose ancestors supposedly assisted the founding king Dravya Shah in conquering Gorkha and were considered the protectors of the throne and lawfulness.[12] Also, the next six buffaloes are each killed by a dignitary of the Gorkhali court, one even representing the king (Bhaṭṭarāī 1997, 70; Unbescheid 1996, 122). The climactic sacrifice occurs on Mahānavamī with that of the *satāra* buffalo, "the big one." This extraordinarily large exemplar is said to represent Mahiṣāsura. It is chosen and taken care of by special procedures, its selection even marking the official onset of the preparatory phase of the palace Dasaĩ rituals (Bhaṭṭarāī 1997, 34–35). In contrast to the other buffaloes, which are to be beheaded with a single stroke, this one is to be decapitated with at least three (Unbescheid 1996, 123) or seven (Bhaṭṭarāī 1997, 76) strokes. The sacrifices are audibly framed and highlighted by music. Special tunes are performed by low-caste male musicians and high-caste female singers (Tingey 1997). Conch, bell, and *ḍamarū* are sounded (Bhaṭṭarāī 1997, 68). The sacrifice of the *satāra* is especially highlighted by the special "tune for cutting the *satāra*" (*satāra khāṭne bākya*).

Another part of the palace rituals is the *nisānāpūjā*, the "worship of the military banners," each carried by a member of one of the clans who helped Prithvinarayan Shah conquer Nepal (Bhaṭṭarāī 1997, 78; Unbescheid 1996, 117–18). In the Dasaĩ rituals carried out in military units, these *nisānas* seem to be the central objects for and receivers of blood sacrifices, simultaneously representing forms of the goddess Durgā and the major divisions of the army (Chaulagain 2013, 180–83). These sacrifices in the compounds of the security forces are known as *maulopūjā*, referring to the sacrificial post (*maulo*) to which the animals are tied, or as *koṭapūjā*, referring to their preferred venue, the *koṭas*, "forts" or "military headquarters."

In the capital of the newly formed empire, Kathmandu, the Gorkhalis' buffalo sacrifices took place in different arenas. The most famous stage for the massive army sacrifices was and indeed still is the *koṭa*, the military headquarters adjacent to the royal palace. Oldfield (1880, 345), who depicted it around 1856,[13] speaks of the king's presence; Brown (1912, 118–20) and others report the prime minister's attendance. Moreover, the Gorkhalis sacrificed buffaloes at the Mulchowk, the "main courtyard" of the palace, to which the goddess of the former Malla dynasty was brought for Navarātra and where the Shah kings' royal "house for Dasaĩ" (*dasaĩghara*) was located. There, in addition to the buffaloes sacrificed at the *maulo*, specialists of the previously reigning Malla dynasty performed their own sacrifices (see below).

The Gorkhalis' buffalo sacrifices at the power centers, replicated all over the country, are conducted according to fixed ritual procedure and by skillful method.[14] This includes the preparation of the sacrificial ground around the *maulo* by the Brahmin priest and his consecration of the sacrificial swords (figure 8.2) and of the animals (figure 8.3). After

Figure 8.2. Before the blood sacrifices of Caite Dasaĩ at the Mulchowk of Patan palace, the Brahmin priest squats near the sacrificial post (*maulo*) to consecrate a pumpkin and the sacrificial swords—the larger *khũḍā* is laid out, ready for sacrificing the he-buffaloes and the smaller *khukuri* for the he-goats (March 25, 2018). Photo by author.

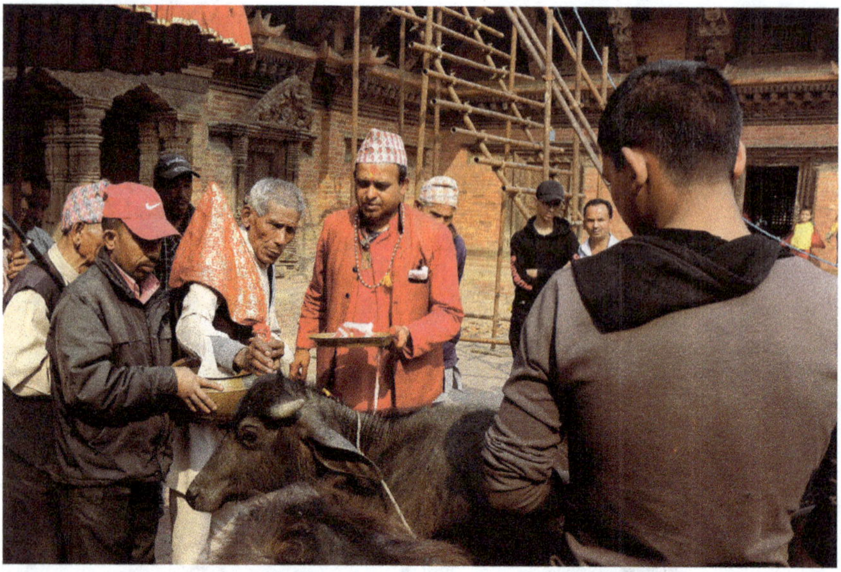

Figure 8.3. Under the guidance of the Brahmin priest, the sacrificial patron, who represents the former Malla king of Patan and carries the latter's sword wrapped in red cloth on his shoulder, consecrates the sacrificial buffaloes (March 25, 2018). Photo by author.

the sacrifice of a pumpkin by a Kshatriya sacrificer, the Brahmin priest usually withdraws from the scene, and other experts take over. Servants of lower social standing—at Gorkha, a member of the butcher caste—help to bring the buffalo into the right position under the supervision of the executioner. In order to fix the animal immobile in front of the sacrificial post, its headgear is bound with a rope drawn through a hole in the *maulo*, and the animal's forefront is firmly fastened to the post. Thus, the buffalo's neck is stretched in order to enable its beheading with one stroke. As soon as the animal is in the proper position, the executioner steps forward. After raising the sword to his forehead in a gesture of homage, the executioner beheads the animal with a powerful single blow (figure 8.4). The headless carcass is dragged three times around the post by way of *pradakṣiṇā* and put aside. Only the head is offered to the goddess.

From the Rana period it is reported that "every regimental officer is expected to present a victim (the higher officers giving two or three) as an offering to the colours of his own corps" (Brown 1912, 117; see also Oldfield 1880, 344) and to perform this spectacular task of beheading with a single stroke. Thus, as also mirrored in the documentation of

Figure 8.4. After paying homage to the sword, the sacrificer decapitates the buffaloes, which are made to stand immobile in front of the *maulo* with their necks overstretched, each by a single blow of a *khũḍā* sword, while journalists and other spectators capture the moment visually (March 25, 2018). Photo by author.

procurement and the eyewitness accounts, in the heyday of the Gorkhali kingdom, the buffalo sacrifices must have assumed a massive scale.

The importance of the sacrificial act repeated over and over again, as carried out by each army officer individually, is underlined by the fact that it was recorded in writing. Letters from the early Shah period disclose that, together with *prasāda* from the Dasaĩ *pūjās*, lists recording details of those who sacrificed buffaloes were dispatched from each army unit to the central authorities (Zotter 2018a, 508). For the Kathmandu palace, a series of such documents has survived pertaining to the buffalo sacrifices at the Mulchowk from the period 1829 to 1851, with numbers quickly increasing from twenty buffaloes beheaded on Mahānavamī 1829 to fifty-two on Mahāṣṭamī/Kālarātri, fifty-seven on Mahānavamī, and fifty-four on Caturdaśī in 1851.[15] The types of the buffaloes as well as the full names and titles of those performing the sacrifice are listed. The family names corroborate what has been said above about Gorkha Palace. The executioners solely consisted of members of the Gorkhali Kshatriya ranks.[16] Moreover, with the exception of the 1829 list, all feature at least one *cautariyā*. This was a title exclusively granted to collateral members of the Shah family. Thus, the royal family took direct part in the sacrifice, not only as patron and VIP spectator but also among the executioners. In this regard, the list from 1845—the year preceding the Kot Massacre through which Jang Bahadur Kunvar (later Rana) advanced to power—is particularly interesting. It mentions two royal princes, half-brothers of the soon-to-be king Surendra—at that time boys of eight and nine years of age—thus confirming that "sacrificial decapitation was a sort of initiation for young princes" (Lecomte-Tilouine 2013, 48). Moreover, Jang Bahadur Kunvar and his brother Dhir Shumsher Jang Kunvar—the founding fathers of the dynasty of Rana prime ministers—figure in the list.

Furthermore, the lists specify the number of hands and the blades used. The weapons mentioned and used to this day are the typical Gorkhali warrior weapons, notably the *khũḍā* and the *khukuri* (figure 8.5).[17] Last but not least, the lists record whether the beheading was accomplished by the single stroke demanded or not. One may speculate what consequences those who missed this target faced if the victim were another than the *satāra* buffalo. From his observation in the 1940s, Filchner reports a public disavowal and the humiliation such a mistake entailed: "The crowd grumbles and ridicules the inept executioner and smears his face with the victim's blood" (Filchner and Maráṭhe 1953, 133, translation mine).

What is going on here clearly speaks for the public staging of warrior bravery through a peculiar sacrificial practice. "Buffalo sacrifice is considered to be the Kshatriyas' ritual" (Lecomte-Tilouine 2013, 52). In documenting names and weapons of the ruling elite, other sacrificial practices (see below) and other ritual agents—notably, the Brahmins present on the occasion—were silenced, their names remaining unrecorded. This is in line with ethnographic reports on the Dasaĩ performances at Gorkha Palace and elsewhere. While the Brahmin specialists act inside the

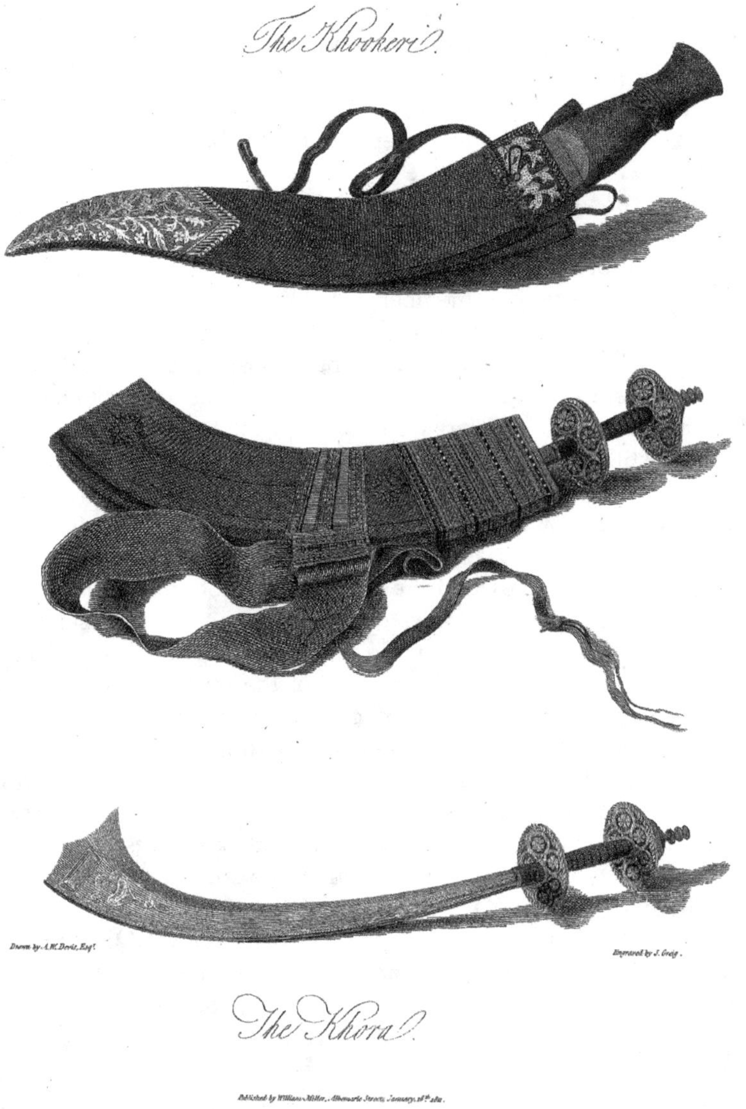

Figure 8.5. Among the fifteen plates in William Kirkpatrick's *An Account of the Kingdom of Nepaul, Being the Substance of Observations Made during a Mission to That Country, in the Year 1793*, which was published in 1811 and is one of the foundational travelogues on Nepal, featuring the very first engravings of Nepalese places and objects based on firsthand observation (Gutschow 2016, 10), is one that shows *"The Khookeri"* and *"The Khora"*—the two typical Nepalese warrior weapons, *khukuri* and *khũḍā* (Kirkpatrick 1811, plate opposite p. 118).

temple, often behind closed doors, the sacrifices are performed outdoors in the publicly accessible courtyards and attract spectators. The buffalo sacrifice is a real crowd puller; moreover, it is audibly announced and orchestrated by music. Even if, on the same occasion, he-goats were sacrificed—probably in even larger numbers—the killing of the buffalo seems to have been the major feat.

Moreover, apart from the general display of Gorkhali warrior bravery, with its attendant monopoly of ritual agency, the sacrificial scene is pregnant with performative rhetoric. In it, warriorness does not remain a claim only; the individual member of the elite is actually put to the test annually. Thus, through the Dasaĩ sacrifices, members of the dominant group in society—and, at its apex, the king—construct and stage themselves as capable masters over life and death. David Holmberg (2006) has argued that, in the sacrifice, the overt violence from the battlefield is transferred into ritual, still maintaining its potential to turn against humans. If His Majesty's soldiers can kill buffaloes with a single stroke, be reminded of what awaits those who dare to affront state authority! Similarly, Marie Lecomte-Tilouine (2013) has argued for a continuum of violence between ritual and battle that provided the war rhetoric not only for Hindu rulers but also for the Nepalese Maoists' revolution against the state. Today, too, after the Nepalese state's monopoly of violence has been framed in republican and secular terms, the scene of the buffalo sacrifice in Dasaĩ remains a performative flagship among lovers of Nepalese martial arts and is visually represented in such contexts (figure 8.6).

The explicit staging of the act of killing and the reservation of its agency for the ruling elite are in remarkable contrast to neighboring groups' practices (see below). There, as well as in other regions of South Asia, the actual killing of the sacrificial animal is a low-caste business. What has been called the "violent impurity of sacrificial killing" (Hiltebeitel 2011, 544) goes hand in hand with the low-caste status of the executioner in buffalo sacrifice in South Indian villages. For the Gorkhali warriors, the value attached to sacrificial killing is of another sort. Rather than downgrading them, it appears as an elevating act. It blends well into the overall imagery of Gorkhali Kshatriya bravery and masculinity[18]—one that differs from what Jeremy Saul (in this volume) describes for young men in Rajasthan today and that has parallels in the sacrificial practices of the Rajputs (see Vergati 1994, 136). Very tangibly, it blends into the heroic mode of worship of Durgā by South Asian rulers as part of a "warrior-culture that prioritized a readiness to face mortality" (Sarkar 2017, 273). Viewed this way, the killing of the sacrificial animal with one's own hands is not only a violent act and military skill enacted on a ritual stage but also an act of exclusively male devotion. The warrior, in killing the buffalo, reenacts Durgā's killing of Mahiṣāsura and so acts

Figure 8.6. Photograph of a bloody *khukuri* sword leaning on a lavishly ornamented *maulo* after the Dasaĩ buffalo sacrifices, on display in the Gurkhas Khukuri House, a shop in the tourist quarter Thamel in Kathmandu (April 12, 2018). Photo by author.

in imitatio Dei. For onlookers, the sacrifice is a devotional act as well. It is believed that through seeing the *satāra* buffalo having its head cut off, one's entire sins are cut off, and merits are acquired (Bhaṭṭarāī 1997, 74).

Partitioning Buffaloes: Blood, Meat, and Hierarchies

The main point of the sacrifice is the blood (Michaels 2016; Sarkar 2017, 249–50). The buffaloes' blood is collected and offered to the goddess. Blood is offered to the regimental colors in the form of handprints (Brown 1912, 119). Bloody handprints are imprinted on houses. Blood is connected not only with appeasing the thirst of the goddess "always fond of buffalo blood" (Sarkar 2017, 55) but also with fertility. Barren women drink the blood; it is also taken to the fields (Unbescheid 1996, 122).

Following textual injunctions, the only part of the buffalo offered to the goddess is the head. But what is done with the carcass? After it is dragged around the sacrificial post, its life stage as sacrificial material ends and its afterlife starts. The typical reuse of sacrificial animals is consumption. This also applies to Nepal, where Dasaĩ is one of the few occasions on which all people, including Brahmins, take meat. But, as said above, from a high-caste point of view buffalo meat constitutes a problem. Traditionally, high-caste status was intimately connected with food avoidances, including alcohol and certain types of meat. The *Mulukī Ain* (1854, §4), the legal code of Nepal promulgated in 1854, prohibits the consumption of beef, pork, chicken, and buffalo meat for all cord-wearing castes. So the cord-wearing Kshatriyas, who, as argued above, sacrificed buffaloes as part of their self-identification as warriors and heroic devotees, would not consume the animals sacrificed.

What was actually done with the carcasses after sacrifice is seemingly less well documented. It may be by pure accident that, so far, I have encountered documents on the afterlife of the sacrificial buffaloes much less frequently than those on procurement and sacrifice. It would, however, align with the observation that warrior-class members' agency around sacrificial buffaloes is more often documented than that of others, as the meat of the buffaloes sacrificed was "offered as food to members of the so-called 'impure' castes" (Lecomte-Tilouine 2013, 50). As documents show, carcasses could be allocated to service castes for counterservice. Thus, in 1813 potters of Thimi, a small town in the Kathmandu Valley, were allocated a buffalo carcass on each of the two Dasaĩs and in return had to provide earthenware for the royal household (Regmi 1982, 63). In a *jogīcakrapūjā* in 1907, the buffalo carcass was auctioned off.[19] For the buffaloes sacrificed at the palaces—and probably for other key places, too—there were fixed distribution schemes that also reflect the caste hierarchy. Though there is a certain overlap between sacrificers and receivers of meat still to be explained,[20] from the perspective officially promoted by the state, the consumption of buffalo meat downgraded, while the act of publicly killing elevated. As Lecome-Tilouine (2013, 50) notes, "This official transaction is thus unbalanced, with some involved in sanctifying and killing the animal while others merely have the role of eating the impure remains of the offering. The sacrifice thus stages the way Hinduism is globally organized and highlights its fundamentally sacrificial order." The exchange practices around the sacrificial buffaloes not only stage but also constitute and reinforce the organizational principles of state Hinduism. The public acceptance of a prescribed share of impure meat belittles the receivers in comparison to the sacrificers. This has parallels in South India, where "those of the lowest rank" consume the flesh of the buffalo (Hiltebeitel 2011, 541).

Reappropriating Buffaloes: Countering State Perspectives

On the one hand, the state would force subjects to provide sacrificial animals and would prescribe and document ritual procedure and agency within the sacrificial grounds it maintained. By publicly and routinely enacting the killing and distributing of buffaloes, it could possibly reinforce the attendant ideologies of status and difference. On the other hand, apart from the commandment that Dasaĩ sacrifices of buffaloes and goats be carried out, the administration did not interfere with the actual sacrificial procedures followed outside these privileged grounds, nor could it "control the meanings that the holiday would hold for local populations" (Hangen 2005, 113). Examples of sacrificial practices that existed parallel, in reaction to, or in the shadow of the officially enacted version illustrate this point.

There are groups that had already celebrated Navarātra with buffalo sacrifices prior to Gorkhali conquest. Thus, the Newars provided the elites under the Mallas, the dynasty ruling Kathmandu Valley from 1200 until the Shah conquest in 1768/69. Newar specialists continued to be involved in the buffalo sacrifices at Dasaĩ—prominently, for the Mallas' tutelary goddess Taleju, worshipped in the Malla palaces. It is difficult to judge what these sacrifices had looked like earlier, but what is enacted now contrasts with the Gorkhali way of sacrificing. The most obvious difference pertains to method. The buffalo's neck is not cut, but the animal is bound, its head bent back, and the carotid artery is slit so that blood splashes in the direction of the blood-receiving deity.[21] Then only the head is cut off and offered to the goddess. This is not done with a sword, a warrior's weapon, but with a knife, a tool in the hands of low-caste butchers. It cannot, of course, be precluded that in Malla times swords were used to decapitate buffaloes—the Newar butchers are also known under their honorific name as Khaḍgī, thus evoking the presence of a sword (Sanskrit: *khaḍga*)—but the absence of swords in blood sacrifices by Newar specialists today is striking. In the Mulchowk at Kathmandu, eight buffaloes are sacrificed in this way (Hoek 2014, 108–9). These also appear in the lists of buffalo sacrifices mentioned above, at least in that from 1851, which accounts for eight buffaloes killed according to this different mode (*reṭiyāko* instead of *chinyāko*). But they only occur in the summarizing account. The sacrificers' names remain unrecorded.

Not only the method and agency but also the communal dimension of the sacrifices is different among the Newars. In Bhaktapur, the main sacrificial buffalo that stands for Mahiṣāsura is intoxicated and chased beyond the city limits, there being killed in a nocturnal rite by the troupe of nine Durgās embodied in humans. The next day, on Vijayadaśamī, Bhaktapur's inhabitants visit the sacrificial site and receive a piece of buffalo meat as *prasāda* (Levy 1990, 535–39, 548). Moreover, this tenth is a major day on which funeral associations each sacrifice a buffalo and share its meat among their members (Gutschow and Michaels 2005, 83). The eating of buffalo meat was commonplace in Newar society, highlighted from early on as one of this community's distinguishing features (e.g., Kirkpatrick 1811, 119). The sharing of buffalo meat on Dasaĩ constitutes an important social tie.

Far from accepting the consumption of buffalo meat as a stigma, the Newars have their own mythology, according to which, when the Mallas' royal goddess Taleju was brought to Nepal, one day people were starving. In a dream, the goddess ordered the king to bring the first animal he saw. This happened to be a wild buffalo. It was sacrificed at the goddess's command. She ordered,

> "Let me drink its blood. You eat the remaining meat as my *prasāda*. A lot has been written in the Tantras. Have no doubt about it. There is no success without buffalo meat." All the people became happy and consumed it as *prasāda*.
>
> From this day onwards, Newars began eating buffalo meat and became initiated (into tantric *dīkṣā*). (Bajracharya and Michaels 2016, 80)

Here, eating buffalo meat is represented as a gift of the goddess in explicitly relating it to a textual form of high religion, the Tantric one. So, an act that defiles the performer when looked at from the Gorkhali side becomes a divine grace, a sign of elevation, from the Newar perspective.

Apart from groups who already practiced Dasaĩ before the conquest, there were those on whom Dasaĩ with buffalo sacrifices was imposed by the Gorkhali state. It is not easy to pin down exactly when, but seemingly already at the beginning of the Rana period (1846–1951) the state staged

Dasaĩ all over the country and forced subjects to participate and, notably, to sacrifice.[22] As still remembered by villagers, under Rana rule officials toured the country to check on the completion of the required sacrifices (Hangen 2005, 120). As a visible proof, heads of households and local communities had to imprint their bloody handprints on the walls of their houses (Holmberg 2016, 308). Notably, the stress was not on what was believed, what the sacrifice symbolized, or how it was practiced, but on the material—namely, that an animal of a particular species (not a cow or yak but a buffalo or goat) and of male (not female) sex was killed.

Groups found different ways to adjust the sacrifices to their own settings (Hangen 2005, 113–14). Arbitrations on the ground included adding rites to atone for the negative karma created by animal sacrifice among the Sherpa or performing funeral rites for the buffalo among the Tamang.

The Dasaĩ buffalo sacrifices were also reinterpreted. Marie Lecomte-Tilouine (2013, 50–51) has noted a general tendency among lower castes and groups with a tribal background to identify with the victim. Susan Hangen (2005), working on the modern anti-Dasaĩ movement in East Nepal in the 1990s, has discussed such counternarratives. In them, the reading of the dominant myth of Durgā killing the buffalo demon is inverse—comparable to what the recent Mahiṣāsura Commemoration Day movement promotes (Simmons and Sen 2018, 7–8): the defeat of Mahiṣāsura is represented as actually being the story of the conquering Gorkhalis in disguise. In this reading of history, the buffalo sacrifices into which the conquered were forced by the state become a forced murder and cannibalism of their own ancestors.

Conclusion

The Nepalese state set up sacrificial arenas all over the country and retained authority over them. In these arenas, a peculiar sacrificial practice was staged and documented; thus, ritual agency was controlled and monitored. Individual members of the dominant group—at its apex, the king—performed their warriorness by slaying buffaloes as the goddess they worshipped slayed her demon enemy, the two arenas of war and ritual being closely interwoven. Focusing public attention and documentation of the Dasaĩ rituals on the buffalo sacrifices, and fielding in them abundant materiality, overshadowed other agents' ritual activities—for example, those of the Brahmin priests.

The massive public display of violent power and heroic masculine devotion evoked a peculiar performative rhetoric to the advantage of the warrior elites, and it was also interwoven with an unbalanced exchange system that channeled buffaloes under state control and in which other groups were made to relate to the buffalo.

The officially organized supply of buffaloes and goats reinforced state power and belonging. The whole realm was made to feed the sacrificial arenas with animals and thus to materially participate in the sacrifices. When comparing the documentation practices, remarkably, the sacrificers are recorded with their names and titles, while the buffalo suppliers remain unnamed, known only by their localities' names. Documents stipulating compulsory modes of exchange for buffalo supply can also be read as charters for territorial integration. By supplying buffaloes and goats, localities were compelled to demonstrate their material commitment to state religion and therewith their belonging to the Gorkhali kingdom.

The distribution of the buffalo meat after sacrifice makes other statements about the officially endorsed social organization. It was a regular occasion to publicly affirm the socially inferior position of the receivers. The distributing of (from the high-caste perspective) impure buffalo meat constituted, perpetuated, and thus reinforced Hindu notions of ritual impurity. The consumption of buffalo meat was one of the touchstones for officially allocating caste status; thus, publicly accepting it at Dasaĩ cemented a group's status in the state-promoted hierarchy.

The state-managed logistics of the buffalo sacrifice can thus be viewed as a vehicle for the consolidation of economic and political integration and social stratification. Rather than by promoting ideas and doctrines, these processes were brought about by exercising authority over agency vis-à-vis an animal species that was a prominent sacrificial victim in the prime ritual practice staged at, and so highlighting, the centers of state power. Just as much as the Gorkhali warrior elites stylized themselves as protectors of the cow (*gorakṣa*), in Dasaĩ they also acted as the killers of the buffalo, distancing and elevating themselves over those for whom buffalo constituted food.

The Nepalese government probably neither had the means nor would develop too much interest in tightly monitoring what happened outside the state-managed sacrificial arenas. When prescribing Dasaĩ sacrifices for subjects, the official stress was on the material—male buffaloes and goats had to be killed—and less on the practical dimension, apart from the fact that sacrifice had to take place in the right time frame, not touching on its interpretation. Rather than imposing their own sacrificial technique on all subjects, the ruling elite claimed this very technique and the agency in it for themselves, while alternate practices and interpretations developed to solidify other groups' identities. For the questions of who was to provide, who was to sacrifice, and who was to eat the buffalo, dominant answers were inscribed in the performative rhetoric of state-sponsored practice, but these could not preclude their subversion.

Notes

This contribution is a result of my ongoing research in the Documents on the History of Religion and Law of Premodern Nepal research unit, run since 2014 by the Heidelberg Academy of Sciences and Humanities. My sincere gratitude for their comments on earlier versions of this paper is to Simon Cubelic, Marie Lecomte-Tilouine, Axel Michaels, Caleb Simmons, Christof Zotter, and the two anonymous reviewers; to Douglas Fear for correcting the English; and to the SUNY Press team for copyediting and typesetting. All remaining mistakes are mine.

Unless indicated otherwise, all technical terms are in Nepali. Rather than using a transcription, I follow the International Alphabet of Sanskrit Transliteration scheme, i.e., with the silent *a* not dropped. For personal and place names, no diacritics are used.

Editions and translations of most documents referred to in this chapter can be found in the *Documenta Nepalica* database (https://www.hadw-bw.de/documents-dasai). For the sake of space, only those cited verbatim are listed in this chapter's references. All digital references to these documents have last been accessed in February 2019.

1. For a concise introduction to the study of material religion, see Meyer and Houtman (2011).

2. See also Krauskopff and Lecomte-Tilouine (1996b, 9) for E. Alexander Powell's similar account from 1938; Oldfield (1880, 344–50); Filchner and Maráṭhe (1953, 132–37).

3. See, for example, the April 10, 2018, release of the United States Department of Agriculture Foreign Agricultural Service's biannual report, *Livestock and Poultry: World Markets and Trade*, available under https://www.fas.usda.gov/data/livestock-and-poultry-world-markets-and-trade.

4. The rejection of the buffalo in Vedic sacrifice is maybe not as absolute and pronounced as sometimes suggested and should be investigated with more nuance. Though Parpola (2018) diagnoses that "after the Ṛgveda, water buffalo sacrifice totally disappears from vedic literature, excepting its inclusion in the *aśvamedha* catalogue of manifold subsidiary animal victims," this alone need not speak to outright rejection but could also indicate neglect.

5. All sacrificial animals had to be male, as ruled by Nepal's legal code of 1854 (*Mulukī Ain* 1854, §§14–17, 22).

6. Actually, in most documents on acquisition, the number of goats outnumbers that of buffaloes.

7. See the *lālamohara* from King Gīrvāṇayuddha granting land to Badhuvā Nagārci for conducting rituals (https://doi.org/10.11588/diglit.44587).

8. Relevant documents have been published, for example, from the years 1796 (Regmi 1985, 150), 1830 (Regmi 1975, 51), and 1850 (Regmi 1980, 62).

9. See, for example, a *rukkā* to the officers of the Rautahat and Sarlahi districts ordering the provision of sacrificial animals for Dasaĩ (https://doi.org/10.11588/diglit.36826); a *purjī* regarding goats and buffaloes to be brought to the capital (https://abhilekha.adw.uni-heidelberg.de/nepal/catitems/viewitem/24687).

10. A list of expenditures for sacrificial animals for Dasaĩ (https://abhilekha.adw.uni-heidelberg.de/nepal/editions/show/25808) records the acquisition of 247 he-buffaloes and 468 he-goats in 1905 (Vikrama Samvat [VS] 1962).

11. For this description, I follow Bhaṭṭarāī (1997, 68–76); Chaulagain (2013, 160–66); and Unbescheid (1996, 119–26).

12. Bhaṭṭarāī (1997, 135) assumes that the Ranas hold this privilege in all major sacrifices at the Gorkha palace because they were descendants of the head of the chief of the army of Dravya Shah. The (Magar) Rānās should not be confused with the (Kunvar) Rāṇās, who were the prime ministers and de facto rulers between 1846 and 1951.

13. At 37 x 50 cm, *The Kôt at Kathmandoo during the Dussera* (1856; British Library, no. WD3280) is the largest among the watercolors made by Henry Ambrose Oldfield during his tenure from 1850 to 1863 or 1864 as surgeon at the Kathmandu Residency (Gutschow 2016, 15, plate 58). Unlike other exemplars of this collection, now kept at the British Library, it was not printed in Oldfield's (1880) two-volume work *Sketches from Nipal*. The image shows a sacrificial scene wherein a sacrificer uses a *khũḍā* sword one-handedly against a buffalo tied to a *maulo* in the presence of dignitaries, army personnel, Brahmin priests, and others.

14. In addition to the available literature, what follows is based on personal observations of the buffalo sacrifices at Patan Mulchowk on the occasions of the autumnal Dasaĩ in 2007 and the Caite Dasaĩ on March 25, 2018.

15. See a document listing the buffaloes sacrificed during Dasaĩ at the royal palace, dated 1829 (VS 1886), https://doi.org/10.11588/diglit.32507; similar lists from 1831 (VS 1888), https://doi.org/10.11588/diglit.37016; 1843 (VS 1900), https://abhilekha.adw.uni-heidelberg.de/nepal/editions/show/17769; 1845 (VS 1902), https://abhilekha.adw.uni-heidelberg.de/nepal/editions/show/17825; and 1851 (VS 1908), https://abhilekha.adw.uni-heidelberg.de/nepal/catitems/viewitem/26631.

16. These prominently include typical Kshatriya names, such as Basnyat, Baniya, Khatri, Pande, or Thapa. Some of these could be Magars (e.g., Thapa). An exception still to be investigated is the mention of two Padhyas (i.e., Brahmins) among the sacrificers in 1851.

17. Occasionally, other swords, the curved *tarovāra* and the straight *kati*, are mentioned.

18. For constructions of Gorkhali bravery and masculinity, see, for example, Onta 1996; Uprety 2017, 81–84.

19. See https://abhilekha.adw.uni-heidelberg.de/nepal/catitems/viewitem/13968.

20. For example, the four thighs of the *satāra* buffalo sacrificed at Gorkha Palace are given to four of the sacrificers (Unbescheid 1996, 124–25; cf. Bhaṭṭarāī 1997, 82), at least some of them being Magars. The Magars, who "seem to have

acted as right-hand men" (Lecomte-Tilouine 2011, 135) for the Gorkhali upper clans, pose an especially interesting case, as they rank both among the sacrificers and among the receivers of meat. In their own pattern of social stratification, eating buffalo meat was indeed a threshold in commensality, with those eating it being of lower rank (Lecomte-Tilouine 1993, 68).

21. Notably, due to purity restrictions, the image of Taleju itself does not receive the blood directly, but two men representing the blood-receiving deities stand at either side of the gate of the goddess's worship room and are sprayed with the sacrificial blood (Levy 1992, 537).

22. That such orders must have existed is attested by an exception permit issued to local officials in the Nubri Valley in 1878 (letter from Jagata Jaṅga Rāṇā to officials in Kutāṅbhoṭ regarding Dasaĩ practices, dated VS 1934, https://abhilekha.adw.uni-heidelberg.de/nepal/editions/show/26792).

References

Adhikari, Krishna P., and David N. Gellner. 2016. "Ancestor Worship and Sacrifice: Debates over Bahun-Chhetri Clan Rituals (Kul Puja) in Nepal." In Gellner, Hausner, and Letizia 2016, 226–61.

Appadurai, Arjun, ed. 1986. *The Social Life of Things: Commodities in Cultural Perspective*. Cambridge: Cambridge University Press.

Bajracharya, Manik, and Axel Michaels, trans. 2016. *Nepālikabhūpavaṃśāvalī: History of the Kings of Nepal: A Buddhist Chronicle: Introduction and Translation*. Kathmandu: Himal Books for Social Science Baha.

Bhaṭṭarāī, Lokaprasāda Śarmā. 1997. *Aitihāsika ra sāmājika sandarbhamā Gorakhādarabārakṣetrako sāṃskṛtika pakṣaḥ: Yasako udbhava ra vikāsa: samājaśāstrīya-mānavaśastrīya adhyayana*. Belajhuṇḍī, Nepal: Mahendra-Saṃskṛta-Viśvavidyālaya.

Biardeau, Madeleine. 1984. "The Śamitree and the Sacrificial Buffalo." *Contributions to Indian Sociology* 18 (1): 1–23. https://doi.org/10.1177/006996678401800102.

Brown, Percy. 1912. *Picturesque Nepal*. London: Adam and Charles Black.

Chaulagain, Nawaraj. 2013. "Hindu Kingship: Ritual, Power and History." PhD diss., Harvard University. ProQuest. http://search.proquest.com/pqdthss/docview/1465060094/abstract/D3385A2CE5A04496PQ/14.

Filchner, Wilhelm, and Shrîdhar Maráṭhe. 1953. *Hindustan im Festgewand*. Celle, Germany: Giesel.

Gellner, David N., Sondra L. Hausner, and Chiara Letizia, eds. 2016. *Religion, Secularism, and Ethnicity in Contemporary Nepal*. Delhi: Oxford University Press.

Gutschow, Niels, ed. 2016. *Nepālikabhūpavaṃśāvalī: History of the Kings of Nepal: A Buddhist Chronicle: Maps and Historical Illustrations*. Kathmandu: Himal Books for Social Science Baha.

Gutschow, Niels, and Axel Michaels. 2005. *Handling Death: The Dynamics of Death and Ancestor Rituals among the Newars of Bhaktapur, Nepal*. Wiesbaden, Germany: Harrassowitz.

Hangen, Susan. 2005. "Boycotting Dasain: History, Memory, and Ethnic Politics in Nepal." *Studies in Nepali History and Society* 10 (1): 105–33.

Hiltebeitel, Alf. 2011. "On the Handling of the Meat and Related Matters: Two South Indian Buffalo Sacrifices." In *When the Goddess Was a Woman*, vol. 2 of Mahābhārata *Ethnographies—Essays by Alf Hiltebeitel*, edited by Vishwa Adluri and Joydeep Bagchee, 517–45. Leiden, Netherlands: Brill.

Hoek, A. W. van den. 2014. *Caturmāsa: Celebrations of Death in Kathmandu, Nepal.* Kathmandu: Vajra Books.

Hoffpauir, Robert. 1982. "The Water Buffalo: India's Other Bovine." *Anthropos* 77 (1/2): 215–38.

Holmberg, David. 2006. "Violence, Non-violence, Sacrifice, Rebellion, and the State." *Studies in Nepali History and Society* 11 (1): 31–64.

———. 2016. "Tamang Lhochhar and the New Nepal." In Gellner, Hausner, and Letizia 2016, 302–25.

King Gīrvāṇayuddha. 1806 (VS 1863). Copy of a *lālamohara* regarding the purchase of rams and he-goats for Dasaĩ rituals in Gorkha. Edited and translated by Astrid Zotter. *Documenta Nepalica,* Heidelberger Akademie der Wissenschaften, 2017. https://doi.org/10.11588/diglit.34877.

Kirkpatrick, William. 1811. *An Account of the Kingdom of Nepaul, Being the Substance of Observations Made during a Mission to That Country, in the Year 1793: Illustrated with a Map, and Other Engravings.* London: W. Bulmer.

Krauskopff, Gisèle, and Marie Lecomte-Tilouine, eds. 1996a. *Célébrer le pouvoir: Dasaĩ, une fête royale au Népal.* Paris: CNRS.

———. 1996b. "Introduction: Un rituel dans tous ses états." In Krauskopff and Lecomte-Tilouine 1996a, 9–45.

Landon, Perceval. 1928. *Nepal.* Vol. 2. London: Constable.

Lecomte-Tilouine, Marie. 1993. *Les dieux du pouvoir: Les Magar et l'Hindouisme au Népal central.* Paris: CNRS.

———. 2011. *Hindu Kingship, Ethnic Revival, and Maoist Rebellion in Nepal.* Oxford: Oxford University Press.

———. 2013. "Does Sacrifice Avert Violence? Reflections from Nepal and the People's War." *Antropologia* 16:37–56. https://doi.org/http://dx.doi.org/10.14672/ada2013197%25p.

Letizia, Chiara, and Blandine Ripert. Forthcoming. "'Not in the Name of Dharma': A Judgement of the Supreme Court of Nepal on Mass Sacrifices at the Gadhimai Mela." In *Animal Sacrifice on Trial: Cases from South Asia,* edited by Daniela Berti and Anthony Good.

Levy, Robert I. 1990. *Mesocosm: Hinduism and the Organization of a Traditional Newar City in Nepal.* Berkeley: University of California Press.

Meyer, Birgit, and Dick Houtman. 2011. "Introduction: Material Religion—How Things Matter." In *Things: Religion and the Question of Materiality,* edited by Birgit Meyer and Dick Houtman, 1–23. New York: Fordham University Press.

Michaels, Axel. 1997. "The King and the Cow: On a Crucial Symbol of Hinduization in Nepal." In *Nationalism and Ethnicity in a Hindu Kingdom: The Politics of Culture in Contemporary Nepal,* edited by David N. Gellner, Joanna Pfaff-Czarnecka, and John Whelpton, 79–100. Amsterdam: Harwood.

———. 2016. "Blood Sacrifice in Nepal: Transformations and Criticism." In Gellner, Hausner, and Letizia 2016, 192–225.

Mulukī Ain. 1854. In *Śrī 5 surendra vikrama śāhadevakā śāsanakālamā baneko mulukī aina*, edited by Kānūna tathā Nyāya Maṃtrālaya. Kathmandu: Kānūna Kitaba Vyavasthā Samiti, 1965 (VS 2022).

Oldfield, Henry Ambrose. 1880. *Sketches from Nipal, Historical and Descriptive, with Anecdotes of the Court Life and Wild Sports of the Country in the Time of Maharaja Jang Bahadur, G. C. B., to Which Is Added an Essay on Nipalese Buddhism and Illustrations of Religious Monuments, Architecture, and Scenery from the Author's Own Drawings*. Vol. 2. London: W. H. Allen.

Onta, Pratyoush Raj. 1996. "The Politics of Bravery: A History of Nepali Nationalism." PhD diss., University of Pennsylvania. ProQuest. https://search.proquest.com/docview/304308290?accountid=11359.

Osti, N. P. 2007. "Nepalese Buffalo Production Trend and Future Prospective." In "Proceedings of the 8th World Buffalo Congress, Caserta, October 19–22, 2007," supplement, *Italian Journal of Animal Science* 6 (S2): 1294–97. https://doi.org/10.4081/ijas.2007.s2.1294.

Panta, Dineśarāja. 1988. *Gorakhāko itihāsa*. Vol. 3. Kathmandu: printed by the author.

Parpola, Asko. 2018. "Indus Civilization (–1750 BCE)." In *Brill's Encyclopedia of Hinduism*, edited by Knut A. Jacobsen et al. Accessed December 18, 2020. https://referenceworks.brillonline.com/entries/brill-s-encyclopedia-of-hinduism/indus-civilization-1750-bce-COM_9000000086?s.num=0&s.rows=20&s.f.s2_parent=s.f.book.brill-s-encyclopedia-of-hinduism&s.q=indus+civilization.

Raṇa Uddīpasiṃha Kũvara Rāṇā. 1859 (VS 1916). Copy of a letter directing persons to pay for animals procured for Dasaĩ. Edited and translated by Astrid Zotter. *Documenta Nepalica*, Heidelberger Akademie der Wissenschaften, 2017. https://doi.org/10.11588/diglit.34497.

Regmi, Mahesh C. 1975. "Selected Documents of Shrawan-Aswin 1887 Vikrama." *Regmi Research Series* 7 (2): 45–58.

———. 1980. "Miscellaneous Documents of 1907." *Regmi Research Series* 12 (4): 62–64.

———. 1982. "Remission of Jhara Obligations." *Regmi Research Series* 14 (3–4): 54–63.

———. 1984. "Some Reform Measures of Prime Minister Chandra Shumshere." *Regmi Research Series* 16 (1): 8–14.

———. 1985. "Royal Orders of Shrawan 1853." *Regmi Research Series* 17 (10): 147–54.

Sarkar, Bihani. 2017. *Heroic Shāktism: The Cult of Durgā in Ancient Indian Kingship*. Oxford: Oxford University Press.

Simmons, Caleb, and Moumita Sen. 2018. "Introduction: Movements of Navarātri." In Simmons, Sen, and Rodrigues 2018, 1–19.

Simmons, Caleb, Moumita Sen, and Hillary Rodrigues, eds. 2018. *Nine Nights of the Goddess: The Navarātri Festival in South Asia*. Albany: State University of New York Press.

Simoons, Frederick J. 1994. *Eat Not This Flesh: Food Avoidances from Prehistory to the Present*. 2nd rev. and enl. ed. Madison: University of Wisconsin Press.

Stietencron, Heinrich von. 1983. "Die Göttin Durgā Mahiṣāsuramardinī: Mythos, Darstellung und geschichtliche Rolle bei der Hinduisierung Indiens." In *Representations of Gods*, 118–66. Vol. 2 of *Visible Religion*. Leiden, Netherlands: Brill.

Tingey, Carol. 1997. "Music for the Royal Dasaĩ: Gorkhā and Nuwākot." *European Bulletin of Himalayan Research* 12–13:81–120.

Unbescheid, Günter. 1996. "Dépendance mythologique et liberté rituelle: La celebration de Dasaĩ au temple de Kālikā à Gorkha." In Krauskopff and Lecomte-Tilouine 1996a, 103–51.

Uprety, Sanjeev. 2017. "Masculinities of Jang Bahadur and Chandra Shumsher: British and Nepali Representations." *European Bulletin of Himalayan Research* 50–51:76–110.

Urban, Hugh B. 2001. "The Path of Power: Impurity, Kingship, and Sacrifice in Assamese Tantra." *Journal of the American Academy of Religion* 69 (4): 777–816.

Vajrācārya, Dhanavajra, and Ṭekabahādura Śreṣṭha. 1980. *Śāhakālakā abhilekha*. Vol. 1. Kathmandu: CNAS.

Vergati, Anne. 1994. "Le roi et les déesses: La fête de Navarātri et Dasahra au Rajasthan." *Journal Asiatique* 282 (1): 125–46. https://doi.org/10.2143/JA.282.1.2006118.

Zotter, Astrid. 2018a. "Conquering Navarātra: Documents on the Reorganisation of a State Festival." In *Studies in Historical Documents from Nepal and India*, edited by Simon Cubelic, Axel Michaels, and Astrid Zotter, 493–531. Heidelberg: Heidelberg University Publishing. https://doi.org/10.17885/heiup.331.454.

———. 2018b. "What Durgā, Which Navarātra? Remarks on Reconfigurations of Royal Rituals in the Kathmandu Valley." In Simmons, Sen, and Rodrigues 2018, 39–62.

9

Domains of Dasara

Reflections on the Struggle for Significance in Contemporary Mysore

CALEB SIMMONS

Dasara in contemporary Mysore is a period of celebration of Indian, Karnataka, and Mysore pride. Dasara, which refers to both the nine-night festival of Navarātri and its culmination on the tenth day (Sanskrit: *daśamī*; Kannada: *dasara*), is a state-sponsored festival (*nāḍahabba*; lit. "festival of the territory / state") where people come together to watch artists perform various classical and folk arts and enjoy fun family-oriented activities and delicious foods in many of the cultural exhibitions throughout the city (figure 9.1).[1] Simultaneously and largely outside of the public gaze, however, there exists a ritual world of goddess-oriented devotion and royalty that forms the basis of the festival and moves it through the ten-day cycle. In this chapter, I am interested in these activities that take place within the ritual landscape, how they demonstrate the multiple identities of the festival, and how those identities are contested and negotiated within the modern Indian state structure. While not immediately evident to the casual observer, there exists a tension constantly bubbling under the surface in which old and new forms of power and authority compete, with democratically elected politicians serving a vital role and providing the funding and infrastructure for the festival and its events but the erstwhile mahārāja playing the necessary role for most of the festival's rituals. The goddess of Mysore, Cāmuṇḍēśvari, the traditional *auctor* of sovereign power, is caught in the middle of this struggle, as her role in the festival's ritual becomes the site through which this struggle manifests. In the first section, I highlight the ritual overlap between the royal and goddess domains of Dasara in order to demonstrate the analogy between the king and the deity during the festival's ritual (Simmons 2020, 190; cf. Stein 1984; Dirks 1993, 38–43). By *domains of Dasara,* I refer to the separate but overlapping ritual apparatuses that took place in the temple and in the court through which divine and royal sovereignty were constituted for the goddess and for the king, respectively. In order to demonstrate how these domains became sites for the negotiation of power in modern-day Mysore, I ground contemporary Dasara rituals in the medieval celebration of Mahānavami (Sanskrit: Mahānavamī) in the Vijayanagara Empire—after which Mysore claims to have based its Dasara celebration—and in the early modern struggle against colonialism during the reign of Kṛṣṇarāja Woḍeyar III (r. 1799–1868).[2] I argue that the rituals themselves are constitutive for the production of power for the king because they demonstrate his and his lineage's divine election and place the king within a broad cosmological complex of political power.

Contemporary Dasara continues to be a site where political and administrative power are mediated vis-à-vis the cultural power of the mahārāja. Therefore, in the next section of this chapter, I explore Mysore's Dasara as a site through which various kinds of social power are negotiated, drawing upon ethnographic work conducted during Mysore's 2013 celebration of Dasara.[3] I describe and analyze the movements of the

Figure 9.1. Collage of cultural performances at the Dasara procession (Mysore, 2013). Photos by author.

festival and the festival image (*mūrti*) of the goddess from the palace to the temple and back to the palace from the beginning of the festival to its close on Vijayadaśami (Sanskrit: Vijayadaśamī). This includes a careful consideration of the traditional rituals performed in both the temple and the palace between the temple priests and the mahārāja's staff. I argue that contemporary Dasara reflects medieval and early modern political theology, but the rituals continue to be dynamic sites for the negotiation and contestation of political authority and local sovereignty between goddess, king, and elected officials within contemporary Indian political structures. Through this case study, I suggest that Navarātri remains an important time in which various powerful institutions continue to carve out socially significant domains of power and authority.

Performing the Past: Mahānavami and Dasara in Vijayanagara and Woḍeyar Mysore

Contemporary Dasara in Mysore is rooted in medieval and early modern forms of the festival that were dynamic sites through which political power was constituted, negotiated, and performed. In these past forms of the festival, we can trace the genealogy of contemporary Dasara and see how the festival and its rituals were central to the construction and the affirmation of graduated and nested forms of local and regional sovereignty. Indeed, they were the physical performance of a broad cosmological political and devotional structure that reflected claims to overlordship and local site-based authority.

The Mysore kingdom from its inception has fashioned its identity as the successor and continuation of the Vijayanagara Empire. Since the early modern period, especially during the reign of Kṛṣṇarāja Woḍeyar III, the courtly literature has portrayed the transfer of power from the Vijayanagara kings to the Mysore Woḍeyar kings as taking place in 1610 when the Vijayanagara viceroy (*mahāmaṇḍaḷēśvara*) Tirumala selected Rāja Woḍeyar as his replacement as the ruler of Śrīraṅgapaṭṭaṇa, which was the regional seat of power within the broader Vijayanagara Empire.[4] This transfer of regional sovereignty was inaugurated when Rāja Woḍeyar ascended the throne during Mahānavami that same year. Therefore, it is important to look to the Vijayanagara celebration of the festival to understand the ritual antecedents of Dasara and their political-theological implications.

While Vijayanagara is the model on which the Mysore Woḍeyars based their celebration of Dasara, Vijayanagara was not the first kingdom to celebrate Mahānavami as a political and military festival. Indeed, textual references to the celebration and its connection with kingship can be found in the *Mahābhārata*, *Rāmāyaṇa*, and *Devīmāhātmya* (see Simmons and

Sen 2018, 3–5; Sarkar 2017, 214–21). Additionally, since the *Devī Bhāgavata Purāṇa* and the *Kālikā Purāṇa*, Sanskritic accounts of Mahānavamī/Navarātri and Vijayadaśamī, have been fully articulated as royal ritual cycles that were central within the royal ritual calendar (see Simmons and Sen 2018, 5–7).[5] Furthermore, the format of Vijayanagara's celebration of the festival was adopted from other imperial rituals within the Kannada-speaking region—now the modern state of Karnataka—that flourished during the Rāṣṭrakuṭa period (ca. eighth to tenth centuries) and were adapted to suit Vijayanagara's political needs (see Inden 1981). Navarātri or Mahānavami functioned as the prime festival of the state under the Vijayanagara rulers, and it continued as the central political ritual in the ritual calendar of many of the empire's successor states throughout South India that adapted it further to suit their political situations and needs.

In Vijayanagara, the celebration of the ritual was extremely diverse, involving multiple processions, rituals, and other events aimed to entertain, to demonstrate the military nature of the festival, and to negotiate political hierarchies.[6] The overarching ritual, however, was the *pūje* in which the emperor (*mahārājādhirāja*) abdicated his throne in favor of the goddess (see Dirks 1993, 41–42). The king not only gave the goddess the premiere position of power within the kingdom (i.e., the throne), but he also relinquished his scepter, the physical symbol of his sovereign power, laying it at her feet. Over the course of the festival, the king, along with his Brahmin ministers and temple priests, performed rituals of devotion to the goddess. After these rituals, the king accepted the scepter as *prasāda* that was imbued with the power of the goddess, the cosmic overlord from whom the king derived his authority and under whom he served.

The imperial *pūje* (Sanskrit: *pūjā*) was inherently connected with the political order of the imperium, as the power that the king had been given by the goddess was further diffused throughout the kingdom at the royal *darbār*. As an extension of the *pūje* and the *prasāda* that accompanied it, the emperor's *darbār* paralleled the devotional relationship between the cosmic sovereign (i.e., the goddess) and her earthly agent (i.e., the Vijayanagara king). In this case, however, the earthly sovereign bestowed royal authority and its attendant power to his subordinates by accepting their offerings of tribute and taxes and bestowing upon them royal emblems (usually in the form of weapons or insignia) similarly imbued with royal power (Dirks 1993, 41). Both the emperor's *pūje* to the goddess and the honor gifting between the emperor and his subordinates were analogous rituals through which sovereign power was diffused from its cosmic source to the earthly sovereign and then throughout the kingdom through the dissemination of the royal authority via emblems of royal power. These rituals, therefore, formed a continuum of divine and earthly sovereignty in which the hierarchies were ritually performed during the celebration of Mahānavami as the king served the important function of the channel through which the grace and authority of the goddess was brokered from its divine source to his subordinates and subjects.

The various levels of political hierarchy were not simply ritual imaginings but were displayed in the very space and structure of the festival upon the Mahānavami *dibba*, the platform on which the aforementioned rituals were conducted (figure 9.2). The Mahānavami platform was one of the largest and tallest structures in what has been called the "royal center" of Vijayanagara, and it was critical for the physical performance and arrangement of the political hierarchy that was constituted during the rituals (Fritz, Michell, and Rao 1984; see also Rao 1991). Indeed, the various levels of political hierarchy (*mahārājādhirāja, mahārāja / mahāmaṇḍaḷēśvara, nāyaka / oḍeyar / pāḷēgāra*) were mapped unto the levels of the *dibba* concretizing the political structure from the goddess on the throne, to the emperor, and to the various outlying and peripheral kingdoms and territories. The spatial arrangement of the *darbār* remains an important aspect of the Dasara celebration in Mysore, in which VIP status is enacted through proximity to the mahārāja as he sits on his golden throne during his twice-daily private *darbār*. Additionally, as Vasudha Narayanan (2018, 279–81) and Aya Ikegame (2013) have shown, the spatial arrangement of the Mahānavami *dibba* seems to have been the inspiration for the widespread phenomena of domestic pyramidal *kolus*, which have been discussed elsewhere in this volume (see Hüsken's and Ilkama's chapters) and which continue to display the hierarchical relationship between deities, kings, and their subordinates. Thus, the Mahānavami *darbār* and its *dibba* were sites within which political hierarchy and power were constituted and displayed, and they continue to be relevant in a variety of public and domestic contexts.

Vijayanagara's celebration of Mahānavami was both a festival of goddess devotion and an annual enactment of political hierarchy. It therefore served as a site through which the status of overlord and subordinate were

Figure 9.2. Mahānavami *dibba* at Vijayanagara. Photo by author.

renewed and the various positions of the subordinates were negotiated through rituals and displayed upon the ritual platform. This ritual and spatial constitution and arrangement of the political structure continued within the Mysore kingdom in the festival practices of the Woḍeyars.

Beginning in 1610 CE, Mysore began to fashion itself as an independent kingdom after Rāja Woḍeyar (r. 1610–17) conquered Śrīraṅgapaṭṭaṇa, the regional seat of Vijayanagara viceroyalty. The Mysore kingdom remained under nominal suzerainty of the Vijayanagara state, at least until the reign of Kaṇṭhīrava Narasarāja Woḍeyar (r. 1638–59), who in 1642 adopted the imperial titles of the Vijayanagara kings and in 1645 began issuing his own coins (*Epigraphia Carnatica* 1898, 4.2 Yd.5; Thurston 1888, 19, 82). The strength of the Mysore state in relation to the Vijayanagara kingdom was further demonstrated in 1650 when the erstwhile king of Vijayanagara took refuge in Śrīraṅgapaṭṭaṇa under Woḍeyar protection. By the colonial period, however, the transfer of power from the Vijayanagara kings to the Mysore Woḍeyars was explicitly connected with Rāja Woḍeyar's ascension upon the throne of Śrīraṅgapaṭṭaṇa. Within courtly productions from this period, we can see the ways that Mahānavami rituals functioned as the enactment of royal power and proof of the transfer of sovereignty from one lineage to the next.

The role of Mahānavami as the proof of one's sovereign authority in colonial Mysore is exemplified in the Kannada history of the kingdom, the *Śrīmanmahārājavara Vaṃśāvaḷi* (ca. 1860s; henceforth *SMV*), which is attributed to its contemporaneous king Kṛṣṇarāja Woḍeyar III (r. 1799–1868) (Woḍeyar 1916, 29–40). The fourth chapter of the *SMV* tells the story of Rāja Woḍeyar, his ascension upon the throne of Śrīraṅgapaṭṭaṇa, and his deeds as king. The beginning of this chapter is important for understanding how Kṛṣṇarāja III and his court envisioned the emergence of the Woḍeyars as the political successors to Vijayanagara kingship and the vital role of Mahānavami in the constitution of political supremacy. In the *SMV*, Śrīraṅgapaṭṭaṇa was not conquered by Rāja Woḍeyar; instead, he came to the aid of Tirumala, the Vijayanagara viceroy, when the city was attacked by armies from Bijapur. During the battle to defend the capital, however, Tirumala had been injured. As a result of his injury, he decided to abdicate the throne and retire to Talakāḍu, and he selected Rāja Woḍeyar as the new king of Śrīraṅgapaṭṭaṇa, which was confirmed by the emperor of Vijayanagara. Rāja subsequently received his *abhiṣēka* (royal unction) and ascended the throne of Śrīraṅgapaṭṭaṇa inaugurating the Mysore kingdom as the dominant political force within the region.

After two short subnarratives, the *SMV* turns to the celebration of Mahānavami six months later, through which the early modern text marks Mysore's independence through the ritual performance.[7] In the text, Rāja Woḍeyar consults the brahmin ministers of his court about the propriety of holding his Dasara *darbār*.[8] The Brahmin ministers, who are said to have consulted various *dharmaśāstras*, tell the king that since he had received his unction and ascended the throne he should also conduct the Mahānavami rituals. Thereafter, Rāja Woḍeyar commences the first Mysore Dasara and decrees that every king in his line ought to conduct them in the same manner. This portion of the narrative is quite telling because Rāja Woḍeyar holds his own Mahānavami *darbār* instead of being ordered within the ritual exchange and space of the *dibba* at the Vijayanagara performance of the festival. The narrative clearly depicts the Mysore court as an independent entity that is not part of the Vijayanagara imperial hierarchy. Furthermore, it demonstrates that the early modern Mysore court fashioned themselves as successors of Vijayanagara as the new host of the Mahānavami festival in the region. Thus, in the *SMV*, Mahānavami, or more aptly the Mysore Dasara, provided the ritual context for the enactment of independent kingship and the transfer of sovereignty from the old guard to the new, in which the political hierarchy was rearranged.

The display of hierarchy during the celebration of Dasara was critical for Mysore during the reign of Kṛṣṇarāja Woḍeyar III (r. 1799–1868). Indeed, his *darbār* was fraught with contestations between the king and the British colonial officers in his court (see Ikegame 2013; Fisher 1990).[9] This contestation over the power of Mysore kingship can be seen in artistic renderings of Kṛṣṇarāja III during his Dasara *darbār* by Mysorean (figure 9.3, *left*) and British artists (figure 9.3, *right*). The image reproduced in figure 9.3 (*left*) is a Mysorean example of Kṛṣṇarāja III in his Dasara *darbār* from the mural in the Raṅgamahal of the Jaganmōhan Palace and shows

Figure 9.3. Kṛṣṇarāja Woḍeyar III represented on the throne in the Raṅgamahal of the Jaganmōhan Palace (*left;* courtesy of Jayachamarajendra Art Gallery) and in an engraving by Frederick Christian Lewis (*right;* photo by author).

the king seated confidently on his golden throne. Kṛṣṇarāja III is bedecked with fine clothing and jewelry, and his royal sword is sheathed through his cloth belt. Around this image in the larger mural (not depicted here), the king is surrounded by important rulers from India's past, including Kṛṣṇa, Ṭipū Sultān, and Aurangzeb. By contrast, in the British example (figure 9.3, *right*), by Frederick Christian Lewis, a noted engraver who depicted the the Mysore *darbār* after he visited the kingdom in either 1848 or 1849, we see the king sheepishly seated on the throne as his royal scepter lays flaccid on the rug beneath his throne. Furthermore, the king is not surrounded by the great kings of India but instead by the British officers, who sit and stand confidently, in marked contrast to Kṛṣṇarāja III. Indeed, after Kṛṣṇarāja III lost his administrative and military power with the institution of indirect rule in 1831, the meaning behind the Dasara *darbār* changed from a display of power to an allusion to the latent power of Indian kingship (see Simmons 2020). The *darbār* and its rituals were an act of memory in which the past glories of India and Mysore were celebrated over and against contemporaneous political realities. The rituals performed during the *darbār*, however, were not merely powerless illusions or symbolic acts that were meaningless reenactments; instead, the performance of court and the ritual hierarchies and its attendant honor gifting stood as a subtle subversion against the rising British hegemony in the subcontinent and enacted a form of Indian sovereignty that was rooted within the medieval context and within the devotional rituals of Mahānavami.

During the same period in which the contestation over sovereignty in Mysore was taking place in the *darbār*, the emphasis on the king's devotional relationship to the goddess and the public Dasara procession began to grow in importance, which led to a marked increase of textual and visual representations of the king's devotion and processions. The importance of the devotional rituals during Navarātri is quite evident from Kṛṣṇarāja III's portrayal of Rāja Woḍeyar's orders about the format of the daily routine of Dasara in the *SMV* (Woḍeyar 1916, 38–40). In the text's description of the Dasara celebration, which certainly reflects the festival at the time of Kṛṣṇarāja III's reign, the Woḍeyars are instructed to have recitations performed at Cāmuṇḍēśvari's temple on Cāmuṇḍi Hill, and it describes various *pūjes* that are to be performed throughout the course of the festival to the goddess, who is repeatedly referred to as the Woḍeyar family deity (*kuladēvate*). Additionally, perhaps as an innovative way to diffuse the divine power of the goddess received by the king, on the final day of Dasara, Kṛṣṇarāja III would exit the palace and be paraded through the streets of the city in a carriage pulled by six royal elephants, providing *darśana* of the royal body for all the citizens of the city (figure 9.4). According to the *SMV*, after this procession the king would distribute honors "as had been done in olden times" (Woḍeyar 1916, 39).

Figure 9.4. Kṛṣṇarāja Woḍeyar III's Jaṃbū Savāri from the Jaganmōhan Palace Raṅgamahal. Photo by author.

Throughout the remainder of the colonial period, the Mysore princely state continued its celebration of Dasara, focusing less of its attention on the *darbār* and its negotiation of the political hierarchy and more toward the pomp and pageantry of the procession that celebrated the Woḍeyar king. This included the construction of a 750-kilogram golden *hōḍa* (palanquin), which was placed on top of a royal elephant. The Woḍeyar king would sit inside the palanquin as he was paraded through the city on the final day of the festival for all of his subjects to see, finally arriving at the *banni* (Sanskrit: *śamī*; *Prosopis cineraria* [L.] Druce) *maṇṭapa* to perform ritual worship to the tree (figure 9.5). This royal *darśana* continued even after Indian independence, until Jayacāmarājēndra Woḍeyar (b. 1919–d. 1974) ended the practice in 1970 in light of the state of emergency declared by Indira Gandhi, just before the abolition of the mahārājas' privy purses in 1971 (Ikegame 2013, 163). Since 1970, the Mysore tutelary deity and goddess of the city Cāmuṇḍēśvari has been

Figure 9.5. Kṛṣṇarāja Woḍeyar IV on the golden *hōḍa* (mural in Mysore Palace). Photo by author.

placed within the *hōḍa* and is carried through the city. While the procession has continued to gain in popularity and has become a spectacle visited by both Indian and international tourists, the Mysore mahārājas have continued to hold their *darbārs*, during which they are praised with medieval encomia and exchange gifts of honor to the descendants of their former subordinates. The Woḍeyar *darbārs*, however, are no longer public events; now the *darbār* is only a private affair, restricted to only a few invited VIPs, which reflects the diminished role of the king in postindependence Indian politics. In 2014, during the recent interregnum between the death of Śrīkaṇṭhadatta Narasiṃharāja Woḍeyar and the installation of Yaduvīra Kṛṣṇadatta Woḍeyar, the *darbār* was still held, with the royal sword (*paṭṭada katti*) placed on the throne.

Since the medieval period, Mahānavami / Dasara has been an important ritual occasion for the negotiation and demonstration of political hierarchy. The rituals of the festival were extremely important for the constitution of the political structure, and they worked to display the rulers' relationship with the divine and with other political powers throughout the region. The celebration of Dasara in Mysore is built upon the foundations of the Mahānavami festival of the Vijayanagara Empire (and at times even contested its overlordship); however, through the changing political circumstances of British colonialism and Indian independence, the public emphasis shifted from the ritual construction of political hierarchies to the grandiose displays of the Dasara procession. If we look more closely at Dasara in contemporary Mysore, however, we see that similar negotiations and contestations over political hierarchies are still very much alive within the festival and its performance.

Contemporary Contestation: The Movements of Dasara (as Observed in 2013)

Despite the many political changes that have brought about adaptations in the performance of royal Dasara rituals, many of the same implications persist. Therefore, in this section I focus on my observations of the Dasara rituals in both the Mysore palace and the Cāmuṇḍēśvari temple on top of Cāmuṇḍi Hill. The rituals display a shared performative and visual rhetoric between the goddess and the king through which we can see the analogous positions of divine and earthly sovereignty. These rituals, however, also display several changes that reflect the new contestation within democratic electoral politics. Through this case study, I demonstrate the dynamic nature of Navarātri and its relevance as a site through which various domains of significance are negotiated.

Temple Ritual Cycle

The first day of Dasara is a busy day for both the goddess Cāmuṇḍēśvari and the mahārāja of Mysore. Early in the morning, the image of Cāmuṇḍēśvari that normally resides in Mysore Palace is delivered to her temple atop Cāmuṇḍi Hill. The temple's head priest takes special care to dress the image and adorn it with garlands of jasmine and roses, preparing her for the Dasara inauguration ceremony, which features important regional politicians and other VIPs and takes place outside the temple during the midmorning (figure 9.6).

Figure 9.6. The Cāmuṇḍēśvari *utsava mūrti* is dressed by the temple's head priest, Śaśiśēkhara Dīkṣita (Cāmuṇḍi Hill, 2013). Photo by author.

Inside the temple, the priests begin daily rituals that will continue through the first nine days of the ritual cycle (table 9.1). The day starts with the goddess's *abhiṣēka*, which is followed by her regular daily *pūje*. Next, the priests circumambulate the temple performing *bali pīṭha pūje* by offering cooked rice to the deities of the different directions. Immediately following *bali pīṭha pūje*, the small *nityōtsava vigraha* (lit. "image for the festival [that takes place] regularly [i.e., daily]") is brought out from the *ardhamaṇṭapa* (lit. "half pavilion"; i.e., the small room just outside the *garbha gṛha*, or sanctum). The image is then taken on procession around the main temple, circumambulating between the temple and the *prakāra* wall as devotees normally do. The image of the goddess is accompanied by a troupe of musicians playing various drums and trumpets. Both the *bali pīṭha* and the *nityōtsava pradakṣina* (Sanskrit: *pradakṣiṇā*; circumambulation) are repeated every morning (approx. 9:15 a.m.) and night (approx. 8:30 p.m.) with times that vary in relation to other Navarātri rituals. After this procession, *ārati pūje* (lamp offering) is performed by the priests to the temple's primary image (*mūla mūrti*).

Then the larger *utsava vigraha* (lit. "festival image"), which has been dressed and adorned for the day, is taken outside the temple and placed on top of one of her nine vehicles (see figure 9.7 and table 9.2). She is then taken on procession around the top of the hill at noon on the first day of Navarātri as people line the street to receive *darśana* of the goddess. Throughout the festival, this is also performed twice daily, at approximately 10:30 a.m. and 5:00 p.m., with the times also changing in relation to other Navarātri rituals, such as the special rituals that occurred on the seventh night (Kālarātri *pūje*). During the evening procession, the goddess is carried on a palanquin by the temple priests. This procession is longer and more elaborate than the morning session, and it includes several special *pūjes* along the way. The most elaborate of the special *pūjes* takes place

Table 9.1. Approximate timetable of regular Navarātri events at Cāmuṇḍi Hill in 2013

Time	Event
6:00–7:30 a.m.	*abhiṣēka* of the primary *mūrti*
9:10–9:15 a.m.	*bali pīṭha pūje*
9:15 a.m.	*nityōtsava vigraha* procession
10:30 a.m.	*utsava vigraha* procession
5:00 p.m.	Large *utsava vigraha* procession with *dore maṇṭapa pūje*
8:15 p.m.	*bali pīṭha pūje*
8:30 p.m.	*nityōtsava vigraha* procession

Figure 9.7. Cāmuṇḍēśvari's *utsava mūrti* on her lion vehicle during Navarātri/ Dasara (Cāmuṇḍi Hill, 2013).

Table 9.2. Forms of the goddess during her procession around Cāmuṇḍi Hills for each day of Dasara

Day	Form of the Goddess	Vehicle
Day 1	Brāhmi	Haṃsa (swan)
Day 2	Mahēśvari	Ṛṣibha (bull)
Day 3	Kaumāri	Navilu (peacock)
Day 4	Vaiṣṇavi	Garuda (eagle)
Day 5	Varāhi	Siṃha (lion)[11]
Day 6	Indraṇi	Gaja (elephant)
Day 7	Sarasvati	Bhūta (ghost) [Navilu (peacock) with *vīṇe*]
Day 8	Cāmuṇḍi	Siṃha (lion)[12]
Day 9	Cāmuṇḍēśvari	Śēṣa (snake)

in the *dore maṇṭapa* (lit. "royal pavilion;" i.e., *darbār*). After receiving her *pūje* in the pavilion, the image of the goddess holds court, during which one temple priest performs a roll call of the various Brahmin castes (e.g., Hoysaḷa Karṇaṭaka, Dīkṣita, Liṅgāyata) and temple-worker castes (Rāja Parivāra, Śivārcaka, etc.). As their caste name is called, representatives of the group step forward, perform one self-circumambulation (*ātma pradakṣiṇa*), and then lie prostrate (*aṣṭāṅga namaskāra*) in front of the image. Everyone who attends the goddess's court is expected to pay obeisance when their group is called, even foreign researchers observing the *pūje*. In many ways, this practice reflects the same enactment of hierarchy that we saw in the Vijayanagara Mahānavami festival, though, in this case, the goddess is the sovereign domain, and the flow of power is restricted to the temple community.

On each day of the festival, the goddess is displayed in her different forms and is mounted upon different vehicles as she goes out on procession. During the first six days, the goddess is portrayed as the *śakti* associated with various male deities and rides the vehicles attributed to that form. Before the morning procession on the sixth day, however, the head temple priest takes an invitation from the goddess to the mahārāja summoning the king to her "great festival" (*mahōtsava*) to perform *pūje* and help pull her chariot on the day of her *rathōtsava* (lit. "chariot festival"), four days after Dasara.[10] On the seventh day of Navarātri, Sarasvati *pūje* is performed, and all of my informants from the temple told me that Cāmuṇḍēśvari's *utsava vigraha* would be given the attributes of the goddess of speech and learning, including her *vīṇe* (Sanskrit: *vīṇā*; lute), and placed upon a peacock mount; however, when the goddess appeared for her procession she was not dressed as Sarasvati but as Cāmuṇḍi, and she was placed upon her *bhūta* (ghost) vehicle. This iconic transformation signaled the transition of the goddess from regal/docile form to the violent form that would kill the buffalo demon. This coincided with a rupture in the normal Dasara schedule of rituals, as happens when the daily *pūjes* are altered for a special Tantric Kālarātri *pūje* during the night. On the eighth day, the goddess appears in her regal form and is mounted upon her lion vehicle. That night, however, the goddess is transformed into a fierce goddess who has long, matted hair, wears a garland of skulls, and stands upon a fierce red *bhūta*. This fierce form is of particular interest to the goddess's devotees, who swoon over her gruesome form during the evening procession of the eighth day, wherein they can see the goddess's dramatic makeover. On the final day of Navarātri, Āyudha Pūje, the temple's head priest performs a fire ritual to the goddess (*caṇḍi hōma*) after the morning *abhiṣēka*, and the goddess is placed atop the cosmic serpent Śēṣa for her final procession of the festival.

Throughout the course of the festival and while all of these rituals are taking place in the temple, the image of Cāmuṇḍi that has been brought from the palace remains in the temple office located inside the temple's *prākāra* wall. The palace image receives daily *abhiṣēka* and *pūje* and is dressed in beautiful silk saris and jasmine garlands; all the while, this image is charged with the divine power of the goddess through proximity to the main temple image and the daily festival rituals. On the morning of Dasara, however, the palace image is dressed by the head priest of Cāmuṇḍēśvari one final time, then she is loaded on the back of a truck and taken down from the hill to the palace. A few *pūjāris*, temple workers, and musicians join the goddess in the bed of the truck for this procession, and the musicians sound the triumphant arrival of the goddess. As the truck slowly descends the hill, cars pull over to the side to view the goddess and to receive *prasāda* of sweets and flowers that is being distributed by the *pūjāris* and temple workers. At the base of the hill, throngs of eager devotees pack the streets between the hill and the palace, barely making space for the truck to slowly proceed along its route (figure 9.8). The demand for *prasāda* is so great that the musicians temporarily stop their music to distribute the *prasāda* until the truck passes the security checkpoint at the Jayamārtaṇḍa Gate of Mysore Palace.[13]

Palace Ritual Cycle

Within the palace, similar rituals are performed throughout the ten-day festival that show the clear analogy between the goddess and the king, who represents her sovereignty in earthly form. The first day sets the paradigm for the royal rituals, though, like the rituals at the top of the hill, they change over the course of the festival to accommodate various special *pūjes* and other rituals.

Figure 9.8. Crowds engulf the goddess as she nears Mysore Palace (2013).

During morning hours of the opening day of Navarātri, the mahārāja prepares to ascend the golden *siṃhāsana* (lit. "lion throne") within Mysore Palace. At around the same time as the goddess receives her morning *abhiṣēka*, the mahārāja begins his daily Navarātri rituals during the *kanya lagnāha* (auspicious ritual time) with an oil bath/anointing (*abhisēka*). He then proceeds to the throne room during *tula lagnāha* to perform *pūje* to the throne, and the palace priest ties the sacred thread (*kaṅkaṇa*) around his wrist. The king finally ascends the throne for his first private *darbār* of the Dasara during the *dhanus lagnāha*. For the rest of Navarātri, the mahārāja ascends the throne twice daily (approx. 11:15 a.m. and 6:00 p.m.). Interestingly, the mahārāja's ascension on the lion throne of Mysore always takes place shortly after the conclusion of her *utsava mūrti*'s procession around the top of her hill.

The *darbār* of the mahārāja of Mysore begins after the king completes *pūje* in the palace Gaṇapati shrine. As the mahārāja enters the *darbār* hall, he walks through a crowd of courtiers, who wave brightly colored flags and sound trumpets announcing the king's presence in the hall. As the king proceeds to the golden throne, the *hogaḷubhaṭṭaru* (court eulogist) praises the king with the medieval epithets of the Mysore Woḍeyar lineage, including Conqueror of Coorg and Protector of the Territory, clear allu-

Table 9.3. Timetable of royal rituals from the first day of Dasara 2013

Time	**Event**
6:12–6:28 a.m.	Mahārāja *abhiṣēka* and the fixing of the throne
7:30–8:40 a.m.	Throne *pūje*
8:46–9:09 a.m.	Tying of the *kaṅkaṇa*
11:15 a.m.	Throne ascension for morning *darbār*
12:30–1:25 p.m.	The Cāmuṇḍēśvari *mūrti* that is used for the mahārāja's rituals is moved from the *darbār* hall to the mirror (*kannaḍi*) hall
6:00 p.m.	Throne ascension for evening *darbār*

sions to a long-lost period of Mysore kingship in which military prowess was a key part of their identity.[14] Then the Mahārāja ascends the throne and salutes those in attendance. After he is seated, the court poet again shouts the encomia of the king, and various hereditary members of the traditional *darbār,* who are dressed in traditional costumes of the court and stand in front of the mahārāja, present themselves before the king and offer him gifts as he stoically stares forward (figure 9.9). The *darbār* is private, so the rest of those in attendance have been invited either by the royal family or by the Karnataka State Department of Archaeology and Museums, which is in charge of the majority of Mysore Palace.[15] The arrangement of the Mysore *darbār* mimics the medieval emphasis on hierarchy and proximity that was displayed upon the Vijayanagara Mahānavami *dibba,* as the royal invitees and VIPs are seated closest to the throne in seats on his right and left side and all others stand near the walls outside of the central corridor in which the *darbāris* are seated.

At the completion of the *darbār,* the king exits with all the same pomp and circumstance. At this point, however, those in attendance are allowed to follow him to the balcony that overlooks the *kalyāṇi maṇṭapa* (marriage pavilion). There, the mahārāja again takes a seat, and the mahārāṇi proceeds to wash and perform *pūje* to his feet while everyone watching takes photos and videos with their phones (figure 9.10). With the completion of this *pūje,* the *darbār* is concluded, and the mahārāja and his wife return to their private quarters.

The only day of Navarātri in which the *darbār* timing deviates from this schedule is the ninth day, or Āyudha Pūje. Āyudha Pūje, or the worship of weapons/implements, is one of the most visible *pūjes* of the festival, as everything from buses and motorcycles to office cabinets and windows are marked with white paste made from *vibhūti* (sacred ash) and a red *kumkuma tilaka* ("mark"). Within the royal context, the mahārāja observes Āyudha Pūje by worshipping weapons from the royal armory and his

Figure 9.9. Mahārāja on the throne (Mysore Palace, 2013). Photo by author.

Figure 9.10. After the *darbār*, the mahārāṇi performs *pūje* to the mahārāja (Mysore Palace, 2013). Photo by author.

various vehicles, which traditionally was reserved for royal elephants, horses, and camels but now, as one of the most evident displays of the continued dynamics of the rituals, also includes the king's Mercedes-Benz, BMWs, and other luxury automobiles (figure 9.11). The worship of the royal weapons also serves as the most important *darbār* of the festival, as the king rewards the faithful services of his *darbāris* with gifts (here, cash) as they proceed according to rank before the mahārāja, his weapons, and the mural of the goddess that overlooks the exchange (figure 9.12).

Figure 9.11. Āyudha Pūje is performed to both traditional and contemporary royal vehicles (Mysore Palace, 2013). Photos by author.

Figure 9.12. The mahārāja performs Āyudha Pūje in front of a mural of Āyudha Pūje in Mysore Palace (2013). Photo by author.

In this *pūje* and its subsequent exchange, we see the continuation of the medieval forms of sovereignty and hierarchy discussed above. Notably, however, in this contemporary performance, the *mūrti* of the goddess is absent, and the royal emblems that were imbued with divine and sovereign power and given as *prasāda* are now exchanged with cash. These changes reflect the position of the king in the current political system as well as significant changes in economics. As with the holdover epithets for the mahārāja in the daily *darbār*, the emphasis on the royal weaponry of Āyudha Pūje points at the kingdom's medieval past, but many more elements—luxury automobiles and gifts of cash—signal that these rituals not only create sovereign hierarchies but also serve as a display of success and the mahārāja's economic means.

Dasara (lit. the "tenth"), the final day of the celebration, begins with a traditional Mysore wrestling match in which the wrestlers (*jaṭṭi*) wear spiked brass knuckles. The wrestlers fight until a drop of blood hits the red earth that has been brought into the courtyard of the palace, at which time Dasara officially begins. It is at this point that the image of the goddess begins her descent from the hill temple toward Mysore Palace. After the wrestling match, the king goes on an adumbrated version of the medieval and colonial Mysore Vijayadaśami/Dasara procession. Instead of traveling from the palace to the *banni maṇṭapa*, as the king had done prior to the dissolution of princely states, the erstwhile mahārāja goes from the main palace to the small Bhuvanēśvara temple inside the palace-fort grounds and performs *banni pūje* to the large *banni* tree on the temple grounds. After the *banni pūje*, the maharāja returns to the palace, performs *pūje* with the mahārāṇi, and removes the sacred thread that was tied on the first day of Navarātri, thereby ending the royal Dasara rituals.

Throughout the Navarātri and Dasara ritual cycle in both the temple and royal contexts, analogous ritual worlds place the king and the goddess within complementary spheres of significance (cf. Stein 1984; Dirks 1993). For both the goddess and the king, Dasara begins around the same time with their unction (*abhiṣēka*) at approximately 6:00 a.m., after which both are dressed with special ornaments that are specifically for the Navarātri festival. Both Cāmuṇḍēśvari and the mahārāja go on processions around their temple and palace, give *darśana* to eager devotees, and ascend their seats of power (i.e., the goddess's vehicles and the king's throne), the mahārāja taking his throne at 11:15 a.m. and 6:00 p.m., shortly after the goddess reenters her temple after her processions at 10:30 a.m. and 5:00 p.m. Both the deity and the mahārāja are accompanied by symbols of Indian royalty including musicians, vehicles, and umbrellas displaying the significance of the protagonist of the moving ritual. In visual rhetoric of their processions, one can see the overlapping imagery between the king and the goddess that demonstrates the analogy between divine and earthly sovereignty that is rooted in the medieval and early modern political theology described above (figure 9.13). In the far left of the collage,

Figure 9.13. The analogous royal rhetoric is seen in the overlapping ritual performances in the palace (*top*; Mysore Palace, 2013) and the temple (*bottom*; Cāmuṇḍi Hill, 2013).

we see the mahārāja at the end of his shortened Dasara procession. He is accompanied by his attendants, one of whom holds an umbrella, a symbol of honor and prestige in India. Similarly, we see the *utsava mūrti* as she begins her procession, leaving her seat in the temple before mounting her vehicle for the circumambulation. In the middle images, we see the palace (*top*) and temple (*bottom*) musicians who lead the royal and temple processions. Notice, here, the accoutrements they and the other attendants hold as they lead the processions, especially the scepters. Finally, in the image on the far right, we see both the goddess (in her *dore maṇṭapa*) and the mahārāja (in his *darbār* hall) holding court.

The Goddess, the King, and Politicians in the Contemporary Dasara Procession

The centrality of the procession to the performance of kingship in the Mysorean courtly tradition can be seen very clearly in the *Mysūru Arasugaḷu Pūrvābhyūdhayagaḷu* from 1714. In this text, the royal procession, specifically the accompaniment of drums and trumpets, is equated with royal rank and political hierarchy. In one portion of the text the Mysore king even refuses to proceed with his procession because an inferior neighboring king has performed a similar procession. The implication of this eighteenth-century Mysorean text is that procession is a declaration of power and a proclamation of one's place atop the political hierarchy. The performance of power is not solely constituted through militarism or its display, as one might expect; the royal procession shares its performative rhetoric and practical discourse with the procession of the goddess on the hill, through which the king is constituted as the divine sovereign's reflection on earth. While the procession served as a clear display of sovereignty in the medieval and early modern periods, this was transformed when Jayacāmarājēndra Woḍeyar was replaced in the procession by the goddess Cāmuṇḍēśvari. Therefore, it is important that we look to the Dasara procession as the final site for the contestation and negotiation of significance in contemporary Dasara.

The Dasara procession is far and away the most famous aspect of the entire Navarātri festival in Mysore, and it draws tens of thousands of visitors from the city, from the state of Karnataka, from India, and internationally, who all come to see the amazing display of performing arts and cultural tableaux that are synonymous with the contemporary celebration. The procession serves as the pinnacle and the culmination of the ten-day-long affair, redoubling the other nine days' energy and spectacle. The display of local, regional, and national pride, however, masks the significance of the event for the political agents involved. Indeed, the Dasara, or Vijayadaśamī, processions traditionally have been the moment at which the king displays his position as the earthly sovereign (see Simmons 2020). In preindependence iterations of the ritual cycle, the Mysorean mahārāja's sovereignty was renewed through the course of Navarātri rituals, particularly the king's acceptance of the royal sword as *prasāda* from the goddess, through which she transferred her surplus sovereign power to her earthly subordinate (see Simmons 2020). It was through the procession that the mahārāja could diffuse and display that divine power throughout his kingdom. As a result of the integration of princely states into the Indian nation (1949) and the eventual revocation of privy purses (1971), in contemporary Mysore, the mahārāja is removed from this significant ritual, replaced by the goddess on the *hōḍa* and politicians in the *pūje*.

As the royal rituals conclude and the goddess enters the palace grounds, the large space in front of the Mysore palace is in the final stage of its transformation into a performance arena, with a path lined with stadium bleachers leading from the main gate, in front of the palace, and out into the streets via the Balarāma gate on the northern side of the fort walls. The grounds themselves are filled with performers, who are putting the final touches on their costumes before taking their place in line with the various cultural and social tableaux that make up the bulk of the procession. The procession lasts a couple of hours before it reaches its crescendo with the Jaṃbū Savāri (elephant procession). The final elephant is laden with the large golden *hōḍa*, upon which the palace image of Cāmuṇḍēśvari has been fixed.[16] This elephant does not continue ahead with the pack but is led to a temporary platform from which the mayor of Mysore and the chief minister of Karnataka perform flower *pūje* to the goddess on her processional throne (figure 9.14). In this final ritual act of the festival, the king is removed from his place of significance, and his sovereign power is openly appropriated by heads of the new political hierarchy, democratically elected politicians. While most of the crowd gleefully watches the parade and the *pūje*, the political significance is palpable in the tension between the mahārāja and the chief minister; displeasure was readily apparent on the face of the mahārāja, who was clearly not amused and left for the palace in the moments just before the final *pūje* (figure 9.15).

After the *pūje* to the goddess, the procession continues to the *banni maṇṭapa*, which now is housed inside a large stadium. Instead of performing a *pūje*, the procession ends in a celebration of the state in which state and local police troop their colors and the crowd is entertained by acrobats, stunt drivers, and fireworks displays. In this final culmination of the ten-day festival, neither the king nor the goddess is present (she

Figure 9.14. The chief minister of Karnataka and the mayor of Mysore offer the goddess flowers before she begins her Dasara procession (Mysore, 2013). Photo by author.

Figure 9.15. Mahārāja Śrīkanthadatta Narasiṃharāja Woḍeyar (*left*) is a mere spectator during the contemporary Dasara procession. He is shown here seated beside Chief Minister Siddaramaiah (Mysore, 2013). Photo by author.

is returned to the palace shortly after she reaches the stadium), and the festival ends with a spectacle of modern democratic India.

Conclusion

The rituals of Navarātri and Dasara have long been constitutive of sovereign power. In its medieval and early modern iterations in Vijayanagara and Mysore, the ritual cycle of the festival renewed the sovereign power of the king through analogous ritual rhetoric and through the diffusion of the goddess's sovereign power into the king through the central act of *pūje*. The earthly sovereignty of the king was then diffused throughout the political hierarchy via the *darbār* and displayed in the royal processions through the kingdom's capital. The rituals, however, were never stagnant and were adapted and altered according to the king's status in the political hierarchy, whether it was as the emperor of a vast empire, the king of a regionally significant kingdom, or a king wading against the changing political tide of colonialism.

Over the course of time, Mysore's celebration of Dasara and the relationship between sovereignty, power, and its display evolved along with the shifting dynamics of political and economic systems and the changing roles of its actors (goddess, king, British administrators, elected politicians, etc.). What remains, however, is the function of Dasara and Navarātri within the articulation and display of power and importance. While they are now removed from one another and their Dasara rituals happen in different physical spaces, the significance of the analogous relationship between the goddess and royals has persisted into the contemporary celebration of the festival. The timing and performance of the temple and palace rituals demonstrate the overlapping concerns between the divine and earthly sovereigns. This relationship, however, was curtailed with Indian independence and the dissolution of the mahārāja's privy purse. Indeed, at the point when the king's sovereign power would be displayed and performed through the triumphant march to the *banni maṇṭapa*, the king is deposed in favor of the new sovereigns of Mysore, the elected politicians.

Notes

I would like to thank Ute Hüsken, Vasudha Narayanan, and Astrid Zotter, the editors of this volume, for all of the hard work that they have put into making this collection. Further, I am deeply indebted to the American Institute of Indian Studies and their generous donors, who provided funding for my fieldwork in Mysore in 2013–14 through the Daniel H. H. Ingalls Memorial Fellowship. I am also extremely thankful to the Department of Religious Studies and Classics at the University of Arizona and the Käte Hamburger Kolleg at Ruhr Universität-Bochum for providing financial support for various stages of research and writing.

1. Unless stated otherwise, all non-English words that appear in this chapter are from Kannada. At times, however, I give the Sanskrit equivalents for terms that either are derived from Sanskrit or appear elsewhere in this volume.

2. For justification concerning the use of *early modern* in the context of colonial Mysore, see Simmons (2020).

3. Most sincere gratitude must be paid to the temple priests, *pūjāris*, and workers at the Cāmuṇḍēśvari temple for their aid and assistance throughout the 2013 Navarātri. Special thanks are due to the head priest, Śaśiśēkhara Dīkṣita, who gave me access to every ritual that was performed in the temple and who insisted that I accompany the palace image of Cāmuṇḍēśvari in her procession down the hill on Dasara, and to Abhilāṣa Dīkṣita, Mōhan Kumar, and Mañjunātha, who all made sure that I knew what rituals would be performed and who graciously explained them to me. I would also like to thank the late mahārāja and his family for allowing me to attend the private *darbār* throughout the festival and for the invitation to the observe Āyudha Pūje and the Karnataka State Department of Archaeology and Museums for their assistance navigating the various levels of security and permissions required to undertake this study.

4. Prior to the early modern period, the transfer of sovereignty was through the right of conquest, represented in Rāja Woḍeyar defeating Tirumala and conquering the throne. Śrīraṅgapaṭṭana remained the capital of the Mysore kingdom from 1610 to 1799, when Kṛṣṇarāja Woḍeyar III was installed as king by the British and the capital was moved to Mysore city.

5. For more on the historical processes in the development of the ritual cycles of Navarātri, see Sarkar (2017, 210–71).

6. According to most later Woḍeyar accounts of the Vijayanagara festival, wrestling was among the other events that were part of the festivities. In these sources, Mysore wrestlers are commonly described as the champions of the tournaments, which causes them to receive greater authority within the Vijayanagara imperium. This continues to be part of the festival in Mysore: the city hosts a major wrestling tournament, and the final day of the festival is inaugurated with a traditional wrestling match.

7. The subnarratives—the Curse of Talakāḍu and the death of Rāja Woḍeyar's son Narasarāja—are extremely important for the story and for understanding lineage succession in the early modern Mysore court; however, for the sake of space I will not discuss them here. For more see Simmons (2020, 119–20; 2018, 70–77).

8. In the text, this conference is called because he was still under ritual prohibition as a result of his son's death.

9. Since the installation of Kṛṣṇarāja Woḍeyar III by the British in 1799, a British Resident was present in the Mysore court. After the peasant insurgency in 1830–31, however, the Resident was given power over all administrative matters in the kingdom. From this point, the British presence in the royal rituals, such as Navarātri, increased steadily throughout the remainder of Kṛṣṇarāja Woḍeyar III's reign.

10. The *mahōtsava* began in the afternoon three days after Dasara with the *kalaśa pūje*; however, the *rathōtsava* acts as the major inauguration of the festival. It is followed two days later by the boat festival (*teppōtsava*). Then on the fifth day the goddess is put to rest for one night during the *śayanōtsava*, receives *mahābhiṣēka* on the sixth, and is crowned queen on with seventh during the *muḍiyutsava* (crown festival).

11. During this celebration of Navarātri, the lion vehicle was also used on the fifth day as the transport for the goddess's manifestation as Varāhi. For Varāhi, I had initially been told that the vehicle would be a *koṇa* (water buffalo), but, when the procession started, she was placed on the lion vehicle. While perhaps a small detail, *koṇa* is the Kannada term used for the Sanskrit term *mahiṣa* and is central in the foundation narrative of the city of Mysore, the Mysore kingdom, and the Cāmuṇḍēśvari temple. I am not sure why this would be connected to Cāmuṇḍēśvari in her form as Varāhi, but the buffalo vehicle does highlight the connection between Navarātri ritual practice and buffaloes, which is significant in many parts of South Asia, especially in Nepal (see Zotter, this volume).

12. The night before is Kālarātri, in which the fierce goddess is worshipped behind the closed door of the temple. The next day, this form is used for the procession; so "that people can see the beauty of the fierce goddess" (interview with Śaśiśēkhara Dīkṣita). I was told that the goddess rides the *bhūta*, or ghost, of Mahiṣāsura as well as her lion in this form.

13. At one point, when the procession stopped at the Ittige Guḍu Viṣṇu temple, the demand for *prasāda* was so great that the temple workers asked me to stop taking photos and start distributing *prasāda*.

14. Special thanks are due to Mr. Jayaramaraja of Mandakalli, the *hogaḷu-bhaṭṭaru*, for reciting the encomia of the mahārāja to me in a less dramatic and more understandable voice after the *darbār*.

15. The *darbār* hall is technically a part of Mysore Palace that belongs to the state (i.e., not the royal family's personal quarters). There is a small space with seats at the front of the *darbār* hall that is reserved for the royal invitees, who must enter from the royal family's quarters; those that enter from the state-owned side stand on either side of the hall.

16. In 2013, the elephant that was given this distinction was named Arjuna. He had been selected the previous year based on his strength and demeanor to replace Balarāma, who was retired from royal service just before the 2012 Dasara.

References

Dirks, Nicholas B. 1993. *The Hollow Crown: Ethnohistory of an Indian Kingdom*. Ann Arbor: University of Michigan Press.

Epigraphia Carnatica. 1898. Vol. 4, part 2. Bangalore: Government of Mysore.

Fisher, Michael H. 1990. "The Resident in Court Ritual, 1764–1858." *Modern Asian Studies* 24 (3): 419–58.

Fritz, John M., George Michell, and M. S. Nagaraja Rao. 1984. *Where Kings and Gods Meet: The Royal Centre at Vijayanagara, India*. Tucson: University of Arizona Press.

Ikegame, Aya. 2013. *Princely India Re-imagined: A Historical Anthropology of Mysore from 1799 to the Present*. London: Routledge.

Inden, Ronald B. 1981. "Hierarchies of Kings in Early Medieval India." *Contributions to Indian Sociology* 15 (1–2): 99–125.

Narayanan, Vasudha. 2018. "Royal *Darbār* and Domestic *Kolus*: Social Order, Creation, Procreation, and Re-Creation." In Simmons, Sen, and Rodrigues 2018, 275–97.

Rao, Nalini N. 1991. "Royal Artistic Imagery at Vijayanagara." PhD diss., University of California, Los Angeles. ProQuest (303919815).

Sarkar, Bihani. 2017. *Heroic Shāktism: The Cult of Durgā in Ancient Indian Kingship*. New York: Oxford University Press.

Simmons, Caleb. 2018. "The King and the Yadu Line: Performing Lineage through Dasara in Nineteenth-Century Mysore." In Simmons, Sen, and Rodrigues 2018, 63–82.

———. 2020. *Devotional Sovereignty: Kingship and Religion in India*. New York: Oxford University Press.

Simmons, Caleb, and Moumita Sen. 2018. "Introduction: Movements of Navarātri." In Simmons, Sen, and Rodrigues 2018, 1–22.

Simmons, Caleb, Moumita Sen, and Hillary Rodrigues, eds. 2018. *Nine Nights of the Goddess: The Navarātri Festival in South Asia*. Albany: State University of New York Press.

Stein, Burton. 1984. *All the Kings' Mana: Papers on Medieval South Indian History*. Madras: New Era Publications.

Thurston, Edgar. 1888. *Coins: Catalogue No. 1: Mysore*. Madras: R. Hill, at the Government Press.

Woḍeyar, Mummaḍi Kṛṣṇarāja. 1916. *Maisūru Saṃsthānada Prabhugaḷu Śrīmanmahārājavara Vaṃśāvaḷi or the Annals of the Mysore Royal Family*. Mysore: Government Branch Press.

10

The Ups and Downs of Competing Power Rituals

Dasarā and Durgā Pūjā in a Former Princely State of Odisha

UWE SKODA

Introduction

With reference to Dasarā rituals in Nepal, Joanna Pfaff-Czarnecka (1998, 577) proposes that "power rituals" in complex sociopolitical orders "express and dramatize social realities, but also . . . organize social groups by relating them with one another. One important element in relating social groups is the establishment of symbolic means for expressing the supremacy of one group and the subordination of others. However, there always remains a large scope for ambiguity . . . and for disagreement existing between various participants who may attach multiple meanings to a religious celebration at different ritual levels." Building on her insights, I introduce three competing, simultaneously performed power rituals in the former princely state in Bonai, now a subdivision of Sundargarh District in Odisha.

First, the raja's Dasarā as a royal tradition expresses a sacrificial polity that integrates and ranks communities, including the Adibasis and the Bhuiyans in particular. Performed inside the fort, it revolves around the goddess Durgā in the form of swords worshipped together with the Bhuiyan goddess Kant Debī, also considered to be Bandurgā (forest Durgā), who visits the raja on this occasion. Second, Durgā Pūjā in the market, relatively more recent and lately increasingly aggrandized, is closer to the temporary Bengali-inspired Mahiṣāsuramardinī style with a clay idol at the center. It combines middle-class-cum-Brahmanical sentiments about a vegetarian style of worship with ideas of a community *pūjā* generously supported by industrialists. Third, the worship of Durgā is linked directly to Bhārat Mātā by the Hindu-nationalist Rashtriya Svayamsevak Sangh (RSS; "National Volunteer Corps"), which is propagating and staging a more martial style of training of the Hindu community in defense of Mother India. All these public-arena activities take place in close proximity and culminate on the day of Vijayadaśamī, and they refer to Goddess Durgā as a pivotal symbol. All actors claim a special relationship to the goddess, compete with one another for audiences, and thus dramatize power as well as the fissures within a local society.

From a historical angle, Bonai as a kingdom, transformed into a princely state under colonial rule, merged with the Indian Union in 1948—a process generally referred to as *merger*. Though they were initially allowed to keep their privy purses after the formal loss of power, the abolition of all appanages in the early 1970s had clear financial implications for the former rulers. In many cases it led to a further decline of pomp, though rituals for the goddess Durgā continue, especially during Dasarā. While the raja's economic capacity decreased, the area's mineral resources attracted industrialists and the state, keen to mine this wealth. Mining booms in the 1940s and 1950s, when the nearby Rourkela Steel Plant was set up, and again from the early 2000s, fueled by a global demand for steel, which also led to the mushrooming of sponge-iron factories in Bonai, brought new power holders into the area. They in turn became patrons and sponsors of Durgā Pūjā as another power ritual. Their economic might increasingly overshadows the raja's diminished capacity to perform lavish rituals, which ascribe to him a central position to him, and thus challenges the raja's claims to privileged access to the goddess.

In the following, building on my recent work on Dasarā rituals as a sacrificial polity (Skoda 2018), I provide an outline of these power rituals, not only Dasarā but also Durgā Pūjā, and focus on changes occurring over decades, thus making the point that these power rituals have had noticeable ups and downs, while the RSS has just started its own version very recently. Rather than demonstrating a straightforward decline of royal rituals, the situation in Bonai and its capital Bonaigarh is more complex and dynamic. The relative rise of Durgā Pūjā depends on donations from industrialists and mining companies, which are influenced by their economic situations. Mining, in turn, threatens the habitat of the Bhuiyans and Goddess Kant Debī's abode as a crucial and increasingly popular element in the royal tradition. Attempts to resist new mines also appear to render the alliance with the raja, expressed through the goddess's visit, meaningful in new ways, in that Bhuiyans turn to the raja for support. Thus, instead of one power ritual simply declining and another arising, Dasarā and Durgā Pūjā coexist and elements in their respective traditions become more popular or disappear while a third player is trying to make inroads.

Dasarā in the Fort: A Sacrificial Polity after Merger

Outline of the Rituals and Sacrificial Polity

During Dasarā, goddesses with different names are worshipped, including Mā Kumārī as the raja's tutelary goddess and Kant Debī (also known as Kant Kumārī) as a goddess residing in the hills but visiting the palace annually. All are linked to or considered to be manifestations of the goddess Durgā; they belong to a category of rather fierce, potentially destructive, but also benevolent mother goddesses (Biardieu 1989, 140; Michaels 1998, 247). As elsewhere in Odisha, their material manifestations include swords (Schnepel 2002; Mallebrein 2004) but also bracelets (e.g., *nabadurgā kaṅkaṇa*) or anthropomorphic idols, though the latter are of secondary importance. For example, the raja is believed to have received the sword *kumārī prasād* as a blessing from Mā Kumārī, and, with reference to the raja's main sword (*pātkhaṇḍā*), the royal priest (*rājpurohit*) emphasizes that the goddess has a permanent seat (*pīṭha*) inside the fort, stressing her localization and her literal grounding (see Kinsley 1987, 186; Galey 1990).[1]

Dasarā rituals in Bonai connect these goddesses, the (former) ruler, and communities in a sacrificial polity as described by Nicholas (2013, 176–77): Goddess worship "aligns the symbols of legitimacy with its substance. The goddess possesses weapons and uses them to destroy those who upend the proper order of heavens. Durga Puja, with a role for dependents and graded responsibilities for various castes, physically assembles the prajas in ranked roles"—and this is also true of Dasarā.[2] Various communities continue to participate in the rituals. For example, the royal swords are washed and sharpened by the Khati, belonging to the Maharona community, while the Behera, belonging to the Hansi community (known as weavers), prepare an umbrella (*suti chatra*) for Mā Kumārī. However, other communities no longer perform their duty, indicating a certain disintegration of the sacrificial polity.[3] These communities supplement the roles of the Brahmanical *rājpurohit*, the Paudi Bhuiyan ritual specialist in charge of Goddess Kant Debī (*dehuri*), and the non-Brahmanical priest belonging to the Sud community (*amat*) as the main

Figure 10.1. The Kathi washing and sharpening the royal swords (2016). Photo by author.

actors in Dasarā, apart from the raja. In different ways, all of them are entitled to customary payments (*dastūrī*) or even sacrificial meat, which also plays a crucial role in maintaining connections between the raja, his clan, and ritual specialists.[4]

Arguably the most important group taking part in Dasarā rituals nowadays, both from an Adibasi perspective and also in terms of the audience attracted, are the Paudi Bhuiyans, who carry the idol of Goddess Kant Debī. In her form of a *sāma*, or the iron part of a village grinder (*dhinki*), she travels in a fortnight-long procession during the bright fortnight of the month Āśvin from her abode to the fort and back.[5] On the eighth day, the Raja meets the Paudi Bhuiyans just outside the fort to receive the goddess—a ritual known as *kant bheṭ*.[6] The close tie between the raja and the Paudi Bhuiyans, mediated through the goddess, is expressed on this occasion when both sides enquire about each other's well-being. Roy (1935, 109–10) documented this ritualized dialogue for the 1930s, and it is also publicly performed nowadays:

> The Dihuri . . . comes up to the Raja with the image [of the goddess], salutes him, and enquires of him about the health and welfare, first of himself, then of his Rani, then of his chil-

> dren, then of his servants, then of his elephants, then of his horses, and last of all about the welfare of the land (Prithvi or Earth). The Raja answers "yes" to every question; and then in his turn, the Raja asks the Dihuri about the welfare of himself and his children and then of the Pauris generally; and to every question the Dihuri replies in the affirmative.

Having received the goddess, the raja passes her on to the *amat*, who in turn worships her and arranges a meeting with her sister, the raja's tutelary goddess Mā Kumārī.[7] Subsequently, the *amat* proceeds with Kant Debī toward the palace but stops at platforms (*maṇḍal*) along the way, to which the public flocks in order to take *darśan*, to hold the goddess, and to offer sacrifices. In the *darbār* hall (formerly the armory), she is placed in a rice pot (*hāṇḍī*) filled with rice (*chaul*) next to two swords, *pātkhaṇḍā* and *kumārī prasād*, and Nabadurgā in the form of bracelets already installed and worshipped there. It is widely believed that this pot, referred to as *rakta hāṇḍī*, used to be filled with blood (*rakta*).[8] Similarly to supposedly secret rituals such as *sandhi pūjā*, performed exactly between *aṣṭamī* and *nabamī*, the eighth and ninth days, by the *rājpurohit*, some people believe that the *rakta hāṇḍī* was linked to human sacrifices in the past.

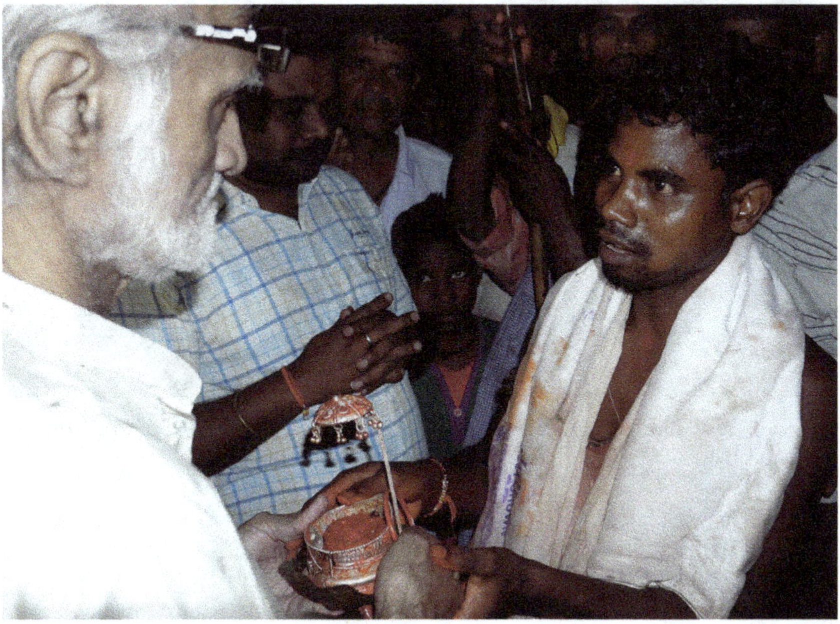

Figure 10.2. *Kant bheṭ*: Paudi Bhuiyan *dehuri* handing over Goddess Kant Debī to the raja (2016). Photo by author.

Figure 10.3. *Amat* holding the goddess after *kant bheṭ* (2016). Photo by author.

After taking *darśan* first of Kant Debī, *pātkhaṇḍā/kumārī prasād*, and Nabadurgā, the raja personally carries Goddess Kant Debī into the inner palace, where she is again worshipped by the *amat*, who places her in pot filled with *mahuli* wine. It used to be produced by the traditionally low-caste Parida, who no longer provide this service, which is considered

Figure 10.4. Paudi Bhuiyans and Goddess Kant Debī leaving Bonaigarh by crossing the river Brahmani (2016). Photo by author.

degrading. However, later the alcohol is distributed as a *prasād* among the public, marking a climax in the palace. Subsequently, the goddess is handed back to the *dehuri*. Just before leaving the town, a special cake (*chakuli*) is offered to her made of bitter neem leaves, expressing the bitterness of farewell. After the Paudi Bhuiyans and the goddess have left, Dasarā *pūjā* is performed by the raja and *rājpurohit* on the veranda of the former Rajmahal, wherein the *pātkhaṇḍā* is held by the raja in order to perform *buliba* by moving it in all directions as a symbolic renewal of the kingdom's conquest.

Declining Palace Rituals and the Increasingly Popular Worship of Kant Debī?

While palace rituals, broadly speaking, seem to be in a state of decline and have been reduced, the importance and popularity of Kant Debī appears to be increasing. Therefore, decline, though clearly perceived, is not linear. Rather, palace rituals have undergone various ups and downs. For instance, when I revisited the rituals in 2016 after detailed observations in 2007 and inquired about the differences, major actors pointed out that the new raja, who took over in 2011, was behind certain changes—for example, a reduction in the number of animal sacrifices. As the *amat* argued, "Oh, at that time the father of the king was alive. . . . His idea or knowledge was different. He [the new king] is different. Whatever he will announce, that is principle. At that time whatever the old king announced was the principle." With some regret, he referred to the *kant bheṭ*, during which two blindfolded he-goats tied together used to be sacrificed—supposedly done in one stroke—but this ritual has been abolished under the current raja. In fact, many people believe the current situation is only a shadow of the previous splendor and royal largesse, when more goats or even buffaloes used to be sacrificed, instead of coconuts nowadays.[9]

Yet the substitution of he-goats by coconuts during *kant bheṭ*, the *kant dehuri* reasoned, was not only the raja's individual decision. Rather, he saw a foreign collector, understood to be an officer from outside of Bonai, as instrumental for this new restriction: "The [current raja's] father told that a collector has come from a foreign place. Twin *bukas* were [beheaded] . . . when the collector visited the goddess. He saw those two heads. He told that this should not be done. . . . What the foreign collector or subcollector did, I don't know. He detained the king ten to twelve hours at the police station. . . . [But] whatever has happened we should not leave the tradition. This is our tradition. This is the Goddess of our 16 Pradhani Paudi Bhuiyan." Interestingly, the *dehuri* considered the "collector" an outsider while acknowledging his power vis-à-vis the raja and regretting the end of blood sacrifices during *kant bheṭ*. In contrast, the raja's version referred to legal prohibitions and campaigns for animal rights that have gathered steam in the region lately. The raja denies any detention; there were, however, consultations between the subcollector and the raja on the performance of such customary sacrifices. The raja is aware of the fact that he has to tread carefully while maintaining a tradition, even though personally he might not be fond of animal sacrifices. This small example of a shift from he-goat to coconut during *kant bheṭ* illustrates how complex change is and how many different actors are involved—including those beyond Bonai (animal-rights activists, etc.). A reduction of sacrifices—seen by some as a decline but by others as progress—relates to financial, ethical, and other reasons and not only to a raja's limited funds. Similarly, the *amat* stated in 2016 that an increased price of meat was the main reason for fewer goats being sacrificed by locals in the royal tradition—poor people could not afford it, though they might have wished to offer it.

A reduction of other things, such as musical performances, could also be cited, but arguably the most radical change concerns the procession to the Dasarā field, which, according to most people, ended in the 1960s—that is, prior to the abolition of the privy purses under Indira Gandhi in the early 1970s. Recently, the old Dasarā field has also disappeared with the construction of new court buildings on the very same ground. However, the royal chronicles written before 1948 describe these rituals (Dasarā Parba) in the following way:

> Arms and ammunitions are worshipped at the armoury [*khaṇḍa ghar*] and the Brahmins are given food [*bhojana*]. . . . the groups [*dala*] of [all Zamindars/Jagirdars] . . . come to the Rajbati. . . . The Raja goes to the Dasarā Parba with silver sedan [*tamajan*] and sword at the hand. Beside Raja, . . . [his sons] go sitting on the elephant with silver palanquin [*palanki*]. British police also escort them in front and behind the Raja's group and all go for Dasarā Parba. At the Dasarā field wrestling, exercise [*kasrat*] and archery play is observed among the different groups of soldiers. At the end Raja distributes the prizes. While returning from the Dasarā field the Raja is given a welcome with dance and song and is worshipped [*bandapana*] with incense at every square. Returning to the Rajbati all the soldiers from different places are given a big feast [*bhoji*]. (Adapted from Pramanik and Skoda 2013, 42)

Photographs taken in 1935/36 depict Dasarā, including *kant bheṭ*, in this way and show the king in state. Yet only a few photos like the *kant bheṭ* picture still show similarities to the current situation. The procession with its pomp and the royal symbols, such as the umbrella (*chattar*) and the Paiks (warrior peasants) holding bows and arrows, have largely disappeared. Many locals believe that a proper performance of all customary rituals is required to ensure the kingdom's prosperity and that, occasionally, a decline of kingship is causally linked to reduced rituals rather than to political changes. The raja, who funds all these activities personally, has been unable or unwilling to continue this grand celebration but has cut it to a bare minimum and even beyond. For example, the *khaṇḍa ghar* (armory) collapsed a few years ago, so the rituals had to be shifted to the former *sabhā ghar*, or *darbār* hall, which also needs repair. Besides, Nabadurgā was worshipped there on a half-broken wooden platform. Given the fact that many ritual sequences have also been tightened, sometimes observers refer to the present-day arrangements as simply a "shortcut *pūjā*."

However, such reductions should not lead to the conclusion that premerger rituals were performed in a static way or that accelerated change is only a postmerger phenomenon. In fact, one might rather expect constant changes, depending on the financial situation or on the presence of a photographer, as mentioned above. A case in point is the evidence for considerable fluctuations in expenditure just around the time of the merger. According to a report from 1948, the raja, enjoying a new but short-lived financial freedom from paramountcy, considerably inflated the budget for rituals, before the Indian state officials subsequently reduced it again. The newly appointed administrator of Bonai, apparently not very familiar with the rituals in Bonai (as depicted in old photographs), wrote to the additional secretary to the government in Cuttack on September 20, 1948: "Prior to the merger in the year 1947 the Ruler drew a sum of Rs. 3.000/– for all his religious ceremonies and festivals for that year. Before that the annual grant from the State for Dessehra [*sic*] was Rs. 26/– only as sanctioned by the Political Agent from year to year. This amount was being drawn by the Ruler. All the celebrations were done inside the Rajbati [palace]. It thus appears that the Dessehra was being celebrated by the Ruler in his private capacity."[10] However, apart from these fluctuations and the tangible decline of palace pomp nowadays, Kant Debī rituals seem to be increasingly popular. More and more locals flock to her rituals—a process also aided by a generally improved infrastructure and communication facilities, such as bridges crossing the river Brahmani, enabling villagers and a growing town population to attend the rituals easily. To streamline her growing procession, the late Rajasahib K. K. C. Deo (who "ruled" from 1948 to 2011) had already introduced a new rite of worship of Kant Debī. According to the royal chronicles, "a change was made. . . . Instead of worshipping her in every household, it was done at a mandala" (adapted from Pramanik and Skoda 2013, 55)—in other words, at fewer platforms. Still, her procession is often delayed—reaching the palace late for the *kant bheṭ*. For example, in 2007 the raja's grandson, as his representative, had to wait. The raja became furious and scolded the Paudi Bhuiyan later on. In 2016, the goddess also did not reach her cave at the full moon after Dasarā as is customary, and this delay also expressed her popularity and the desire of many devotees to be included in the worship. As the *dehuri* complained to the raja, in certain places villagers insisted on a night halt or a longer presence of the goddess. In one case, a village officially petitioned the raja to be included in the goddess's route, though the raja politely refused, pointing at already existing delays.

Many devotees explicitly wish to hold the goddess. Though the *dehuri* argued that the goddess should not be held by others, it happens frequently: "As per the mantras of *dehuri* the wish of all the others are fulfilled. Taking the goddess in the hand after the *pūjā* is not good." However, he also agreed that he could hardly refuse to pass the goddess into a devotee's hands if somebody had a wish to do so, and many indeed cherished the physical connection. This growing popularity is often also linked to indiscipline. As the *amat*'s *barik* (sacrificer) said, "Under kingship all the *pūjās* were celebrated in a very disciplined way. People were fearing to do mischievous activities," whereas nowadays, without permission, they take the goddess inside their houses or even grab the head of the sacrificial goat after sacrifice, though it should go to the *kant dehuri* (and *barik*). Such things, the lament conveyed, would not have happened in the old days when people feared the goddess more, but they are possible in a dark age (Kali Yuga).

Seventy years after the state merger, times may not be good for royalty, but the alliance between the raja and Paudi Bhuiyan mediated by Goddess Kant Debī continues. In fact, it becomes meaningful in novel ways. From 2007 onward, the link between the Paudi Bhuiyan and the raja was additionally strengthened when the South Korean steelmaker POSCO proposed an iron-ore mine in the area. The Paudi Bhuiyan feared that it would threaten the goddess's divine abode and be a severe blow to, if not extinguish outright, the Paudi Bhuiyan community. They turned to the raja, and subsequently the raja participated in protest rallies, which also foregrounded the goddess, similarly to other resistance movements, such as that in the Niyamgiri Hills.[11] Dasarā and the raja's position were implicitly highlighted by this, both of which would be significantly diminished without his central role vis-à-vis Kant Debī.[12] The outcome of the resistance movement remains to be seen, and other players, such as politicians, are, no doubt, increasingly important.[13] However, the raja's stress on the link with the Bhuiyans and opposition to new mines might also have been influenced by the fact that the owners of existing mines and sponge-iron factories often support a relatively new local Durgā Pūjā in the market, which tends to overshadow the royal Dasarā in terms of spectacle.

Durgā Pūjā in the Market

Outlining the Pūjā

The worship of Goddess Durgā in the market area—commonly referred to as *Durgā Pūjā*—shares with the royal Dasarā the overall schedule between *ṣaṣṭhī*, the sixth day, and Vijayadaśamī, the tenth day of victory—a period that coincides with the well-known Durgā Pūjā celebrated in Bengal (Östör 2004; Nicholas 2013) Within both ritual cycles, elements such as *bel barni pūjā* (*bel* invitation) and *bisarjan* (immersion), though different in form, are crucial parts and are often also seen as typical Bengali elements (McDermott 2011, 13). Unlike Dasarā, however, Durgā Pūjā ends with Vijayadaśamī,[14] and Brahmins officiate in all its rituals. Arguably, the most important distinctions between both traditions relate to the form of the idol as well as the conception of the deity's presence. In contrast to swords or other aniconic and permanently present *mūrtis*, Durgā Pūjā revolves around the *mṛnmaya mūrti*—*mṛnmaya* meaning "made of clay." Here the goddess appears as a temporary and ideally biodegradable unfired clay (*mati*) idol. Iconographically, it depicts Durgā in her widely known anthropomorphic yet ten-armed form, slaying the demon (Mahiṣāsuramardinī Durgā). She is surrounded by her four children, Lakṣmī, Sarasvatī, Gaṇeś, and Kartik, completely absent in the royal tradition, and thus combines the "martial with the maternal image" (Guha-Thakurta 2015, 1; see also Ray 2017). Her motherly representation lets her appear as a milder form (Michaels, Vogelsanger, and Wilke 1997) differing from her relatively

Figure 10.5. Durgā Pūjā *maṇḍap* in the market (2007). Photo by author.

fierce manifestation inside the fort. Yet, here too, the killing of the demon Mahiṣāsura and "the display of life and death, with weapons, bloodshed, and apprehension, makes explicit the force behind the authority," as Nicholas (2013, 185) has pointed out.

Similar to her worship in Kolkata (Guha-Thakurta 2015, 2), the goddess Durgā is seen as visiting Bonai, and the main rituals are performed in her equally temporary temple or *maṇḍap* in the market, as the ritual center. However, two processions lead her to the Brahmani River. First, on *saptamī* (seventh day), a *mūrti* of Nabadurgā is created, consisting of nine elements (e.g., banana leaves) representing nine deities.[15] Not only in Bonai but also in Bengal and elsewhere, this *mūrti* is known as *nabapatrikā* and indicates a close association of Durgā with land, agriculture, and fertility in the wider sense (see Khanna 2000). Armed with a sugarcane stick and wrapped in a sari symbolizing womanhood, Nabadurgā takes her bath, which is combined with a reading of the sacred *Devīmāhātmya* text presenting the goddess as a warrior.[16] Moreover, a flower known as *aparājitā* (undefeated) is offered, pointing to her epithet as "victorious." Afterward, in her *maṇḍap* an offering known as *māso* (meat) is made for her, consisting of lentils, rice, and honey—the name indicating a substitute for a blood sacrifice, although all offerings are strictly vegetarian. On the same day, the *mṛnmaya mūrti* is brought to life in several steps (giving

Figure 10.6. *Nabapatrikā* at the river Brahmani (2007). Photo by author.

Figure 10.7. *Mūrti* of Goddess Durgā before her immersion (2016). Photo by author.

of the eyes, giving of life/*jīban*, etc.), triumphing over the demon and thus protecting the world from evil. Her daily worship culminates on Vijayadaśamī, after which the *mūrti* is dismantled and finally immersed in the river, bidding farewell to the goddess.[17]

History, Organization, and Sponsorship of Durgā Pūjā in Bonaigarh

Unlike the older Dasarā in the fort, Durgā Pūjā in Bonai has a relatively short and traceable history with a steady rise and a recent cutback.[18] In fact, shortly after merging the former princely state with the Indian Union in 1948, the Home Department of the government of Odisha inquired about the "Celebration of Durga Puja or Dussera."[19] In his reply, Mr. Das, the newly appointed administrator of Bonai, wrote on September 20, 1948, "It appears that in the past there was no elaborate religious celebration of Deshera [*sic*] in Bonai. No image is prepared and worshipped according to the customs prevailing in the coastal area. The image of the goddess has been installed in the local Jagarnath temple. It appears that during the Dessehra the image is taken to the Rajbati where the ruler offers Pūjā."[20] Unfamiliar with local customs, the outsider administrator apparently mixed coastal Durgā Pūjā with local Dasarā celebrations as depicted in photos or vividly remembered by interlocutors. However, he was probably right that no image was "prepared," because, according to my interviews, in September 1948 there simply was no Durgā Pūjā according to the customs prevailing in the coastal area. It transpired that this form of worship with a *mṛnmaya mūrti* was celebrated in Bonai for the first time only in October 1948. Despite this rather clear beginning, the question of who took the initiative to celebrate Durgā Pūjā is contested. Some point at Mr. Das himself, but most others, including the current leaders of the organizing committee and the late Rajasahib Sri K. K. C. Deo, believe that Mangovind Mohanty was the driving force behind the establishment of Durgā Pūjā in Bonai.

Most people consider Mohanty a Katki—a person coming either from Cuttack itself or from the coastal area in the wider sense—pointing to the frequent migration from coastal Odisha to the hinterland in the early twentieth century. He is seen as a newcomer who settled down in Bonai a few years prior to independence. With his background, Mohanty was apparently familiar with Durgā Pūjā in Cuttack or coastal Odisha, where it had already been performed for a longer period.[21] Although most people would probably agree that Durgā Pūjā originated in Bengal, Mohanty's migration, as well as the historical roots of many families involved in the rituals nowadays, also point to a process of Odiaization. In fact, the design of the *mūrti* in 2015, with Lord Jagannath as a towering figure behind Durgā, can be seen as an example. Rather than simply indicating a postmerger Bengalization of Bonai, it is important to note that this tradition was mediated by ritual patrons coming from the coastal belt.[22]

Before the merger, as the late Rajasahib remembered, Mohanty visited the palace frequently and, as a loyal subject, read out English newspapers to his father. He was a clever and educated person—a graduate of Benares Hindu University. Just before the merger, Mohanty approached the raja for permission to establish a *Durgā maṇḍal*. The Raja agreed but demanded a continuous performance for twelve years. Accordingly, Mohanty performed it from 1948 to 1960, and some people believe that Mohanty not only initiated the rituals but also brought Brahmins from the coastal belt to do the *pūjā*—at least for the initial worship—though in 2007 the president and secretary of the Universal Durgā Pūjā Committee could not confirm this. After Mohanty's initial worship, the responsibility passed on to others, though the period after 1960 remains somewhat obscure. However, subsequently, Durgā Pūjā was transformed, involving a broader group of people, and at present the worship is organized through the Universal Durgā Pūjā Committee, which arranges meetings, makes plans for a budget, and so on. While in bigger cities such committees are frequently tied to specific neighborhoods (*para*) (Guha-Thakurta 2015, 15), in Bonaigarh this remains the only committee.[23] According to its president and secretary, in 2007 it had around two hundred members, of whom only around fifteen were active, and the Working Committee had six members—all involved in the organization, with preparations starting at least a month before the *pūjā*. Though figures generally vary, the idea of community *pūjā* was expressed by a member of the committee in 2016, who stated that "all are doing unitedly. We collect money. The mine owners also donate to the *pūjā*. Someone tells he shall provide the tent. Someone tells he shall give the cost of drums. Someone tells he will give the costs of *mūrti*. Someone tells he will give the costs of the *pūjā* [items]. The *pūjā* cannot be performed by a single man. If fifty people are united and they donate, then *pūjā* is performed. There are so many members in our committee." Many members are businessmen, engaged in rather small-scale businesses, or are journalists, lawyers, and so on. They could be described as and would consider themselves middle class, and they belong to very different political parties across the spectrum. In fact, in 2007 it was known that the president had connections to the local Bharatiya Janata Party MP and was regarded by many as a political broker or henchman. Significantly, most members are either relative newcomers to Bonai society or descendants of twentieth-century migrants—for example, children of officers and administrators who had already come during the period as a state and who were hardly integrated in the royal sacrificial polity, with its land grants and the customary services grantees provided. While the committee acknowledges the recent entry of many of their members into Bonai society, it also maintains that everybody in Bonai is a migrant except a few tribal communities (Adibasi). Yet, it is noticeable that the royal family and its collateral lines (*bābus*) are not part of the committee. When asked in 2016 whether there is any *bābu* in the committee, a member said, "Yes, the raja of Bonai," and then added, "Though he is not in the committee, he is welcome everywhere. Wherever the *pūjā* festival is celebrated, he is invited everywhere. That is the first tradition." Though such references are frequently made, especially in the presence of members of the royal family or vis-à-vis people known to be loyal to the raja, the committee remains an independent body that is ostensibly more democratically organized.

Apart from the committee, there is an external factor contributing significantly to the performance over a longer period—namely, mining. As the late Rajasahib also said, Mangovind Mohanty—together with the raja's relatives—applied for a mining lease in the Koira area of Bonai already during the state period and established a company called Bonai Industrial Mines, whose general manager he became. While it is not clear whether Mohanty used profits from the mining venture for the rituals, one can infer that his successful businesses probably helped in funding the new *pūjā* and that the origin of the Durgā Pūjā was already entangled in processes of migration and the emerging mining industry in Bonai in the 1940s. Moreover, as the organizers state, only recently, over the last ten to fifteen years, have the celebrations been aggrandized, because industrialists or owners of mines and factories setting up new enterprises have donated substantial amounts. Bonai's transformations due to an ongoing mining boom and a concomitant process of industrialization, especially the mushrooming of sponge-iron factories, have led—particularly when coupled with illegal forms of mining and violations of environmental norms—to "super-normal profits."[24]

These profits have facilitated the latest boost to and visible rise of Durgā Pūjā. Parallel to the industrial transformation, Durgā Pūjā started growing and its budget multiplied. According to the Universal Durgā Pūjā Committee, before 2007 the budget for the ceremonies was around INR 40,000. Subsequently, it increased to three lakhs (2007–8) and further to five lakhs (2013).[25] As the secretary argued in 2014, Durgā Pūjā is now "celebrated in a big way," with a budget substantially higher than the raja's budget for Dasarā. Around 2007 the organizers started collecting money not only from businessmen and contractors but also from political leaders and officers. However, in 2014 the biggest donor was a sponge-iron factory/integrated steel plant and mine, which some people believe is run by distant relatives of Mangovind Mohanty.

Not all donations might be entirely voluntary, though, and the secretary has described the collection of funds in the following way: "We collect donation from them. We tell them we are cooperating with you and you cooperate with us once in a year. As a result, they donated, and the *pūjā* became bigger." His statement can be read as a not-so-veiled hint at possible protests against the new, polluting factories if the owners don't support local causes. Similarly, a committee member argued in 2016 that "we have to put some pressure on Sub-Collector [and] DFO [Divisional Forest Officer]. DFO is the owner of whole mining. If he puts a signature, mining will be stopped." His words also express the use of pressure tactics involving state agencies keen to avoid any interruptions to the smooth functioning of the industries.

Funds increasingly generated in this way were utilized for the embellishment of rituals, for example, the *maṇḍap*. Its design changes annually, including, for example, a replica of the famous sun temple in Konark in 2007. Designs are usually suggested by artisans from Bengal, as the center of Durgā Pūjā with its spectacular *maṇḍaps*, and then selected by the Universal Durgā Pūjā Committee. Dreaming big, locals also talked about designs like the *Titanic* and the Taj Hotel in Mumbai, which they had seen or heard about and wished to see in Bonai as well. This illustrates aspirations for extravagant theme *pūjās*, as in Kolkata, where over the last few years a significant shift towards "arty" idols or "themed" pavilions has occurred (Guha-Thakurta 2015, 12–13)—even called "Bengal's own installation art" (Ray 2017, 1139).[26] However, even less-spectacular designs in Bonai usually cost several lakhs—for example, in 2013, 2.5 lakhs, or half of the year's entire budget.[27] The attractions also include the *mūrti*, made locally or in nearby Rourkela, and the *maṇḍap*'s surroundings, decorated with carpets and illuminations as impressive and enticing as possible.

The state is complicit in this performance by blocking the main road for this purpose, under the pretext of managing substantial crowds, particularly during the evening ritual, or *arthi*. Locals are also attracted acoustically, as various groups, not only locals, play their music—competing with the devotional music from loudspeakers.[28] In sum, Durgā Pūjā equipment inside and outside is extensive and expensive—far beyond the raja's limited arrangements—and clearly offers a spectacle. The very visible, audible, and tangible aggrandizement of Durgā Pūjā corresponds to a wider Indian pattern of gods and goddesses benefitting from global market forces, as Nanda (2011) argues. Donations from the corporate sector, with thinly veiled state support, help to gentrify their temporary temples, where "a style of worship acceptable to educated middle classes" is promoted (Nanda 2011, 87).

A Temporary Down and a Novelty: Durgā Pūjā 2016

The nexus between temple, business, and state works broadly to the advantage of Durgā in her relatively pan-Indian Mahiṣāsuramardinī form rather than her manifestations inside the fort. Yet, revisiting Durgā Pūjā in 2016, I found the picture was slightly different. Although the overall ritual setup with *maṇḍap*, *mūrti*, and so on remained the same, the design of the temporary temple, the music program, and the crowd appeared less impressive than in previous years. Upon my inquiring about the downsized performance and possible changes, most locals and members of the *pūjā* committee referred to a shortage of funds. One member said that "the orchestra and other programs are not organized for the last two years because the mining companies are not giving much funds," while another explained that "this year the gathering for the immersion was less compared to other years. . . . It was celebrated with one mixed music party only."

Fewer donations meant less music and smaller audiences. Others said the design for the *maṇḍap* was from Rourkela rather than Kolkata, or the *mūrti* was smaller, and many locals drew a direct connection to the condition of the mining industry in Bonai. The statements were corroborated by newspaper articles documenting the closure of industrial units in the Rourkela area, including in Bonai. For example, *The Telegraph* reported under the headline "Industries Exit Sundergarh" that "a large number of industries are closing down" in a district that once "had the largest concentration of sponge iron units (41) in the state"—the closure being caused, it was reasoned, by a "slump in the steel market, a lack of orders from the Rourkela Steel Plant and the non-payment of bills."[29] Thus, the *pūjā*'s scale was affected by reduced donations from a stagnating or downsizing industry, and Durgā rituals were performed in what was hardly a grandiose way.

However, the budget was sufficiently high to start a new spectacle—namely, Rāvaṇ Podi, or the burning of the effigy of the demon-king Rāvaṇ. Initiated three years ago, organized by the same committee, and performed at grounds close to the high school where the Republic Day parade is also usually held, it introduced and popularized a tradition in Bonaigarh which is regarded as coming from North India, where it marks the end of Dasarā without primarily revolving around the goddess Durgā. Apparently, younger committee members, keen on entertaining elements, took the initiative for this novel event in Bonaigarh's ritual calendar. As one young member explained, "More people have joined [Rāvaṇ Podi]. . . . Two thousand, three thousand have come and enjoyed a lot."[30] In the same interview, he also hailed the artist of the Rāvaṇ effigy for his impressive creation, declaring, "It is mind-blowing. You must have seen the Ravan, how he has made it? It took him fifteen days. He has no advisor. He works in his own way"—perhaps echoing the recent "arty" turn in Kolkata's Durgā Pūjā performance, though here projected onto Rāvaṇ's idol. Compared to a somewhat lackluster performance of Durgā Pūjā in the eyes of locals or even the committee members organizing both activities, Ravan Podi seemed to have outshone the worship of the goddess in terms of spectacle and attraction in 2016.

A Third Player: RSS and the Worship of Durgā

The worship of the goddess Durgā in Bonai is not limited to the two main ritual cycles in the market and the fort just presented. For the last few years, the Rashtriya Svayamsevak Sangh (RSS) has been trying to establish itself as a crucial player during this period of heightened ritual activities. Founded in 1925 and active in the region at least since the late 1940s (Kanungo 2003), it promotes its version of Hindu nationalism, which reserves a pivotal place for the goddess or mother—especially in the form of Bhārat Mātā (Mother India). RSS leaders such as Golwalkar ([1966] 1980) have explicitly referred to the work of Bankim Chandra Chatterjee and his praise for Durgā as "the Great Destroyer armed with ten weapons" and considered Bharat as the Hindu nation and "a land which has been to us since hoary times the beloved and sacred Bharat Mata whose very name floods our hearts with waves of pure and sublime devotion to her—well, this is the mother of us all, our glorious motherland" (108). Through the work of Chatterjee and Aurobindo but also Golwalkar, Bhārat Mātā has emerged as a modern goddess clearly linked to the earlier worship of the goddess Durgā, now morphed into a national deity (see also Ramaswamy 2010).

This tie between the Goddess Durgā and Bhārat Mātā was explicitly shown during an RSS function on the day of Vijayadaśamī in 2016. Mobilizing around fifty members, the RSS organized a march through town that connected the fort as a starting point and final destination with the main road, including various neighborhoods and institutions such as the high school. Dressed in their uniforms and armed with sticks, the very disciplined procession, divided into two lines and accompanied by police guards, followed the saffron flag held by the first volunteer. This march, announced beforehand, was occasionally greeted by locals throwing rice, and, especially in the neighborhood outside the fort (*bāharī garh*), several households set up a new *kalas* for a ritual welcome—precisely on the same spot in front of their houses where Kant Debī had been worshipped

Figure 10.8. Announcement for an RSS function in front of the *darbār* hall (2016). Photo by author.

earlier in the day while departing from Bonaigarh. However, unlike the Kant Debī procession, the RSS march was not interrupted for any ritual performance.

After the return to the fort, the main function took place outside the palace in front of the *darbār* hall—a place that no longer plays a major role during the royal Dasarā but where the raja holds a *darbār* during Caitra Parba.[31] As locals said, in the past the RSS had actually organized events on the former Dasarā ground, which has recently largely disappeared as an open field after new court buildings were constructed and another part was converted into a playground. The court extension caused the shift to the new location, but it is intriguing that both places—the old and the new one—are closely linked to kingship and statecraft and could be understood as attempts to appropriate royal spaces.

In this politically and symbolically loaded space, a banner was put up explaining the event as a celebration of the victorious tenth day ("Sri Bijay Dossomi Utsab"). While the day is commonly associated with Goddess Durgā, the accompanying image presented a typical iconography of Bhārat Mātā with a lion and saffron flag projected onto a map of India. Additionally, chairs were used as elevated platforms to venerate the garlanded images of three icons—namely, of Hedgewar, Bhārat Mātā, and Golwalkar (on the left and right: the first and second RSS leaders, respectively). In front of the very neatly arranged rows of members that offered a stark contrast to the far more crowded and far more randomly organized Kant Debī Pūjā, a large poster of the Goddess Durgā was installed. Here, Durgā appeared in her well-known ten-armed Mahiṣāsuramardinī form that was also present in the Durgā Pūjā *maṇḍap*, but without her children and only as a poster. In front of this poster, two swords and a shield were placed—corresponding to her weapons in the picture. However, after the saffron flag was hoisted in a kind of roll-call atmosphere, the goddess was worshipped only with light and incense.

These symbols, Durgā killing the demon combined with the worship of the swords, blended elements of both Durgā Pūjā and Dasarā while claiming an erstwhile royal space. These images and accessories of the warrior goddess were, however, somewhat contradicted by members in attendance explaining this occasion as a ritual of harmony and unity. This very basic worship was followed by speeches—absent in the other events—that equated Bhārat culture and Hindu culture and highlighted national political issues. Apart from the members, hardly any locals showed up, although they were clearly invited to attend and to listen to the speeches. Though invited, the raja also stayed away and later on was not amused when RSS members ventured into the palace compound, which probably indicated that many volunteers were not locals, who would have been more familiar with the location.

Figure 10.9. RSS Dasarā celebration in front of the palace (2016). Photo by author.

Conclusion

Questions about changes to the rituals, be it Dasarā or Durgā Pūjā, often lead to initially dismissive replies from interviewees. Ritual specialists, especially, tend to state, "No, everything is going on as usual." Only when one inquires further by pointing at specific observations of rituals being postponed, merged, or abolished are other explanations offered. These include that it was the order of the raja, or it was done in line with the horoscope (*pañji*), or we live in a dark era (or Kali Yuga) in which rituals, including royal ones, are replaced by shortcut *pūjās*. A façade of continuity is maintained despite the visible transformations such as declining palace facilities or a disintegrating sacrificial polity with fewer communities providing services. A tangible rise of Durgā Pūjā in the market equally brings into question any simple notion of a static situation. Rather, Durgā Pūjā is a local response linked to massive industrialization that is occurring, arguably, during a period of "accelerated change" or even "overheating" (Hylland Eriksen and Schober 2017) with intensified global processes such as the demand for steel. Globalization has indeed been good for the goddess Durgā in the market, as Nanda (2011) argues, but the goddess's manifestation in the fort has not benefitted in the same way, resulting in laments about a bygone era. Change, it seems, is downplayed by representatives of an older, royal order because their position and status are potentially threatened by the larger Durgā Pūjā. Their representatives appear to stress continuity.

One might be tempted to interpret the Dasarā and Durgā Pūjā performances as a somewhat delayed replication of a crucial shift of patronage from rather closed aristocratic circles in palaces to more open community or street celebrations, which occurred earlier in Kolkata, the center of Bengali Durgā worship (Guha-Thakurta 2015, 3). There are certainly spillover effects, in the sense that the Durgā Pūjā committee was inspired by spectacular temple designs used in Kolkata and perhaps also by an increasing emphasis on arty representations of the goddess lately (14). However, the situation in Bonai, and especially in its capital, Bonaigarh, is more complex than any unidirectional power passage from fort to market. Many Dasarā rituals are performed in a public arena, and particularly the Kant Debī worship attracts larger crowds. Besides, the recent beautification of temples linked to the goddess Durgā, including that of the raja's tutelary goddess, contradicts any oversimplistic impression of a continuous, unilinear decline of kingship. Similarly, the ostensibly more democratically organized Durgā Pūjā, driven by the middle class, which challenges the raja's privileged access to the goddess, is not simply on the rise. In 2016, donations to the Durgā Pūjā were reduced following a downsizing of companies and a crackdown on illegal mining, which, in turn, had an impact on the rituals' embellishment. Because the Durgā Pūjā was somewhat less attractive for the audience, fewer people attended, whereas the crowd for the Paudi Bhuiyan goddess Kant Debī coming to the palace remained the same.

Over the last few decades, these two public-arena activities—Dasarā and Durgā Pūjā—have coexisted in Bonai, to which the RSS-led Goddess Durgā–cum–Bhārat Mātā worship has been added recently. These power rituals are tied to different patrons and orders: first, the raja at the center of a sacrificial polity that includes various castes and Adibasi communities; second, a middle class with a relatively strong migrant background, barely integrated in a royal framework but supported by industrialists; and third, a political, cadre-based national organization promoting its Hindutvā ideology. They have very different spending powers but compete with one another, especially on Vijayadaśamī. For example, the RSS challenges both Dasarā and Durgā Pūjā by connecting the goddess Durgā to Bhārat Mātā, the goddess identified with the holy motherland. With its relatively simple ritual of offering incense and light to the goddess, it clearly differs from the pomp and spectacle, found especially in the market, though the iconographic representation of the goddess Durgā as Mahiṣāsuramardinī is shared. It also includes swords in the worship, as in the royal tradition. Moreover, the RSS marching through town before coming to the palace for the final part loosely resembles the earlier, still remembered but now abolished, movement of the raja to the Dasarā field to symbolically reconquer his realm. Yet, while in the royal rituals communities are ranked around the raja as the central figure and an elevated position is imparted to the Paudi Bhuiyan in charge of Goddess Kant Debī, and while the market Durgā Pūjā combines middle-class sensitivities with Brahmanical rituals, the RSS explicitly propagates the need for resurrecting a Hindu nation.

Whereas the RSS function has not found strong traction among locals so far, Dasarā and Durgā Pūjā are popular. And, interestingly, many people, including committee members and ritual specialists, attend both of the latter two ritual cycles. In the case of Kant Debī, there is an opportunity as well as a strong desire to have a physical connection with the goddess, which is not possible in the case of Durgā Pūjā. While some point out that both rituals revolve around the goddess Durgā and both forms can bless and fulfill wishes, it seems the efficacy and power of Kant Debī in the royal tradition is often considered greater. For some, at least, the goddess in the market in her Mahiṣāsuramardinī form, with her strictly Brahmanical worship and vegetarian offerings—that is, her rather milder *śānti* form in contrast to her appearance in the fort—and who continues to accept blood sacrifices, is not as approachable and perhaps not as powerful as Durgā and Kant Debī in the fort. At the same time, the largest attraction in 2016 was the burning of the demon Rāvaṇ, which was done without any major ritual. A member of the organizing Durgā Pūjā committee aptly emphasized the desire for entertainment, which Durgā Pūjā also offers: "people want *melā*, opera, in holidays they want to enjoy."

However, beyond pure enjoyment, the RSS organized their function right in front of the *darbār* hall, exactly where the raja sits on his throne (*gaddī*) during Caitra Parba. It clearly challenged this royal space. Or, as the *rājpurohit* somewhat sarcastically remarked while hinting at the rising power of the RSS, "here all are kings. The people [RSS] who came yesterday also think of themselves as kings." Yet they are aspiring kings who relate power to the goddess. Goddess worship in Bonai offers a focal point to understand the fragmentation of local society, with its constantly changing power equations and newly emerging power holders. Thus, a new power ritual might arise in the future, though the resilience of earlier performances and ideas, despite their downturns, is also clearly recognizable.

Notes

This chapter is based on discontinuous field research in the region starting in 2003, initially funded by the German Research Foundation (DFG) and later with a travel fund provided by Aarhus University. It builds on and expands the earlier work on Dasarā (e.g., Skoda 2018). All emic terms are transcribed from the local Odia language unless indicated otherwise.

1. A third sword, or *mohana khaṇḍa*, was fetched from a tribal chief while the raja conquered the realm (see similar cases in Odisha, e.g., Schnepel 2002, 259) and is also worshipped during Dasarā.

2. Nicholas refers to Durga Pūjā, whereas in Bonai this is more applicable to Dasarā and the royal tradition.

3. For example, the traditionally low-caste Parida, who earlier used to provide alcohol for the goddess Kant Debī, considered it degrading and discontinued this custom.

4. Even more important than the rather nominal amounts spent on *dasturi* is the distribution of sacrificial meat. Almost half of the royal budget is spent on uncastrated male goats (*buka*). Amat, Dehuri, and Rājpurohit claim them as an entitlement, and the *dehuri* also offers heads of sacrificial goats to the raja. While the raja generally distributes meat to close friends or servants, the goat sacrificed for the *mohana khaṇḍa* is prepared jointly by the *biradri*, or male members of the royal family (clan).

5. According to the royal family chronicles, it is called *samā* and is the iron part of a husking pedal/mill, or *dhinki* (see Pramanik and Skoda 2013, 40). The

kant dehuri argued that it is not made of iron nor brass but of earth, bird, tree, leaves, gold, silver, diamond, ruby, and so on, whatever is available in the earth, whereas the *amat* stated, "Nobody could say that" (interview by the author, 2016).

6. On the second day of the fortnight (*dvītiyā*), the goddess leaves her abode in the hills and is carried by a group of Paudi Bhuiyan to Bonaigarh in the plains. She will return to her cave only on the final day of this fortnight (full moon). This procession includes overnight stays in the houses of various headmen (Naik) and a Jagirdar of the Gond community (also Roy 1935, 107) and connects various Adibasi and non-Adibasi communities. Its route is customarily drafted by the raja, and the dehuri carries out the raja's order.

7. His family presumably has taken over this duty from the Bhuiyans generations ago (Roy 1935, 117).

8. In the *darbār* hall, parallel rituals start already from the seventh day of the fortnight, *saptamī*. The swords (*patkhaṇḍa* and *kumārī prasād*) are worshipped by the *amat*, while the *rājpurohit* worships Nabadurgā in the form of the bracelet. The *rājpurohit* characterized these two different forms of worship—non-Brahmanical versus his Brahmanical *pūjā*—also as *tantra* versus *mantra pūjā*.

9. Buffaloes are, in some parts of Odisha, also considered possible substitutes for human sacrifices.

10. Reply (no. 10226) by the administrator of Bonai to the additional secretary to the government, Home Department, States Section, Cuttack, Odisha (September 20, 1948). The report also mentions that subsequently he reduced the amount to 1,000 rupees. This amount, the administrator argued, should be spent on the Bhuiyan *darbār* on Dasarā but not on the ritual activities. Thus, he hints at a ritual of loyalty the Indian state was keen to continue in a transitional phase, although it was abolished some years later.

11. See, for example, Shubhankar Behera, "World Environment Day: Cry to Save Khandadhar Gets Louder," *Odishatv.in*, June 5, 2014, https://odishatv.in/odisha-news/otherstories/world-environment-day-cry-to-save-khandadhar-gets-louder-48792. Behera stressed how his father prevented the Birla company from starting a mine in 1947, though he could not prevent it after independence.

12. Apart from Dasarā, the raja also plays a crucial role in the Caitra Parba rituals in April.

13. While newspapers stressed the participation of the local member of parliament (MP) Jual Oram (now again Union cabinet minister for Tribal Affairs and himself from Bonai), the list of signatures in a petition passed during the rally indicates the esteemed position of the raja by including him as the first signatory, before the MP, followed by the raja's son (Prasanta Varma, "Representation of the Bonaigarh Tribals to the Governor of Orissa," posted January 8, 2007, http://hindtoday.com/blogs/viewblogs.aspx?htadvtid=775&htadvtplacecode=world).

14. The immersion (*bisarjan*) of the idol might be delayed, however.

15. The nine elements are banana, *saru* (a root), *haldī* (turmeric), *jayantī*, *bel*, *dalimba* (a fruit), *aśoka*, *mānasaru*, and *dhān* (paddy). The nine goddesses are Brahmānī, Kālī, Durgā, Kārtikī, Śivā, Raktadantikā, Śokarahitā, Camuṇḍā, and Lakṣmī. For a detailed analysis of the rituals in Bengal, see Khanna (2000).

16. On the text and the various traditions of the feminine sacred merging in it, see Kinsley (1987).

17. Actually, a final Satyanārāyaṇ ritual is performed at the *maṇḍap* by the officiating Brahmins praying for forgiveness in case of mistakes committed during the worship.

18. Dasarā in the fort is not dated by locals, such as by linking it to a specific raja starting rituals. In fact, the royal chronicles locate the appearance of Kant Debī in mythical times without naming any raja.

19. Letter (no. 14939 [23]) from the Government of Orissa, Home Department, inquiring about the "Celebration of Durga Pūjā or Dussera" (September 10, 1948) to all administrators: "Please report whether in your state in the past Durga Pūjā or Dussehra has been celebrated as a State function or as the Ruler's private function. If it was celebrated as a state function the expenditure should have been met from the state revenues and there should have been a budget provision for the purpose. It is likely that though the celebrations were the private celebrations of the Ruler, he used to receive a grant from the state revenues."

20. Reply (no. 10226) by the administrator of Bonai to the additional secretary to the government, Cuttack (September 20, 1948).

21. Frequently, the year 1832 is mentioned as when the first performance of Durgā Pūjā took place in Cuttack. For example, an article in *Incredible Orissa* states that "the earliest Durga Puja was reportedly held in the Kazi Bajaar area of Cuttack in 1832 by both Odia and Bengali employees of the East India Company" ("Cuttack Durga Puja—21 Chandi Medha, 158 Puja Mandaps," October 22, 2015, http://incredibleorissa.com/cuttack-durga-puja-chandi-medha-mandaps/). It is also argued that, for example, the silver filigree work for which Cuttack is so famous became a feature of Durgā Pūjā in Cuttack, which according to other sources dates back to the time of Chaitanya (see Piyush Rout, "Durga Puja the Festival of Autumn Tune," September 23, 2017, https://medium.com/@piyushrout/durga-pūjā-the-festival-of-autumn-tune-b4a3887d782d).

22. Durga Pūjā in Cuttack and Bengal was simultaneously subjected to processes of change. For example, Ghosh (2006) and Chatterjee (2008) mention processes of commercialization or museumization.

23. However, there are other committees in other parts of Bonai, such as in the mining townships.

24. A report and list in the subcollector's office in 2007–8 showed about forty sponge-iron factories and crusher units dotting the former kingdom, several of which have substantially transformed the landscape and environment in the immediate vicinity of Bonaigarh. A boom period was easily observable, particularly between 2003 and 2008 with the rapid growth of coal-based sponge-iron plants. See Centre for Science and Environment (2011); "Sponge Iron Industry Needs Quick Actions for Survival" (*Economic Times*, October 24, 2013, https://economictimes.indiatimes.com/news/politics-and-nation/sponge-iron-industry-needs-quick-actions-for-survival/articleshow/24694957.cms). The term "super-normal profits" is borrowed from Chitrangada Choudhury ("The Keonjhar Take Over," *Outlook*, February 8, 2016, https://www.outlookindia.com/magazine/story/the-keonjhar-take-over/296512).

25. Budget details were, however, not shared beyond the committee itself.

26. On the recent competitiveness, commercialization, but also creativity in Bengal and particularly in Kolkata, see Ghosh (2006) and Chatterjee (2008).

27. While the artisans from Kolkata or other parts of West Bengal contribute their labor and decorations, the basic materials come from local tent houses.

28. Locals as well as drummers from Jharsuguda (the neighboring district's capital, the distance mentioned here as a sign of their high-quality performance) had been invited to play in front of the temple in 2007, and by 2013 three groups, one from Bhubaneshwar, one from Sambalpur, and a local group, competed for attention from the audience.

29. Rajesh Mohanty, "Industries Exit Sundergarh," *The Telegraph*, October 6, 2016.

30. However, while it is a new event in the capital or subdivisional headquarters of Bonai, Ravan Podi has been performed for many years in a village a few kilometers away. Referring to this performance, with which he was clearly familiar, the committee member also stated that "we the young people decided in a meeting that the population of Bonai [Bonaigarh] is more. . . . If we will do it here [Bonaigarh], the name of Bonai will be popular." Thus, the performance was new in the capital but not entirely new in the kingdom.

31. Caitra Parba is often described as "spring Navarātri."

References

Biardieu, Madeleine. 1989. *Hinduism: The Anthropology of a Civilization*. Delhi: Oxford University Press. First published 1981.

Centre for Science and Environment. 2011. *Sponge Iron Industry: The Regulatory Challenge*. Delhi: Centre for Science and Environment. https://cdn.cseindia.org/attachments/0.25223700_1499927364_sponge_iron_layout.pdf.

Chatterjee, Partha. 2008. "Critique of Popular Culture." *Public Culture* 20 (2): 321–44.

Galey, Jean-Claude. 1990. "Reconsidering Kingship in India: An Ethnological Perspective." In *Kingship and the Kings*, edited by Jean-Claude Galey, 123–88. Chur, Switzerland: Harwood Academic.

Ghosh, Anjan. 2006. "Durga Puja: A Consuming Passion." *Seminar* 559 (March). http://www.india-seminar.com/2006/559/559%20anjan%20ghosh.htm.

Gowalkar, Madhav Sadashiv. (1966) 1980. *Bunch of Thoughts*. Bangalore: Jagarana Prakashana.

Guha-Thakurta, Tapati. 2015. *In the Name of the Goddess: The Durga Pujas of Contemporary Kolkata*. Delhi: Primus Books.

Hylland Eriksen, Thomas, and Elisabeth Schober. 2017. *Knowledge and Power in an Overheated World*. Oslo: Department of Social Anthropology, University of Oslo.

Kanungo, Pralay. 2003. "Hindutva's Entry into a 'Hindu Province': Early Years of RSS in Orissa." *Economic and Political Weekly*, August 2, 2003, 3293–303.

Khanna, Madhu. 2000. "The Ritual Capsule of Durgā Pūjā: An Ecological Perspective." In *Hinduism and Ecology: The Intersection of Earth, Sky, and Water*, edited by Christopher Key Chapple and Mary Evelyn Tucker, 469–98. Cambridge, MA: Harvard University Press.

Kinsley, David. 1987. *Hindu Goddesses: Vision of the Divine Feminine in the Hindu Religious Tradition.* New Delhi: Motilal Banarsidass.

Mallebrein, Cornelia. 2004. "Entering the Realm of Durgā: Pātkhandā, a Hinduized Tribal Deity." In *Text and Context in the History, Literature and Religion of Orissa,* edited by Angelika Malinar, Johannes Beltz, and Heiko Frese, 273–306. New Delhi: Manohar.

McDermott, Rachel Fell. 2011. *Revelry, Rivalry, and Longing for the Goddesses of Bengal: The Fortunes of Hindu Festivals.* New York: Columbia University Press.

Michaels, Axel. 1998. *Der Hinduismus: Geschichte und Gegenwart.* Munich: Beck.

Michaels, Axel, Cornelia Vogelsanger, and Annette Wilke, eds. 1997. *Wild Goddesses in India and Nepal.* Bern: Peter Lang.

Nanda, Meera. 2011. *The God Market: How Globalization Is Making India More Hindu.* Delhi: Random House.

Nicholas, Ralph W. 2013. *Night of the Gods: Durgā Pūjā and the Legitimation of Power in Rural Bengal.* Delhi: Orient Blackswan.

Östör, Ákos. 2004. *The Play of Gods: Locality, Ideology, Structure, and Time in the Festivals of a Bengali Town.* New Delhi: Chronicle Books. First published 1980.

Pfaff-Czarnecka, Joanna. 1998. "A Battle of Meanings: Commemorating Goddess Durgā's Victory over Demon Mahisā as a Political Act." *Asiatische Studien: Zeitschrift der Schweizerischen Gesellschaft für Asienkunde* 52 (2): 575–610.

Pramanik, Rashimi, and Uwe Skoda, ed. 2013. *Chronicles of the Royal Family of Bonai, Odisha.* Delhi: Manohar.

Ramaswamy, Sumathi. 2010. *The Goddess and the Nation: Mapping Mother India.* Durham, NC: Duke University Press.

Ray, Manas. 2017. "Goddess in the City: Durga Pujas of Contemporary Kolkata." Review of *In the Name of the Goddess: The Durga Pujas of Contemporary Kolkata,* by Tapati Guha-Thakurta. *Modern Asian Studies* 51 (4): 1126–64.

Roy, Sarat Chandra. 1935. *The Hill Bhuiyas of Orissa.* Ranchi, India: "Man in India" Office.

Schnepel, Burkhard. 2002. *The Jungle Kings: Ethnohistorical Aspects of Politics and Ritual in Orissa.* New Delhi: Manohar.

Skoda, Uwe. 2018. "Dasarā and the Selective Decline of Sacrificial Polity in a Former Princely State of Odisha." In *Nine Nights of the Goddess: The Navarātri Festival in South Asia,* edited by Caleb Simmons, Moumita Sen, and Hillary Rodrigues, 83–102. Albany: State University of New York Press.

Contributors

Ute Hüsken is a professor in the Department of Cultural and Religious History of South Asia (Classical Indology, South Asia Institute), Heidelberg University. Until 2017 she was a professor of South Asia studies (Sanskrit) at Oslo University (Norway), and she was a member of the collaborative research project Dynamics of Ritual at Heidelberg University. Hüsken's main research fields are Buddhist studies, Hindu studies, ritual and festival studies, and gender studies. Her major publications include *Die Vorschriften für die Buddhistische Nonnengemeinde im Vinaya-Piṭaka der Theravādin* (Reimer, 1997), *When Rituals Go Wrong: Mistakes, Failure, and the Dynamics of Ritual* (Brill, 2007), *Viṣṇu's Children: Prenatal Life-Cycle Rituals in South India* (Harrassowitz, 2009), and two edited volumes on the denial of ritual: *The Ambivalence of Denial: Danger and Appeal of Rituals* (ed. with Udo Simon, Harrassowitz, 2016) and a special issue of the *Journal of Ritual Studies* (vol. 27, no. 1, 2013, ed. with Donna L. Seamone). Together with Ronald Grimes and Barry Stephenson, she edits the Oxford Ritual Studies series (Oxford University Press).

Ina Marie Lunde Ilkama is an associate professor of religion and didactics of religion at the University of South Eastern Norway, where she currently works with religion in the education of teachers. She has a PhD in South Asian studies with a specialization in Hinduism from the Department of Cultural Studies and Oriental Languages, University of Oslo (2019). Her dissertation research focuses on aspects of play and roles and images of the feminine (goddesses and women) during Navarātri in Kāñcipuram. With a background in religious studies and Sanskrit, she combines anthropological fieldwork with textual studies. Her academic interests include goddess studies, ritual, mythology, gender and religion, vernacular, and Sanskrit traditions.

Vasudha Narayanan is a distinguished professor in the Department of Religion at the University of Florida and a past president of the American Academy of Religion (2001–2002). She was educated at the Universities of Madras and Bombay in India and at Harvard University. She is the author or editor of seven books and numerous articles, book chapters, and encyclopedia entries. In addition, she is also the associate editor of the six-volume *Brill's Encyclopedia of Hinduism*. Her research has been supported by grants and fellowships from several organizations including the Center for Khmer Studies, the American Council of Learned Societies, the John Simon Guggenheim Memorial Foundation, the National Endowment for the Humanities, the American Institute of Indian Studies / the Smithsonian Institution, and the Social Science Research Council.

Jennifer Ortegren is an assistant professor in the Department of Religion at Middlebury College. She specializes in the ethnographic study of religions in South Asia, particularly Hinduism and Islam, with a focus on women, ritual, and class. She has published on the intersections of religion and class among upwardly mobile Hindu women in Udaipur, Rajasthan, including her forthcoming book with Oxford University Press, *Middle-Class Dharma: Gender, Aspiration, and the Making of Modern Hinduism*, which analyzes how class operates as a category of religious identity. Her current research project examines class mobility among Muslim women and how shifting lifestyles and identities within Muslim communities are reshaping relationships with Hindu neighbors.

Hillary Rodrigues (PhD McMaster) is a professor of religious studies at the University of Lethbridge (Canada). Aligned with his project on the pedagogy of religious studies, he has published *The Study of Religion: A Reader*, and new editions of his *Introduction to the Study of Religion*, *World Religions: A Guide to the Essentials*, *Introducing Hinduism*, and *Hinduism: The eBook* are anticipated soon. He has authored *Ritual Worship of the Great Goddess* and coedited *Nine Nights of the Goddess: The Navarātri Festival in South Asia*, a sister volume to this book, both published by SUNY Press. He has been honored by his institution's Board of Governors Chair in Teaching and Distinguished Teaching Award.

R. Jeremy Saul received his PhD in Asian studies from the University of Michigan in December 2013. He currently teaches about Asian religions and philosophies in the College of Religious Studies, Mahidol University, in Bangkok. His research interests pertain to modern developments in devotion (*bhakti*) in South Asia, with an emphasis on shrine deities in northwestern India. Among his publications, he has written "The Kali

Yuga as the Era of Wealth-Pursuit: Perceptions of Patronage at a Hindu Shrine" (*Nidan*, vol. 26, no. 1, July 2014); "Danger and Devotion: Reflections on Hindu Ecology," in *Ethics, Ecology, and Religion* (ed. Imtiyaz Yusuf, Konrad Adenauer Foundation, 2015); and "Kaila Devi: The Great Goddess as Local Avatar of Miracles," in *Garland of Goddesses* (ed. Michael Slouber, University of California Press, forthcoming). His current book project considers the modern rise and Vaishnavization of miracle deities, particularly those associated with Hanumān, at shrines of northern Rajasthan and the parallel development of devotional organizations dedicated to those deities in urban merchant communities throughout India.

Moumita Sen is a visual studies scholar studying the transnational flows of Hindu-nationalist ideology in addition to the grassroots-level religiopolitical movements against it. Her forthcoming monograph, *The Mahishasur Movement in India: Caste, Religion, and Politics*, is based on her postdoctoral research, which focuses on the intersection of aesthetic discourse, popular religiosity, and organized politics in the Mahishasur movement, in which caste minorities in India publicly venerate a demon in hegemonic Hindu mythology. Her larger research interest is in the field of Indian visual culture. Her doctoral dissertation (2016), which she is in the process of turning into a book, studied the practices of clay modeling in West Bengal, which weave together the worlds of art, religion, and politics. Her dissertation received the Norwegian king's gold medal for outstanding research in 2017. She is a coeditor of *Nine Nights of the Goddess: The Navarātri Festival in South Asia* (SUNY Press, 2018).

Neelima Shukla-Bhatt is a professor of South Asia studies at Wellesley College in Massachusetts. She studies and teaches courses on religion in South Asia. She studies devotional literature of medieval North India with a focus on its performative aspects, goddess traditions of Gujarat, and South Asian religions in the context of globalization, especially as they traverse popular media. She is the author of *Narasinha Mehta of Gujarat: A Legacy of Bhakti in Songs and Stories* (Oxford University Press, 2015) and coauthor, with Surendra Bhana, of *A Fire That Blazed in the Ocean: Gandhi and the Poems of Satyagraha in South Africa, 1909–1911* (Promilla, 2011). She has also published on the female poet Mira of Rajasthan, Hindu perspectives on religious diversity, and commercials for South Asian faith healers in the diaspora.

Caleb Simmons is an associate professor of religious studies at the University of Arizona. He specializes in religion in South Asia, especially Hinduism. His research specialties span religion and state formation in medieval and colonial India to contemporary transnational aspects of Hinduism. His book *Devotional Sovereignty: Kingship and Religion in India* (Oxford University Press, 2020) examines how the late early modern/early colonial court of Mysore reenvisioned notions of kingship, territory, and religion, especially through articulations of devotion. He also edited (with Moumita Sen and Hillary Rodrigues) and contributed to *Nine Nights of the Goddess: The Navarātri Festival in South Asia* (SUNY Press, 2018). He has additional publications examining a broad range of contemporary topics, including ecological issues and sacred geography in India, South Asian diaspora communities, and material and popular cultures that arise as a result of globalization—especially South Asian religions portrayed in comic books and graphic novels. He is currently completing his second monograph, *Singing the Goddess into Place: Folksongs, Myth, and Situated Knowledge in Mysore, India,* which examines popular local folk songs that tell the mythology of Mysore's Chamundeshwari and her consort Nanjundeshwara.

Uwe Skoda is an associate professor of India and South Asia studies in the Department of Global Studies, Aarhus University (Denmark). Currently, he is working on visual culture and photography as well as on themes within the field of political anthropology—particularly, transformations of kingship, indigenous people, and domestic politics. His recent books include *Bonding with the Lord: Jagannath, Popular Culture and Community Formation* (coedited with Jyotirmaya Tripathy, Bloomsbury, 2019), *India and Its Visual Cultures: Community, Class and Gender in a Symbolic Landscape* (coedited with Birgit Lettmann, Sage, 2018), and *Highland Odisha: Life and Society beyond the Coastal World* (with Biswamoy Pati, Primus, 2017).

Astrid Zotter is the project coordinator and deputy leader of the research unit Documents on the History of Religion and Law of Premodern Nepal at the Heidelberg Academy of Sciences and Humanities. She has been researching Hindu traditions in the Kathmandu Valley (Nepal), combining textual studies with fieldwork. Her monograph *Von Blüten, Göttern und Gelehrten: Die Behandlung von pūjā-Blüten im Puṣpacintāmaṇi: Text, Herkunft und Deutung eines nepalischen Kompendiums* deals with a text on the use of flowers in worship from seventeenth-century Nepal. She has also coedited two volumes, *Hindu and Buddhist Initiations in India and Nepal,* together with Christof Zotter, and *Studies in Historical Documents from Nepal and India,* together with Simon Cubelic and Axel Michaels, and is currently preparing a monograph on the Nepalese Dasaĩ festival.

Index

www.ingramcontent.com/pod-product-compliance
Lightning Source LLC
Chambersburg PA
CBHW071839270326
41929CB00013B/2048
9781438484068